DOOMSDAY PROPHECIES

DOOMSDAY PROPHECIES

A COMPLETE
GUIDE TO THE
END OF THE WORLD

JAMES R. LEWIS

Prometheus Books
59 John Glenn Drive
Amherst, New York 14228-2197

Portions of this work rely heavily on the research and writings of others. The information on the Branch Davidians can be found in James Tabor, "The Waco Tragedy: An Autobiographical Account of One Attempt to Avert Disaster," in *From the Ashes: Making Sense of Waco*, edited by James R. Lewis (Lanham, Md.: Rowman & Littlefield, 1994). The information on Father David can be found in David Millikan, "The Children of God, The Family of Love, The Family," in *Sex, Slander, and Salvation: Investigating The Family/Children of God*, edited by James R. Lewis and J. Gordon Melton (Stanford, Calif.: Center for Academic Publication, 1994). Finally, the information on Sister Thedra can be found in Jerome Clark, "Sister Thedra," *Syzygy: Journal of Alternative Religions and Cultures* 6, no. 1 (1997). All are reproduced by permission.

Published 2000 by Prometheus Books

Inquiries should be addressed to
Prometheus Books, 59 John Glenn Drive, Amherst, New York 14228–2197.
VOICE: 716–691–0133, ext. 207.
FAX: 716–564–2711.
WWW.PROMETHEUSBOOKS.COM

04 03 02 01 00   5 4 3 2 1

Library of Congress Cataloging-in-Publication Data

Lewis, James R.
    Doomsday prophecies : a complete guide to the end of the world / James R. Lewis.
        p.   cm.
    Includes bibliographical references and index.
    ISBN 1–57392–690–6 (alk. paper)
    1. Millennialism–Case studies. I. Title.

BL503.2.L49   1999
001.9–dc21
                                                                                    99–050123
                                                                                    CIP

Printed in the United States of America on acid-free paper

CONTENTS

ACKNOWLEDGMENTS

Innumerable people have contributed to the present volume in various ways.

The first person I would like to acknowledge is my agent, Evelyn Oliver, who sold this project. Second, thanks to Steven L. Mitchell at Prometheus Books for his role in bringing this project to fruition. Third, my discussions in certain chapters are heavily indebted to certain colleagues, and I would like to acknowledge this indebtedness. These scholars are James Tabor (the later section of chapter 4), Jerome Clark (chapter 6), and Gordon Melton, Moormon Oliver, and David Millikan (chapter 5).

Finally, I would like to thank the many leaders and members of millennialist groups who have allowed me to question them and to observe their activities at close range over the years. Without this kind of ongoing, open-minded contact, my understanding of such movements would be immeasurably poorer.

1

INTRODUCTION
Blueprints for Doomsday

My day's work started a little before five o'clock yesterday, when I began helping Ed Sanders mix heating oil with the ammonium nitrate fertilizer. . . . We stood the 100-pound bags on end one by one and poked a small hole in the top with a screwdriver, just big enough to insert the end of a funnel. While I held the bag and funnel, Ed poured in a gallon of oil. Then we slapped a big square of adhesive tape over the hole, and I turned the bag end over end to mix the contents while Ed refilled his oil can from the feeder line in their oil furnace. It took us nearly three hours to do all 44 sacks, and the work really wore me out. . . .

Finally, I ran the cable and switch from the detonator through a chink from the cargo area into the cab of the truck. . . . George and I headed for the . . . building in the car, with Henry following in the truck . . . until we found a good spot to park.

. . . The pavement shuddered violently under our feet. An instant later the blast wave hit us—a deafening "ka-whoomp," followed by an enormous roaring, crashing sound, accentuated by the higher-pitched noise of shattering glass all around us.

Overturned trucks and automobiles, smashed office furniture, and building rubble were strewn wildly about—and so were the bodies of a shockingly large number of victims. Over everything hung the pall of black smoke burning our eyes and lungs and

reducing the bright morning to semi-darkness. . . . We gaped with
a mixture of horror and elation at the devastation. . . .

All day yesterday and most of today we watched the TV cov-
erage of rescue crews bringing the dead and injured out of the
building. It is a heavy burden of responsibility for us to bear, since
most of the victims of our bomb were only pawns who were no
more committed to the sick philosophy or the racially destructive
goals of the System than we are. But there is no way we can
destroy the System without hurting many thousands of innocent
people—no way. It is a cancer too deeply rooted in our flesh. And
if we don't destroy the System before it destroys us—if we don't cut
this cancer out of our living flesh—our whole race will die.

Nevertheless, every time the TV camera focuses on the pitiful,
mutilated corpse of some poor girl—or even an FBI agent—being
pulled from the wreckage, my stomach becomes tied in knots and I
cannot breathe. It is a terrible, terrible task we have before us.

Passages from a Timothy McVeigh letter? Excerpts from the diary of Terry Nichols? Citations from a fictionalized version of events in Oklahoma City on April 19, 1995? The correct answer is "None of the above."

While the parallels to the bombing of the Oklahoma City federal building are eerie, this prophetic description of events comes from the 1978 novel *The Turner Diaries*. The narrative of this dark piece of fiction is built around an apocalyptic race war that culminates in the extermination of all nonwhite peoples. The book's twisted tale is told through the eyes of Earl Turner, a white revolutionary who eventually bombs the Pentagon in a final act of redemptive martyrdom (Macdonald 1978).

An underground "classic" within America's racialist subculture, *The Turner Diaries* supplies both a rationale and a prophetic blueprint for white terrorists. While not particularly well-written, there is some strange appeal about this narrative that has inspired a number of different right-wing extremists to take direct, violent action against "the System." The bombing of the federal building in Oklahoma City is merely the most dramatic case in point. Also of note are the activities of the Order, also known as the Silent Brotherhood, a group of white revolutionaries similarly inspired by *The Turner Diaries*. In 1983–84 the Order engaged in a wave of crimes, mostly in the West, preparatory to the launching of attacks on the federal government. Between 1984 and 1986 the members of the Order were captured and tried, and its leader, Robert Matthews, was killed in a shootout with the FBI (Barkun 1998).

While William L. Pierce, the presumed author of the *Diaries*,* may not have intended such literalistic readings of his fiction, it is clear that he did envision a future race war for which he wished his Aryan brethren to be prepared. Although not fitting the stereotype of the robed and bearded recluse familiar from Hollywood adaptations of the Bible, he was, in a very real sense, a modern doomsday prophet. The major difference was that, rather than simply predicting events, Pierce, perhaps inadvertently, became involved in inspiring them.

Closer to the biblical model was a prophecy put forth in 1954 predicting a very different kind of doomsday that was to have taken place on December 21 of that year:

> Earthlings will awaken to . . . the lake seething and the great destruction of tall buildings. . . . The scenes of that day will be as mad . . . the event will begin at dawn and end swiftly as a passing cloud. . . . When the resurrected have been resurrected or taken up . . . it will be as a great burst of light. . . . In the midst of this it is to be recorded that a great wave rushes into the mountains. . . . The slopes of the side to the east will be the beginning of a new civilization upon which will be the new order, in light. . . .

In this prophecy one finds many familiar apocalyptic elements, from the theme of universal destruction to the postapocalypse vision of a dawning new order. One can well imagine that these words spilled unbidden from the trembling lips of an ecstatic, Middle Eastern prophet. Alternately, perhaps they were uttered by a fiery preacher in harsh, dramatic tones from the pulpit of some backwoods church.

---

*One reason Pierce is believed to be the author is he is known to be the book's publisher.

Instead, however, this prediction was one of the central transmissions of "Space Brother Sananda" (aka Jesus) to Marian Keech, a middle-aged, middle-class suburbanite who transcribed them via the medium of automatic writing* in the comfort of her own living room. In other messages, Sananda assured Mrs. Keech that she and a select group of followers would be taken up by a flying saucer in a kind of "technological rapture" before the destruction commenced on December 21, 1954. Needless to say, neither the "rapture" nor the predicted apocalypse occurred–a dramatic nonevent, the significance of which was captured in the title of the first and only study of the group, *When Prophecy Fails*. The scenario predicted in Ms. Keech's prophecy is eerily similar to that of the Bo and Peep cult–a group which, in the wake of recent events, is more familiar as Heaven's Gate.

On March 26, 1997, the bodies of thirty-nine men and women were found in a posh mansion outside San Diego, all victims of a mass suicide. Messages left by the group indicate that they believed they were stepping out of their "physical containers" in order to ascend to a UFO that was arriving in the wake of the Hale-Bopp comet. They also asserted that this comet, or parts of it, would subsequently crash into the earth and cause widespread destruction. In a taped message, their leader further noted that our calendars were off–that the year 1997 was really the year 2000, as if everyone was in agreement that the world would end precisely two millennia after the birth of Jesus.

The leader of Heaven's Gate, Marshall Applewhite, taught that aliens had planted the seeds of current humanity millions of years ago and were coming to reap the harvest of their work in the form of spiritually evolved individuals who would join the ranks of flying saucer crews. Only a select few members of humanity would be chosen to advance to this "transhuman" state. The rest would be left to wallow in the spiritually poisoned atmosphere of a corrupt world.

Later in his prophetic career, Applewhite also prophesied that after the elect had been picked up by the Space Brothers, the planet would be engulfed in cataclysmic destruction. When, in 1993, under

---

*Relaxing and allowing one's hand to write, seemingly by itself.

the name of Total Overcomers Anonymous, the group ran an advertisement in *USA Today*, their portrayal of the postrapture world was far more apocalyptic than Applewhite had taught at the beginning of his career as UFO prophet:

> The Earth's present "civilization" is about to be recycled—"spaded under." Its inhabitants are refusing to evolve. The "weeds" have taken over the garden and disturbed its usefulness beyond repair. (Cited in Balch 1995)

The group death of the Heaven's Gate members embodies the same dark side of apocalyptic religiosity that propelled the Oklahoma City bombers to engage in a radical act of preemptive violence as a way of invoking the final end.

Yet another event that seemed to embody the pattern of an apocalyptic group fulfilling its own prophecies involved the Japanese religious group AUM Shinrikyo. On March 20, 1995, a poison gas attack occurred in a Tokyo subway that killed twelve people and injured many others. Within a few days of the attack, AUM Shinrikyo was fingered as the most likely suspect. The leadership was eventually arrested and the religious corporation dissolved.

The group had been founded by Master Shoko Asahara in Tokyo in 1987. A form of Tantric Buddhism, AUM Shinrikyo's teachings emphasized yoga practices and spiritual experiences. Master Asahara, whose original name was Chizuo Matsumoto, had traveled to India seeking enlightenment. Before returning to Japan, he sought out the Dalai Lama and received what he believed was a commission to revive true Buddhism in the land of his birth. By the time of the subway incident, AUM Shinrikyo had acquired a large communal facility near Mt. Fuji and a following of 10,000 members in Japan.

In addition to the usual teachings that go hand in hand with mainline Buddhism, Master Asahara was also fascinated with the future. His preoccupation with divination may have grown out of the weakness of his physical senses, as he was born blind in one eye and had only partial use of the other. Before undertaking yoga and meditation practices, Asahara pursued the study of such divinatory practices as astrology. Like many other Japanese spiritualists, he was fascinated by Western biblical prophecies as well as by the prophecies of Nostradamus, the famous French prophet. Perhaps influenced by the apocalyptic flavor of these predictions, Asahara himself began preaching an apocalyptic message to his followers. In particular, he prophesied a confrontation between Japan and the United States before the end of the century that would in all likelihood decimate his home country.

Asahara was, in fact, so certain of an impending conflict between Japan and the United States that he actually began preparing to wage war. Unable to match the conventional military might of the United States, AUM scientists investigated unconventional weapons, from biological agents to poison gas. This research is reflected in Asahara's final published book, *Disaster Approaches the Land of the Rising Sun,* which contains page after page reflecting a very un-Buddhist interest in various forms of poison gas, including one known as sarin, the gas identified in the Tokyo subway attack.

In the end, it was Asahara's own incautious pronouncements that drew police attention to AUM Shinrikyo. In particular, Master Asahara had predicted that poison gas attacks by terrorists would occur in the not-too-distant future. This made him an obvious target of suspicion and he was eventually arrested.

In addition to these incidents, we might also note that there have been a number of close calls. An organization named the Covenant, the Sword, and the Arm of the Lord, for example, was founded in the mid-1970s by James D. Ellison, a minister in San Antonio, Texas. Ellison had an apocalyptic vision of the coming collapse of the American society and decided to flee the city. He established a survivalist community on a 224-acre tract of land in the Ozark Mountains of Arkansas. The commune was seen as a purging place and given the biblical name Zarephath-Horeb.

In common with the larger Identity Movement, Ellison's teachings identified the white Anglo-Saxon race as the literal descendants of ancient Israel and hence heir to the covenants and promises God made to Israel. They believed that the Anglo-Saxons had been called to be the light of the world, and that black people were created for perpetual servitude. Ellison and his followers also believed that God's spirit would be coming soon in judgment to the earth and that the Covenant, the Sword, and the Arm of the Lord would be the arm of God used to administer that judgment.

The members of the Covenant, the Sword, and the Arm of the Lord, in accordance with Ellison's vision, expected the imminent collapse of America and ensuing war. In that war (Armageddon), they believed that Anglo-Saxons would be set against Jews, blacks, homosexuals, witches, Satanists, and foreign enemies. The settlement in Arkansas would become a Christian haven. In preparation for the difficult times ahead, the community stored food and stockpiled weapons and ammunition.

The community was largely self-supporting. A farm produced most of the food. Educational and medical services were provided internally, and most families lived without electricity or plumbing. Beginning in 1978, the group began to acquire sophisticated weaponry adequate for modern warfare. In 1981, it opened a survival school and gave training to the public in the use of firearms and survivalism.

In 1984, a grand jury was investigating the murder of an Arkansas state trooper. A gun found in the possession of the person accused of the murder was registered to James Ellison. Ellison was ordered to appear before the grand jury and a warrant was issued for his arrest when he failed to appear. In April 1985, FBI agents surrounded Zarephath-Horeb and arrested Ellison and several members on federal racketeering charges. Following the raid, the Covenant, the Sword and the Arm of the Lord disbanded. Subsequently, James Ellison was sentenced to twenty years for racketeering. Three other members received lesser terms (Barkun 1997).

If the above examples are typical of doomsday thinking, then clearly we live in dangerous times. The near approach of the year 2000 has led to widespread interest in the end of the world. While there have been many predictions over the last several centuries that the world is coming to an end, their number has dramatically increased as the end of the second millennium approaches.

To date, all predictions of the end of the world share one important characteristic: They have been wrong. Doomsday prophets have become objects of comic delight. The media, quite apart from the tabloids, have tended to treat news of new predictions as an opportunity for entertainment. In the process, the life and thought of apocalyptic groups is frequently distorted.

In more than one case reporters have deliberately falsified reports for the sake of creating a more sensational story. It should also be noted that, in sharp contrast to the many frightening images created by the media's marked tendency to give one-sided attention to sensational acts of apocalyptic violence, the great majority of religious groups preaching some sort of Armageddon as an integral part of their beliefs about the endtime are decidedly "safe sects." In point of fact, almost every religion in the larger Judeo-Christian-Islamic tradition has an apocalyptic theology, even the traditional peace churches that forbid members from participating in the military. Thus, contrary to the assertions of some contemporary critics, the possession of an apocalyptic theology should not, in itself, be grounds for alarm. This is because in most apocalyptic scenarios it is God and His angels who fight the final battle, not flesh-and-blood human beings. The human role is spiritual, and the "saved" fight a spiritual war, not a literal, physical war. An apocalyptic theology is only dangerous when individual followers believe they are going to be called upon to be foot soldiers in God's army.

Thus, upon closer examination, it turns out that apocalypticism is not a monolithic ideology. We can begin to understand the different varieties of endtime thinking by first learning a basic "doomsday vocabulary." The most general term in this arena of study is *eschatology* (from the Greek *eschaton-logos*), which refers to the study of the end of time—the end of the world as we know it. Eschatology involves the idea of redemption or salvation (*soteriology*), and is a part of the doctrine of most world religions. It can be subdivided into *individual eschatology*, which is concerned with the fate of individual souls or the judgment of the dead and their ultimate destination, and *cosmic eschatology*, which can be either restorative of the old, pure, primordial order, or utopian, in the sense of establishing a perfect system that never before existed.

In South Asian traditions, individual eschatology involves liberation of the soul from the endless cycle of deaths and rebirths that are experienced on the wheel of reincarnation. Hindu and Buddhist cosmic time, which is also cyclic, is divided in four primary ages called *yugas*. We are said to be living in the fourth of these ages (the Kali Yuga). The appearance of an Avatar or of a new Buddha will signal the end of the Kali Yuga and the beginning of a new cosmic cycle. Unlike the Judeo-Christian-Islamic complex of religions, South Asian religions view the *eschaton* (the end of the world as we know it) as a cyclical event which continues ad infinitum.

Zoroastrianism, the dualistic religion of Persia prior to the Islamic invasion, is one of the religions in which individual and cosmic eschatologies merge. The souls of the dead are provisionally assigned a state of bliss or suffering. Their final status is determined at the end of the world. Once the forces of light have completely overturned the forces of darkness, the resurrection of the dead will occur. This optimistic vision of the end of the world is an original contribution to the religious thought of the world, and all of the major Western religions–Judaism, Christianity, and Islam–adopted Zoroastrian eschatology.

Early Jewish eschatology as documented in the prophecies of the Hebrew scriptures (the Old Testament) aimed at the restoration of a golden age. Persian and Hellenistic ideas influenced Judaism during the first diasporas (the scattering of Jews into countries outside their homeland), leading to the development of a number of different messianic and/or apocalyptic ideas. These sometimes contradicted each other, and only in later centuries were they harmonized into a coherent system. The Messiah who is expected to come is a descendent of the House of David and/or a divine being referred to as the Son of Man. He represents the redeemer of a peaceful world, while the apocalypse envisions the annihilation of the present age.

Judaism influenced the eschatology of early Christianity, providing the notion of the Messiah as redeemer of a new age. The Messiah will replace the present age with the "kingdom of God" upon the day of judgment and the resurrection of the righteous. Throughout the centuries, various Christian movements have developed their own millenarian doctrines that anticipate the end of the world and the coming of a new golden age.

In the early development of Islam the notion of a final universal judgment and the end of the world (as a historical process) were important elements in the religious experience of Mohammed. In the later history of Islam, the messianic figure of the "Mahdi" (prophet) was introduced as a figure inaugurating the beginnings of a new age, especially in Shiite Islamic groups.*

Apocalypse, a Greek word for "revelation," originally referred to a literary genre in which mysterious revelations were given or explained by a supernatural figure such as an angel. Apocalyptic literature generally includes an account of an eschatological scenario that includes a final judgment of the living and the dead. Because apocalyptic literature invariably included an account of massive destruction—particularly in the form of Armageddon, the final battle between good and evil—the term "apocalypse" came to refer to complete destruction, as in the title of the popular movie *Apocalypse Now*.

The first work to be formally called an apocalypse was the Apocalypse of John, more familiarly known as the Book of Revelation, well-known for its plagues, wars, and other vehicles for violence and destruction. While the name comes from a Christian composition, the genre is much older, with Jewish apocalyptic literature appearing by at least the third century B.C.E.

Apocalypticism appears in every era and every culture, but has become a uniquely vital theme in American religious life, especially since the rise of the Millerite movement in the 1830s. The failure of William Miller's predictions regarding the end of the world in the 1840s led directly to the Bible Students Movement that was built around the predictions of Charles Taze Russell (1852–1916), which in turn was succeeded by the prophetic proclamation of the Jehovah's Witnesses. Within the emerging fundamentalist movement of the late nineteenth century, prophecy conferences provided hope for the eventual triumph of beleaguered evangelicals locked in a losing confrontation with modernists for control of American Protestant churches. As evangelicalism prospered in the twentieth century, it

---

*Those groups who believe that the leader of the Muslim community should be a biological descendant of Mohammed.

produced literally thousands of books advocating an expectancy of the near end of the world as we know it.

The terms "millenarianism" and "millennialism" are derived from Christian theology, and refer to the paradisiacal thousand-year period—the millennium—in which, according to the Book of Revelation, history and the world as we know it will terminate (it is sometimes conceived of as the re-establishment of the Garden of Eden). The expression "millenarian movement" is applied to groups of people who expect the imminent emergence of the millennium, and whose religious life is saturated by this expectation. Although the term originated in the Christian tradition, by extension other, non-Christian religious movements that are characterized by such an expectation can be referred to as millenarian or millennialist movements. Other terms for these types of groups are "crisis cults" and "messianic movements." Some researchers have argued that all religions with historically specifiable origins began as millenarian movements—movements which, after they became established, lost much or all of their millennial enthusiasm.

Norman Cohn, in his classic study, *The Pursuit of the Millennium*, outlined five traits that characterize the way in which millennialist movements picture salvation. According to Cohn, millenarian salvation is envisioned as

a. collective, in the sense that it is to be enjoyed by the faithful as a collectivity [i.e., community];
b. terrestrial, in the sense that it is to be realized on this earth and not in some otherworldly heaven;
c. imminent, in the sense that it is to come both soon and suddenly;
d. total, in the sense that it is utterly to transform life on earth, so that the new dispensation will be no mere improvement on the past, but perfection itself;
e. miraculous, in the sense that it is to be accomplished by, or with the help of, supernatural agencies. (Cohn 1957, p. 15)

Although formulated in the context of a study of Western millennialism, these characteristics have been found to be generally applicable to similar movements in other parts of the world.

Millenarian movements in the so-called Third World often,
though certainly not invariably, arise in situations of contact between
very different kinds of cultures, as when a Western nation intrudes
into a geographical area in which traditional peoples reside and disrupts the patterns of life such peoples are accustomed to following.
The response to this crisis is frequently a religious one in which the
disrupted culture attempts to apply traditional understandings to a
radically new contact situation. More often than not, this creative
response will be articulated by a single individual (a prophet or a
messiah) who receives a millenarian vision.

In some cases the vision will be a hostile one in which the community is counseled to resist the intruders and to adhere to the tradition of earlier generations (this subcategory is termed a "nativistic
movement"). In other cases the vision is a syncretistic response in
which elements of both cultures are wedded together to form a new
spiritual synthesis. Also, in some visions millenarians are advised to
wait patiently for redemptive, supernatural intervention, while in
others the community or group is encouraged to help bring about the
millennium by some type of action—often religious, but sometimes
political and/or military.

In the traditional Christian understanding of the millennium, the
dead are resurrected in new bodies. The living and the dead are
judged (either at the beginning or at the end of the millennium), with
evil people being either condemned to hell or snuffed out, depending
on one's interpretation of the Book of Revelation. Non-Christian millenarian movements often, though by no means always, include similar return-of-the-dead and final judgment themes in their end time
scenarios. In the Native American Ghost Dance religion, for example, the prophet Wovoka's millennial vision included a renewal of the
earth in which the spirits of the dead returned to earth. The millennium would be preceded by a general catastrophe (an apocalypse)
that would destroy Euro-Americans and their material culture.

Much apocalyptic thought is tied to the Christian New Testament idea of a millennium, the predicted period of a thousand years during which Satan would be chained and not allowed to pursue his evil work on earth. The arrival of the millennium has been a major theme in American Christian thought, and Christians have debated whether the millennium would be brought in by a sudden act of God in the near future (premillennialism), emerge gradually as society became more Christian (postmillennialism), or not be a literal historical period at all (amillennialism).

Within the metaphysical/New Age subculture, one finds a non-biblical form of apocalypticism, built around the theme of drastic upheavals in the earth that will supposedly occur around the year 2000. The most influential figure in this regard has been Edgar Cayce, a psychic who died in 1945, but whose readings were turned into a series of highly popular books by his son, Hugh Lynn Cayce. Followers of Cayce have even produced maps showing how the land-scape of the United States will be changed, with much of what is now California becoming sea bottom. To this basic view, the popular writer Ruth Montgomery (1983) has added the idea, supposedly revealed to her by her spirit guides, that these upheavals will occur because the north and south poles of the earth will shift in 1999. This apocalyptic scenario has become widely accepted within certain seg-ments of the New Age community.

The New Age movement, while often explicitly rejecting Chris-tianity, shares the millennialist emphasis of Christian thought. The movement hopes and expects that the world of the dominant culture will be swept aside and replaced with a golden era. At an earlier stage of the movement the millennium was referred to as the Aquarian Age, which is an astrological notion that the planet is entering a new cosmic cycle in which "higher vibration" energies are being focused on the earth, ushering in a new era of peace and understanding.

It is, of course, the millennial hope of the coming of a golden age of peace and light that gives the New Age movement its name. This millennialism also provides a basis for a social consciousness which has been notably lacking in prior occult-metaphysical thinking. Once articulated, the New Age vision has become grounded in various endeavors designed to assist the transition to the New Age, from environmentalism and lay peace movements to the women's rights movement and cooperative forms of social organization.

In whatever form it takes, millennialism's hopeful view of the future is undeniably attractive. This is especially the case for individuals not doing particularly well under current social conditions, and for whom an ordinary future appears to hold little chance for improvement. The increasingly difficult world and national conditions in which we find ourselves, in combination with the approach of the millennially significant year 2000, will only add to the appeal of millennialism for larger segments of the population in the immediate future. Because of the close association of apocalypticism with millennialism, this means that, for better or for worse, doomsday visions will also become increasingly appealing in the future.

The scope of millennialism/apocalypticism is so broad and so much has been written about this important topic that I have *not* attempted a comprehensive overview of the phenomenon in the following pages. Instead, I have chosen to focus on four widely divergent groups that, in different yet related ways, manifest the "doomsday-impulse": the Branch Davidians, The Family (aka the Children of God), Heaven's Gate, and a lesser known UFO group, the Association of Sananda and Sanat Kumara. The first two organizations adhere to a fairly orthodox version of biblical apocalypticism, while the latter two embrace a New Age, "earth-changes"–type doomsday. These contrasting apocalyptic strands represent the two major types of doomsday thinking one encounters in America today.

All four have a high opinion of themselves, in the sense that each envision their particular group as playing *the* central role in God's– or, for the last two groups, the Space Brothers'–endtime plan. All four have also been highly controversial, with the Branch Davidians and Heaven's Gate being headline news for extended periods of time in the wake of dramatic events involving the deaths of group members. Although the term "cult" is problematic because of its pejorative connotations, all four groups could properly be referred to as doomsday cults. The core chapters of the present book–chapters 4, 5, 6, and 7–deal with each of these four in turn.

The millennialist scholar Norman Cohn argued in his 1993 book,

Cosmos, Chaos and the World to Come, that apocalypticism in the proper sense—by which he means a final, definitive end to linear history as opposed to a cyclic destruction and recreation of the world—is the specific creation of Zoroastrianism. From this relatively small world faith in ancient Persia, Zoroastrian eschatology spread first to the Jews, and then from Judaism to Christianity and Islam. While Cohn's argument seems basically valid, at the same time I feel that he has overemphasized the dissimilarities between linear and cyclical doomsdays. Both are variations on the mythological theme referred to as "Universal Cataclysm" in folklore references—a theme which also encompasses narratives about *past* destructions of the world, such as the Noah story and other universal flood myths.

Another question that emerges from further reflection upon Cohn's discussion is the issue of millenarian movements which arise out of cultures that have had minimal contact with the ideology of the Judeo-Christian-Islamic complex. Some scholars have argued that all cultures giving birth to such movements have had at least some exposure to the Western religious tradition. But, while this exposure might help to explain the *origin* of an apocalyptic vision, it does little to explain the widespread *appeal* of millenarian movements. In other words, if doomsday religiosity is really alien to the religious traditions of a given society, then why are members of that society immediately attracted to a strange and unfamiliar ideology? The responsiveness of the human imagination to doomsday prophecies indicates that there is something universally appealing about millennialist spirituality—something that transcends particular historical formulations such as Zoroastrianism's apocalyptic scenario. This issue and the question of the parallels between apocalypticism and other variations on the theme of universal cataclysm will be discussed in chapters 2 and 3. The final chapter and the epilogue examine the associated phenomenon of opposition to doomsday movements.

2

UNIVERSAL CATACLYSMS AND THE BIRTH OF APOCALYPTIC

HINDUISM—CYCLES OF DESTRUCTION

The atomic age began with the detonation of the first atomic bomb on July 16, 1945, at Los Alamos, New Mexico. When this bomb exploded, two lines from the Bhagavad Gita (11:32) flashed through the mind of Robert Oppenheimer, director of the Los Alamos project, according to his later writings:

> I am become death, the shatterer of worlds;
> Waiting the hour that ripens to their doom.

The corpus of Hindu scriptures of which the Bhagavad Gita is a part constitute a complex, multilayered body of literature that is difficult to describe or characterize in a short space. The oldest layers of this tradition go back thousands of years before the Christian era. The Bhagavad Gita (the "Lord's Song"), one of the more significant and popular of Hindu texts, is a short work that Western scholars speculate was inserted into the Mahabharata, the world's longest epic, sometime between 200 B.C.E. and 200 C.E. The Bhagavad Gita contains a number of evocative passages on the subject of the destructive, apocalyptic side of the divine nature.

The central narrative of the Mahabharata is about a civil war and the events surrounding the culminating battle in an ancient Indian kingdom. Before the great battle begins, Arjuna, the chief protagonist, asks his chariot driver, Krishna, to drive his chariot out between the two armies. Krishna is a complex figure, whom many Hindus regard as the supreme deity himself. The text of the Bhagavad Gita contains a conversation between Arjuna and Krishna that was supposed to have taken place on this battlefield before the fighting broke out.

From his vantage point on the field between the two armies, Arjuna sees all of his closest friends and relatives in both armies, and loses the willingness to fight:

> Arjuna saw in both armies fathers, grandfathers, sons, grandsons; fathers of wives, uncles, masters; brothers, companions and friends. When Arjuna thus saw his kinsmen face to face in both lines of battle, he was overcome by grief and despair. (1:26–28)

He realizes that many of the people dearest to him are about to lay down their lives. After unburdening his heart to Krishna about these matters, Arjuna firmly asserts, "I will not fight."

Krishna smiles, and then responds to his friend with an extended discourse on the nature of life, death, and ultimate reality. With respect to the soul and death, Krishna reminds Arjuna of certain "truths" of classical Hinduism: The real human being, as opposed to our false sense of self, is the soul, not the body. The soul, which reincarnates in different, successive bodies, is eternal and basically changeless. Because we are all eternal souls, who can ever really "die"? And for that matter, who can ever really "kill"?

Krishna also reminds Arjuna that, as someone born into the warrior class, it is his duty to fight, particularly in a righteous war such as this one. Arjuna is encouraged to perform this worldly duty without attachment, keeping his mind fixed on eternal rather than on earthly matters. Krishna notes that, in his own role as God, he performs his duty of maintaining the universe with an attitude of detachment—a model attitude that Arjuna should emulate. If Arjuna can adhere to the eternal perspective, acting only as his social duty dictates, then he can kill without sin.

Krishna further asserts that, as the supreme deity of the universe, he is about to take the lives of Arjuna's enemies anyway. Thus if Arjuna takes up the fight, he will merely be the instrument of God's will. It is in the context of this conversation that, at Arjuna's request, Krishna reveals his divine form—a form that includes the frightening aspect of the divinity which destroys the world at the end of time:

> When I see thy vast form, reaching the sky, burning with many colours, with wide open mouths, with vast flaming eyes, my heart shakes in terror: my power is gone and gone is my peace, O Vishnu [Krishna]! Like the fire at the end of Time which burns all in the last day, I see thy vast mouths and thy terrible teeth. . . . The flames of thy mouths devour all the worlds. Thy glory fills the whole universe. But how terrible thy splendours burn! . . . Who art thou in this form of terror? (11:23–31)

Krishna replies that he is all-powerful time which consumes all things, and that he is about to manifest this aspect of his nature in the midst of the upcoming battle. After these and many other philosophical points have been made, Arjuna agrees to engage in battle.

More than in any other tradition, the Hindu apocalypse is muted and relativized within a never-ending cycle in which the cosmos is periodically destroyed and recreated. Furthermore, these macrocosmic cycles are reflected in the microcosmic life of the individual in the form of reincarnation. A complex tradition with ancient roots, Hinduism has more than one myth of universal destruction. This is partially the result of Hinduism's diversity.

To be considered within the Hindu fold, one must nominally acknowledge the authority of the four Vedas. These are ancient religious texts that express concepts and values bearing little resemblance to current Hinduism, much as the first five books of the Hebrew scriptures express a religious ideology at variance, on many points, from that of current Judaism and Christianity. Indian religions that reject the authority of the Vedas–particularly Jainism, Buddhism, and Sikhism–are regarded as non-Hindu. However, what is left over even after these other religions are subtracted is a broad diversity of beliefs and practices that, at their extremes, bear little resemblance to one another. A naked ascetic tormenting his body is as much a Hindu as the villager abandoning himself to the wildness of the Holi festival or the office worker engaged in quiet meditation in a suburban home.

One characteristic contributing to Hinduism's diversity is that earlier strands of spiritual expression tend to be retained rather than discarded as new religious forms emerge. Thus in the wake of a devotional reform movement,* for example, certain segments of the population might be persuaded to abandon older practices and ideas in favor of something new, but other members of the community will continue in the old ways. As a result of this trait, ideas and practices that are very ancient–sometimes thousands of years old–are still practiced by at least some contemporary Hindus.

The reader may recall from her or his early education the notion that humanity made the transition from tribal lifestyles to the more complex forms of social organization we call "civilization" along four great river basins–in China, India, Egypt, and what is today Iraq. A civilization that thousands of years ago existed along the Indus River in western India left ruins of sophisticated cities. One of the bodies of ruins was uncovered near Harappa; hence this civilization is sometimes referred to as the "Harappan" civilization. Because their written records were apparently composed on perishable materials, we know very little about them or their religious beliefs. Scholars have, however, surmised that some of the basic beliefs of classical Hinduism, such as the doctrines of reincarnation and karma, are probably Harappan in origin.

One of the reasons we know so little about the Harappans is that around 1500 B.C.E. (some Indian scholars say much earlier) a group of aggressive pastoral peoples from central Asia invaded India

---

*Particularly during the Indian "middle ages," Hinduism experienced wave after wave of devotional movements that encouraged Hindus to abandon empty ritualism in favor of religious activities that allowed one to directly express one's love of the divinity.

through the northern mountain passes, conquered the Harappans, and destroyed whatever records might have remained from the original civilization. These peoples, who called themselves Aryans ("Nobles"), originated from around the Caspian Sea. For unknown reasons, during the several millennia before the common era, groups of Aryans took off in every direction, subjugating indigenous peoples in every area of the world from India to Ireland (the words "Iran," "Ireland," and "Aryan" all derive from the same root). The Indo-European family of languages is one of the legacies of this expansion.

The worldview of the Aryan invaders of India was partially preserved in the Vedas. By the time of the Indian classical period (at least a millennium after the initial invasion), the leading gods of the Vedas (e.g., Indra and Varuna) had been demoted to demi-gods, and their status as chief divinities supplanted by non-Vedic deities such as Vishnu and Shiva. It has been hypothesized that this mythological transformation was one phase of the victory of the religious ideology of the indigenous peoples over the religious sensitivity of the Aryan invaders.

Another aspect of this influence may be reflected in the otherworldly orientation of later Hinduism. The religious vision of the Vedas, in sharp contrast to classical Hinduism, had focused very much on this world. The gods were ritually invoked to improve one's situation in this life, so that priests became something approaching magicians. After settling down in the Indian subcontinent, the Aryans became more introspective, started asking questions about the ultimate meaning of life, and developed an ideology centered around release or liberation (*moksha*) from the cycle of death and rebirth (*samsara*). The various disciplines that are collectively referred to as *yoga* developed out of this introspective turn. Because some of the artifacts that survive from the Harappan period appear to be human beings in yogic meditation poses, it seems likely that the Aryans picked up these practices from the indigenous peoples.

To understand the worldview of classical Hinduism it is necessary to understand that the process of reincarnation was viewed negatively, as a cycle that kept the individual soul bound to an endless cycle of suffering. Unlike many Western treatments of reincarnation, which make the idea of coming back into body after body seem exotic, desirable, and even romantic, Hinduism, Buddhism and other South Asian religions portray the samsaric process as unhappy: Life in this world is suffering. Hence, liberation from this process represents the supreme goal of human strivings. Reflecting the diversity of Hinduism, liberation can be attained in a variety of different ways, from the proper performance of certain rituals to highly disciplined forms of yoga.

Reflecting the individual samsaric process, the cosmos itself undergoes periodic dissolutions and recreations. As recorded in the Puranas, the principal mythological texts of classical Hinduism, these macrocosmic cycles take place across vast expanses of time—a spectacle of eternity that seems aimed more at boggling the mind than anything else. The basic building blocks of the Hindu temporal schema are the four yugas—Krita, Treta, Dvapara, and Kali—which roughly correspond with the four ages of the classical Greco-Roman world—the ages of Gold, Silver, Brass, and Iron. Like the Mediterranean ages, the series of Hindu ages reflects a successive degeneration in the moral order.

One complete cycle of four yugas, referred to as a *mahayuga*, is 4,320,000 human years in duration. One thousand mahayugas, in turn, constitute a *kalpa* of 4,320,000,000 human years. The end of each kalpa—also referred to as a day of Brahma—culminates in the dissolution of the cosmos and its return to a state of chaos. This state, referred to as *pralaya*, is symbolically represented by the image of a primordial ocean. Pralaya—the night of Brahma during which the creator is said to "sleep"—lasts as long as a day of Brahma, or another 4,320,000,000 years. At the end of this "night," the cosmos is recreated. Lesser dissolutions occur at the end of every mahayuga.

The dissolution of the cosmos into pralaya is not to be confused with the deluge and the accompanying universal flood which occurs fourteen times each kalpa at the end of temporal periods called *manvantaras*, or "Manu-intervals." The events of each kalpa recur exactly during each day of Brahma. Each Brahma, in turn, lives one hundred years consisting of 360 "days of Brahma" each—very long-lived indeed! Furthermore, successions of different Brahmas become the building blocks for even longer time periods. Scholars such as the late Heinrich Zimmer (1946) have speculated that at least part of the purpose behind delineating such incomprehensibly long cycles is to relativize ordinary human existence, overwhelming the mind with the insignificance of our everyday concerns. In other words, reflecting upon the brevity and transitoriness of life helps one renounce the world and motivates one to seek liberation from the cycle of death and rebirth.

While there are variations in detail from text to text, the endtime events outlined in the *Puranas* are remarkably consistent, and the basic puranic scenario has persisted in contemporary Hindu accounts of the eschaton. The agent of destruction is Shiva or Vishnu in the form of Shiva. In the classical formulation, Brahma, Vishnu, and Shiva constitute a kind of trinity, with Brahma creating the world, Vishnu maintaining the world, and Shiva destroying the world.

At the close of a day of Brahma, the three worlds (heaven, earth, and hell) are first dried out by a scorching sun. This drought is so severe that even the waters of the netherworld are dried out. When everything is so dried out that the earth is parched and cracked, a terrible wind blows through the worlds, drawing the life-breath out of all creatures.

This wind is followed by a universal fire that consumes all of the worlds in a frightful tornado of flame. The source attributed to this fire varies, but of particular importance is the widespread image of a mare with flames issuing out of her mouth (an image that may ultimately be derived from the ancient vedic rite of horse sacrifice) as the source of this doomsday fire. In a well-known mythological episode, Shiva, in a moment of anger, slew Kama, god of desire, with a fiery blast from his third eye. Once set in motion, however, this fire could not be stopped, and threatened to destroy the three worlds before the appointed time of the apocalypse. Brahman therefore transformed the fire into a fire-breathing mare. The mare's fire, which is inextinguishable, is held in check until the endtime by her residence at the bottom of the ocean.

While consuming the three worlds of Hindu cosmology, first with fire and then with water, Shiva dances the Tandava dance in his familiar form as Nataraja, "Lord of the Dance." In the words of the Kurma Purana,

When all the gods are consumed by fire, the mountain-born goddess Parvati [Shiva's consort] stands alone [and] the supreme lord looks at the goddess as he dances the Tandava dance. This goddess of supernal felicity in turn drinks in the nectar of the dance of her husband while she herself, abiding in Yoga, enters the body of the trident-wielding god. Quitting his Tandava dance as he pleases, the blessed Pinaka-bearer [Shiva] whose nature is light burns up the orb of the egg of Brahma [i.e., the manifested cosmos]. Then, while the gods Brahma, Vishnu, and the Pinaka-bearer alone remain, the earth, with all her properties, dissolves into the waters.

Finally, the air fills with great clouds that rain down a ferocious deluge until the world perishes in watery darkness. To cite Zimmer's evocative description from his classic *Myths and Symbols in Indian Art and Civilization,*

The ultimate elements melt into the undifferentiated fluid out of which they once arose. The moon, the stars, dissolve. The mounting tide becomes a limitless sheet of water. This is the interval of a night of Brahma.

The universe is reabsorbed into the ultimate divinity (Vishnu in the puranic texts), who withdraws into inactivity. The deity's static state is traditionally symbolized by the image of Vishnu asleep on the coils of a giant serpent, who floats like a raft on the surface of the primordial waters. At the beginning of the next "day," Brahma then emerges from a lotus flower that sprouts from Vishnu's navel and recreates the cosmos.

MESOPOTAMIA – DESTRUCTION IN THE PAST TENSE

With the first light of dawn a black cloud came from the horizon; it thundered within where Adad, lord of the storm was riding. In front over hill and plain Shullat and Hanish, heralds of the storm, led on. Then the gods of the abyss rose up; Nergal pulled out the dams of the nether waters, Ninurta the war-lord threw down the dykes, and the seven judges of hell, the Annunaki, raised their torches, lighting the land with their livid flame.

This passage from the *Epic of Gilgamesh* is perhaps the most vivid description of the end of the world found in Mesopotamian literature. Unlike more familiar forms of apocalyptic literature, however, the *Epic of Gilgamesh* places this pivotal event in the past rather than the future. And there are other Mesopotamian stories of the mythological past built around the theme of apocalyptic destructiveness.

In common with most traditional religious systems, the Mesopotamians populated the cosmos with an expansive pantheon (some sources say several thousand) of gods and goddesses. Some of these were distinguished as the patron deities of particular city-states, so that the importance of various gods tended to vary in different time periods according to the relative strength of their respective city. Thus Marduk, patron of Babylon, rose from the status of a rather obscure divinity to become king of the gods with the rise of Babylon's political fortunes.

Like the gods of the Greek and Roman pantheons, Mesopotamian divinities were pictured as human beings "drawn large." The gods were, in other words, not much more than strong humans, possessing magical powers and immortality. Humanity, for its part, was created out of clay to serve the gods. Unlike Judaism, Christianity, or Islam, this creation did not include the fashioning of an immortal soul. Hence the afterlife was conceived of as a pale shadow of earthly life, much like the Jewish Sheol or the Greek Hades.

Mesopotamians, like many of the other traditional peoples of the world, imagined the universe as a three-tiered cosmos of heaven, earth, and underworld. Heaven was reserved for deities, most of whom resided there. Living human beings occupied the middle world. The spirits of the dead resided beneath the earth. Gilgamesh, legendary king of Uruk, is unhappy with this state of affairs, and the *Epic of Gilgamesh* tells of story of his quest for immortality.

The first part of the epic relates the events leading up to Gilgamesh's meeting with a wild man, Enkidu, their friendship, and, later, Enkidu's death. Gilgamesh is distraught by the death of his best friend, and begins to consider his own mortality. He has heard that the mortal man Utnapishtim, the Mesopotamian Noah, was granted immortality by the gods. To discover how Utnapishtim obtained such a favor, Gilgamesh undertakes an arduous journey. When he finally arrives, Utnapishtim relates how the gods, in a fit of anger, destroyed all of humankind.

According to Utnapishtim, in the period of time leading up to the great flood, "the people multiplied, and the world bellowed like a wild bull." The great god Enlil, aroused by the clamor, said to the gods in council: "The uproar of humankind is intolerable and sleep is no longer possible because of the ceaseless babel!" So the gods agreed to exterminate humanity. Only the wise divinity Ea had the foresight to warn Utnapishtim, who built a great boat in which he and his family survived. As for the gods, they managed to frighten themselves with their own apocalyptic violence. To continue the account of the end of world from above:

> A stupor of despair went up to heaven when the god of the storm turned daylight to darkness, when he smashed the land like a cup. One whole day the tempest raged, gathering fury as it went, it poured over the people like the tides of babel; a man could not see his brother nor the people be seen from heaven. Even the gods were terrified at the flood, they fled to the highest heaven, the firmament of Anu; they crouched against the walls, cowering like curs. (Sandars 1960, p. 110)

Almost immediately after destroying the human race, the gods realized the error of their ways: Human beings "feed" the gods and, without humanity, celestial beings will starve. Ea then revealed to his fellow divinities that Utnapishtim has survived. After the flood subsides, this remaining mortal and his wife make the appropriate offerings and the gods are able to eat. Out of gratitude, the gods grant them immortality.

As for Gilgamesh, Utnapishtim requires that, as a test to determine his worthiness for immortality, he stay awake for a week. Gilgamesh promptly fails the test and, instead, sleeps for a week. Good host that he is, however, Utnapishtim gives Gilgamesh a "consolation prize," namely a plant with the powers of rejuvenation (the next best thing to immortality). Unfortunately, on the journey back a snake eats the plant, so that Gilgamesh arrives home empty-handed. Although his quest has been a failure, Gilgamesh is able to return to Uruk, seems content to assume his place as a mortal man. The lesson seems to be that death is part of the natural order, and humanity must, as a consequence, accept death as part of life and enjoy this life as best one can.

A number of Mesopotamian myths develop the connection between life and death in such a way that we can perceive the "logic" behind universal destructiveness: To renew the world, the old world must be destroyed. Simultaneously, the myths seem to teach that the forces of death must not claim so much of the realm of life that the spark of life is crushed completely. The principal myths surrounding the underworld make both of these points.

The chief deity of the Mesopotamian underworld was the goddess Ereshkigal. While she could be harsh, Ereshkigal was not a devil or Satan figure. The dead stood before her and she pronounced their death sentence. Simultaneously, their names were entered in the ranks of the dead by the scribe Geshtinana. Rather than enjoying her job, the queen of the underworld was portrayed as saddened by the fate of many of her subjects: "I weep for young men forced to abandon sweethearts. I weep for girls wrenched from their lovers' laps. For the infant child I weep, expelled before its time."

One of the more widespread Mesopotamian stories involves the descent of the goddess Ishtar to the underworld. The first version of this tale was recorded by the Sumerians, whose name for Ishtar was Inanna. The second version was a later, Akkadian text. In all periods of Mesopotamian history, Ishtar is the most important goddess, the parallel of the Mediterranean Aphrodite/Venus. Precisely why Ishtar should have undertaken such a perilous journey is obscure. Some interpreters have speculated that Ishtar wished to usurp her sister (Ereshkigal) and extend her rule to the underworld; others that she simply wished to visit her sister.

Before embarking, she has the wisdom to inform her chief minister that she is about to undertake a journey to the underworld, and instructs him to appeal to the gods in heaven to intervene should it become necessary to retrieve her from her sister's realm. As it turns out, Ishtar is unable to return. Because Inanna/Ishtar is the goddess of sex and therefore the goddess of fertility, her absence from the earth is immediately noticed: "No bull mounted a cow, no donkey impregnated a jenny. No young man impregnated a girl. The young man slept in his private room. The girl slept in the company of her friends." In order to reactivate the natural forces of life and reproduction, the gods in heaven are forced to come to Inanna/Ishtar's aid.

The ancient Mesopotamians also told several variants of another, more upbeat, story of descent to the underworld, the tale of Nergal and Ereshkigal. In this story Nergal, as a consequence of an affront to Ereshkigal's vizier, is required to appear in the queen of the underworld's court to offer an apology. Ereshkigal finds herself attracted to this upper-world god, and attempts to seduce him by allowing Nergal, the Mesopotamian Mars, to see her undress for a bath. He resists her charms at first, but gives in on her second try. After a full week of love-making, Nergal steals away before dawn. When she hears that he has abandoned her, Ereshkigal falls to the ground and cries. She then sends her vizier to heaven, demanding that Nergal be returned to her:

> Ever since I was a child, I have not known the companionship of other girls. I have not known the romping of children. As mistress of the dead, I am not pure enough to take my rightful place among the other great gods. I have dwelt alone in sadness, but the god whom you sent to me has opened my heart to love. Return him to me! Return him to me or I shall raise up the dead, and they will eat the living, until the dead outnumber the living! (Dalley, p. 173)

This threat to upset the balance between the living and the dead would result in an intolerable situation that, like Ishtar's disappearance from the land of the living, would eventually destroy everything, including the gods. It is thus a threat to which the celestial divinities must respond.

In one version of this myth, Ereshkigal threatens to kill Nergal. Nergal responds by invading the underworld, assaulting its queen, and forcing her to marry him. In other versions, however, Nergal returns for a happy reunion: "Laughing joyously, he entered her wide courtyard and approached her. He pulled her from the throne, and began to stoke her tresses. The two embraced, and went passionately to bed" (Dalley, p. 176).

Subsequently, Nergal becomes Ereshkigal's consort. Yet another myth recounts what happens when Nergal tarries so long in his wife's bed that he neglects to perform his function as god of war and killing. This story begins with an image of Nergal (who in this story is referred to by his Akkadian name of Irra or Erra–"scorched earth") lying awake in bed beside his wife, experiencing a rather restless night. At length, the silence of the nuptial chamber is disturbed by the voice of his weapon, Sibittu. Sibittu calls Nergal to embark on a campaign of war, citing the general decline of the world as evidence that the equilibrium of things has been disturbed: Lions and wolves, no longer hunted by Nergal, attack the cattle and carry them away. The shepherds, though watchful, are powerless to stop them. Other creatures invade the fields and carry away the grain. Most importantly, by failing to exercise his function as god of war and death, the population of men and animals has multiplied to the point where the earth groans from the weight of them. The increased population has also made the earth so noisy that the celestial gods cannot get any peace.

Recognizing the truth of Sibittu's observations, Nergal resolves to embark on a campaign of violence, but it is an unusual kind of conflict in which the normal order of things is inverted: "He who knew nothing of weapons drew his dagger. He who knew nothing of projectiles drew back the arrow in his bow. He who knew nothing of war engaged in hand-to-hand conflict. He who did not know how to run flew like a bird. The weak defeated the strong. The cripple outstripped the swift" (Dalley, p. 303).

It is a world turned upside down, in which even sunlight has turned to shadow. After the task of destruction is complete, the cosmos is reborn as a fresh creation. The various inversions in the story, only a few of which are cited above, exemplify the renewal symbolism of reversal that one finds worldwide in the myths and rituals of many traditional societies. The "logic" of such myth/rituals is that the old must be destroyed before the new can grow, and if the old is not periodically obliterated, then the cosmos will decay and run down.

ZOROASTRIANISM: EARLY THINKING ABOUT THE FINAL END

Zoroastrianism was the first religion in the historical record to trade in the mytho-"logic" of periodic destruction and recreation for one big blast at the end of time and the establishment of an eternal paradise. Zoroastrianism was founded in Persia (Iran) by Zarathustra (Greek: Zoroaster) in the sixth century B.C.E. (though some sources say much earlier). Once the state religion of Persia, Zoroastrianism was supplanted by Islam in the seventh century C.E., so that today the majority of surviving Zoroastrians live in India where they are known as Parsis (Persians). Zoroastrianism is, as was indicated in the introduction, the ultimate source for the apocalyptic eschatologies of Judaism, Christianity, and Islam.

The religion of Zoroaster is best known for its dualism. The god of light and the upper world, Ohrmazd or Ahura Mazda ("wise lord") and his angels, are locked in a cosmic struggle with the god of darkness and the lower world, Angra Mainyu or Ahriman ("evil spirit") and his demons. Unlike Christianity, in which the outcome of the war between god and the devil has already been decided, Zoroastrianism portrays the struggle as more or less evenly matched. Individual human beings are urged to align themselves with the forces of light, and are judged according to the predominance of their good or evil deeds.

Zoroaster is remembered as an innovator and reformer, and is often compared to the Hebrew prophets. Like the prophets of Israel, he preached the rejection of ancient practices he regarded as barbaric in favor of an ethical monotheism. Under Cyrus the Great, the Persians conquered the Babylonians in 539 B.C.E. and, under an essentially friendly rule that extended approximately two centuries, restored the Jews to Palestine. Zoroastrianism exercised a powerful influence over Judaism–and, through Judaism, a decisive influence on Christianity and Islam–introducing such ideas as a powerful evil god (the devil) who is locked in conflict with the good god, a final judgment, an apocalypse, hell, and the resurrection of the dead.

One of Zoroastrianism's more compelling images involves the soul's crossing of a bridge following death. According to Zoroastrian belief, for three days after death the soul remains at the head of its former body. All of the individual's good and bad deeds are entered in a sort of accountant's ledger, recording evil actions as debits and good actions as credits. The soul then embarks on a journey to judgment, walking out onto the Chinvat ("accountant's") Bridge. In the middle of the bridge, according to the Pahlevi text the *Bundahishn* (Pahlevi is the ancient language of Persia),

> There is a sharp edge which stands like a sword; and Hell is below the Bridge. Then the soul is carried to where stands a sword. If the soul is righteous, the sword presents its broad side. If the soul be wicked, that sword continues to stand edgewise, and does not give passage. With three steps which the soul takes forward–which are the evil thoughts, words, and deeds that it has performed–it is cut down from the head of the Bridge, and falls headlong to Hell. (Cited in Pavry, pp. 92–93)

If, when weighing bad against good deeds, debits outweigh credits, "even if the difference is only three tiny acts of wrongdoing," the sinner falls off the bridge and into hell. Hell is a dismal realm of torment, where the damned can consume only the foulest food for nourishment. If debits and credits cancel each other out, the soul is placed in Hammistagan ("region of the mixed"), a limbo realm in which souls are neither happy nor sorrowful and in which they will abide until the final apocalypse. In later texts, a person's deeds greet him on the bridge in personified form–a beautiful maiden for a good person; an ugly hag for a bad person–who either leads the soul to paradise ("the luminous mansions of the sky") or embraces the soul and falls into hell, according to whether the person has been good or evil.

After the final battle between good and evil, there will be a general judgment in which everyone will be put through an ordeal of fire (a river of molten metal), in which good individuals will have their dross burned away and evil people will be consumed. Thus the souls of the damned will trade their ongoing torment in hell for a painful annihilation. The souls of the blessed, on the other hand, will be resurrected in physical bodies, which Ahura Mazda will make both immortal and eternally youthful. In a later modification of tradition, both good and evil souls have their dross burned away, so that everyone shares the post-resurrection paradise.

Resurrection (from Latin *re-surgere*, to rise again) is a religious notion that implies the resurgence or revival to life of the body of the dead. In polytheistic religions, resurrection is experienced only by certain gods, often linked to fertility and to the seasonal cycle of the death and rebirth of nature. In the Canaanite religion, Aliyan Baal, god of fertility, is killed by his enemy Mot ("death"), but returns to life upon the intervention of his sister Anat. Similarly, in ancient Egypt the god Osiris, whose body had been killed and dismembered by his brother Set, is brought back to life by his wife, the goddess Isis.

The concept of resurrection as formulated in Zoroastrianism represents one of the earliest efforts to conceive of immortality. It is part of an optimistic vision of the end of the world, in which the forces of light overcome darkness and all humankind rejoices with the renewal of creation. An entire section of the *Avesta* (Zoroastrian scripture) explains how the body is returned to the soul upon the moment of reunion and resurrection.

The final great transformation, called the "making wonderful," is described by Norman Cohn in *Cosmos, Chaos and the World to Come* in the following way:

> The earth will be flattened by the fiery flood, so that its surface will
> be a single level plain: the snow-covered mountains of Iran–first
> thrown up as a result of Angra Mainyu's onslaught–will be no
> more. In this perfect environment the surviving human beings will

live in the most perfect harmony with one another. Husbands and wives and children, including of course the resurrected dead, will be re-united and will live together as they do in this present world–except that there will be no more begetting of children. All mankind will form a single community of devout Zoroastrians, all united in adoration of Ahura Mazda and the Holy Immortals, and all at one in thought, word, and deed. (Cohn 1993, pp. 98–99)

Many of the components of this vision of the endtimes–a final battle between good and evil, judgment of the wicked, resurrection of the dead, etc.–were adopted by Jewish apocalyptic thinkers. From texts composed by these apocalypticists, such notions were adopted into Christianity and Islam.

Zoroastrianism also influenced Christianity through Manicheism, a religious movement that arose in the third century and spread across the Mediterranean world. Founded by Mani (a Persian born into a Christian and Jewish community in Assyria in 215 C.E.), Manicheism was a mixture of Zoroastrianism, Christianity, and other Hellenistic religious movements that spread across the Western world and lasted for the better part of a thousand years. Its central teaching was a severe dualism between spirit and matter, soul and body. St. Augustine, the most influential of the church fathers, converted to Christianity from Manicheism, and some have said that Christianity's antagonism toward the flesh was influenced by Augustine's former religion. While this movement died out during the Western Middle Ages, the term "Manicheism" continued to be used to refer to any sect or teaching that seemed to overemphasize the struggle between good and evil, particularly teachings that make the god of darkness appear as strong or almost as strong as the god of light.

Many contemporary sects and new religions, especially those in the larger Judeo-Christian-Islamic tradition, place particular emphasis on the end times and on the eternal fate of the individual. From a historical perspective, the ultimate source of these notions is Zoroastrianism. Many contemporary new religions also place particular emphasis on the conflict between good and evil in a way that could be called Manichean. Thus, while Zoroastrianism has little, if any, direct influence on contemporary new religions, its indirect influence is vast.

JUDAISM, JUSTICE, AND THE RESURRECTION

Zoroaster's central ideas about the end of time were later adopted by the Jews at least partially because the notion of the resurrection enabled Jewish thinkers to preserve God's justice, insuring that he could fulfill the promises he had made in his covenant with Israel. To understand how this came about, it is first necessary to understand the covenant. At the core of Judaism is a covenant relationship–which is both a contractual agreement and a "marriage" of love–between Yahweh and his chosen people. Because Judaism is built around a relationship involving agreements and promises in *this* life, the afterlife is less essential for Judaism than for other world religions. It would, in fact, be relatively easy to imagine Judaism *without any afterlife beliefs whatsoever*. In marked contrast, the promise of a post-mortem paradise lies at the very core of the believer's religious life in traditions like Christianity and Islam, so that to delete afterlife beliefs would be to delete an ingredient essential to these faiths. Because of the noncentrality of the afterlife for Judaism, this tradition has been able to entertain a wide variety of different afterlife notions through-out its history, more so than perhaps any other religion.

The ancient Hebrews emphasized the importance of the present life over the afterlife. Like both the ancient Greeks and Mesopo-tamians, the afterlife, when it was mentioned at all, was conceived of as a pale shadow of earthly life, much like the Greek Hades. Also like the Greeks, the Hebrews made no distinction between the treatment of the just and the unjust after death. Instead, rewards and punish-ments were meted out in the present life, and in the covenant "con-tract" Yahweh promised to do just that.

The ancient Hebrews, like many of the other traditional peoples of the world, imagined the universe as a three-tiered cosmos of heaven, earth, and underworld. Heaven was reserved for God and the angels. Living human beings occupied the middle world. The spirits of the dead resided beneath the earth in Sheol. As in other cultures, the conceptualization of the realm of the dead as being located beneath the earth's surface probably derives from the custom of burying the dead underground. Again similar to the Mesopotamian underworld, Sheol was not much more than a gloomy pit where the spirits of the dead exist as dim reflections of their earthly selves.

With the exception of the comparatively late apocalyptic book of Daniel, the only stories in Hebrew scriptures (the Old Testament) that refer to afterlife notions are the story of Elijah's bodily ascent to heaven, which was not taken to indicate that all righteous human beings would eventually reside in the sky, and the story of the so-called Witch of Endor. King Saul had banished, under threat of death, "all who trafficked with ghosts and spirits" (1 Sam. 28:3). However, faced with a superior army and feeling himself in a desperate situation, Saul, in disguise, consults a woman whom we would today refer to as a medium. This woman, who lived at Endor, summoned the spirit of the prophet Samuel from Sheol, the Hebrew equivalent of Hades. When he arrived, he asked Saul, "Why have you disturbed me and brought me up?" (1 Sam. 28:15) By making a directional reference ("brought me *up*"), the clear implication is that Sheol is underneath the surface of the earth.

Samuel told Saul that he should never have turned away from God, that he was on the verge of defeat, and, furthermore, that "tomorrow you and your sons will be with me" (1 Sam. 28:19). In other words, tomorrow they would be dead. By asserting that Saul's soul will soon be residing in the same resting place as Samuel's, the clear implication is that moral distinctions do not influence one's afterlife fate–the spirits of the good (Samuel) and the spirits of morally bad people (Saul) both end up in the same place, presumably under much the same conditions.

While this is the general view of the ancient Hebrews, reflection on the inequalities of this life and on the apparent failure of Yahweh to make good on his covenant promises led serious religious thinkers to consider the option of resurrection. The resurrection of ordinary human beings originated, as we have seen, in Zoroastrianism. As a result of several centuries of Persian control of the Middle East, Jews were brought into contact with Zoroastrian religious ideas and the notion of resurrection. Zoroaster had combined resurrection with the idea of a final judgment, in which the entire human race was resurrected and individuals were rewarded or punished. This clearly appealed to Jewish religious thinkers of the time as an adequate way of coming to grips with the injustices that were so apparent in this life, and was incorporated into such late books as the Book of Daniel.

The Book of Daniel was composed around 165 B.C.E., when Judaism was suffering the first major, specifically religious persecution in its history. The Seleucid ruler Antiochus IV, descendant of one of Alexander the Great's generals, attempted to impose Hellenistic (Greek) culture on his subjects in an effort to unify his realm. While Hellenizing measures had been imposed for many years, it was not until 167 B.C.E. that the practice of Judaism was actually forbidden. Outlawed practices included temple sacrifices, circumcision, sabbath observance, kosher restrictions, and possession of sacred books. Jews were even forced to eat foods that the Torah classified as impure and to sacrifice at Greek altars that were set up across the country. The death penalty was imposed upon those who refused to comply with any of these requirements. The final insult occurred in December of the same year when a pig was sacrificed on an altar erected to Zeus in the Jewish temple. A successful revolt, led by the Maccabees, soon followed and the event is celebrated by the holiday of Hanukkah. The Book of Daniel, which addresses these circumstances, incorporated a notion of resurrection into its apocalyptic, final scenario in the following words:

> Many of those who sleep in the dust of the earth shall awake, some to everlasting life, and some to shame and everlasting contempt. (12:2)

While resurrection is a type of afterlife, it is peculiar in that it is an afterlife which returns the deceased to this life. It is thus, in a sense, more of a continuation of the present life than a true afterlife. Because of this peculiarity, it saves the original covenant relationship, and hence divine justice, by allowing Yahweh to reward devout Jews in what amounts to an extension of *this life.* Also, by adopting the notion of resurrection, none of the Jewish notions about the essential goodness of this world and this life need be abandoned.

Resurrection is also mentioned in such apocryphal (noncanonical) books as Second Maccabees, where it is described as a "wonderful reward" (2 Macc. 12:45). In postbiblical Rabbinic Judaism, acceptance of the doctrine of resurrection became one of the essentials of the faith. The Mishnah (a commentary on scripture; part of the Talmud) even states that, "All Israel has a portion in the world-to-come" (the postresurrection world) except "one who says, 'There is no resurrection of the dead.'" (*San.* 10.1) In the standard basic prayer of the Rabbinic liturgy, still recited daily by observant Jews, the second benediction of the Standing Prayer (*Amidah*) praises God for the resurrection:

> You, O Lord, are mighty forever, you give life to the dead, you have great power to save. You sustain the living with loving kindness and revive the dead with great mercy; you support those who fall, heal those who are sick, release those who are captive, and keep your faith with those who sleep in the dust. Who is like you, powerful Master, and who resembles you, O King who kills, gives life, and brings forth salvation? You are faithful to bring the dead to life; blessed are You, O Lord, who revives the dead.

The belief in resurrection deeply affected the Jewish attitude toward burial, so that it was considered a Jew's duty to drop everything else and bury an exposed corpse, should one be encountered along the road. Such untended bodies were referred to by the rabbis as *met mitzvah* which, roughly translated, means an "obligatory corpse" (which one is "obliged" to bury).

The remains of the body were considered a sort of "seed" from which Yahweh would later reconstruct the body. As an extension of this idea, the notion developed that a small bone in the spine, referred to as *luz,* never completely disintegrated, and formed the nucleus around which the body would be resurrected. This notion, in turn, filtered into Jewish folklore, and was elaborated in lore and practices associated with the need to protect the *luz* from accidental destruction. People who perished at sea, for instance, were regarded as having suffered an unspeakable fate, endangering their chances of resurrection. The need to preserve the remnants of the body also explains the Jewish aversion to the practice of cremation.

Christianity derived the idea of resurrection from the Jewish tradition, and that belief is expressed in the New Testament. To the extent that the gospels are adequate guides, Jesus clearly assumed the doctrine of resurrection, as when the Sadducees asked him about the post-resurrection fate of a woman who married another man after her first husband had died (Mark 12:18–27). Jesus also provided concrete evidence for resurrection when he raised Lazarus from the dead, as well as when he was himself resurrected.

Early Christianity arose as a Jewish sect during the period when apocalyptic speculation was popular. The first Christians strongly believed in the imminent second coming of Christ (within their lifetimes), which would be accompanied by the resurrection of the dead, a final judgment and the end of this world. The Book of Revelation mentions resurrection at several points, for example,

> And the sea gave up the dead in it, Death and Hades gave up the dead in them, and all were judged by what they had done. (20:13)

Thus, simple bodily resurrection was the earliest Christians' concept of the afterlife. However, in the course of its propagation to the non-Hebrew world, Christianity was confronted with popular afterlife ideas that were not part of original Christianity. While the Hebrews had viewed the body as being an intimate and essential part of the human being, the Hellenistic notion—one that prevailed throughout the Mediterranean world—was that the essential human being was an immortal soul which was trapped inside a physical body. Upon death, the body was abandoned and the soul continued to exist as an independent entity. In the Gospel of John, Jesus seems to accept this Greek view when he promises believers that he will come to them in the hour of their death and take them to heaven (14:2–3). Why a soul in heaven should need to be resurrected is not explained.

Christianity had to reconcile these two very different notions of the afterlife. As a consequence, we get a scenario in which, immediately after death, sinners go to hell and the saved go to heaven. However, at the end of time the souls of the dead leave heaven and hell, are reunited with physical bodies, and face judgment on the earth—even though, by virtue of their former residence in either heaven or hell, they have already been judged. The unnecessary redundancy resulting from the awkward attempt to reconcile two different schemes of survival after death should be quite evident, and most ordinary, modern-day Christians embrace the Greek view of an immortal soul that goes directly to heaven or hell following death.

While seemingly a dreadful day, many believers throughout the centuries have looked forward to the final judgment as the day on which their suffering for the faith will be vindicated, and their persecutors and ridiculers punished. This "revenge" motif finds expression in, for example, the writings of Church father Tertullian, who "could scarcely wait for the great moment":

> What a panorama of spectacle on that day! What sight shall I turn to first to laugh and applaud? Mighty kings whose ascent to heaven used to be announced publicly, groaning now in the depths with Jupiter himself who used to witness the ascent? Governors who persecuted the name of the Lord melting in flames fiercer than those they kindled for brave Christians? Wise philosophers, blushing before their students as they burn together, the followers to whom they taught that the world is no concern of God's, whom they assured that either they had no souls at all or that what souls they had would never return to their former bodies? Poets, trembling not before the judgment seat of Rhadamanthus or of Minos, but of Christ—a surprise? Tragic actors bellowing in their own melodramas should be worth hearing! Comedians skipping in the fire will be worth praise! The famous charioteer will toast on his fiery wheel. . . . These are things of greater delight, I believe, than a circus, both kinds of theater, and any stadium.

The notions of resurrection, heaven, and hell were also incorporated into Islam. When human beings die, they remain in a sort of interworld (*barzakh*), a realm located closer to the luminous cosmic center, until the day of resurrection. In this interworld, which somewhat resembles dreaming, the soul of the deceased, liberated from its bodily layers, can awaken and become aware of its true nature. The interworld period is important in preparing for the day of resurrection, which occurs at the end of time; that is, when human possibilities and potential have been exhausted. The day of resurrection (referred to as *qiyama*, the return, or *ba'th*, awakening), which constitutes one of the essential beliefs of the Islamic faith, is believed by some to last thousands of years. On this day the souls, rejoined with their bodies, will be assigned eternal life either in paradise (literally the garden) or in hell (the fire), depending on their merits.

Although the figure of the Mahdi is more central to Shiite Islam, it is a popular belief among many Sunni Muslims that a righteous leader (a Mahdi or "rightly guided one") will reign for a brief period in the last days. He will be followed by an imposter messiah (parallel to the Christian notion of an Antichrist) who will attempt to lead the world astray. Finally, however, the prophet Jesus will appear to usher in the final judgment. On Judgment Day the earth will quake and mountains become a "heap of sand":

> When the stars shall be extinguished, when heaven shall be split, when the mountains shall be scattered . . . (Arberry, p. 318)

As in the judgment day scenarios of other Middle Eastern religions, the dead are resurrected:

> Upon the day when the Caller shall call unto a horrible thing, abasing their eyes, they shall come forth from the tombs as if they were scattered grasshoppers, running with outstretched necks to the Caller. The unbelievers shall say, "This is a hard day!" (Arberry, p. 247)

And judged:

Then he whose deeds weigh heavy in the Balance shall inherit a pleasing life, but he whose deeds weigh light in the Balance shall plunge in the womb of the Pit. (Arberry, p. 348)

Paradise (*al-Jannah*) is located at the macrocosmic center of light and is composed of eight levels (or, according to some authorities, as many as the number of souls). This is viewed as a garden where all kinds of delights are prepared for the saved. On the far outer part of the macrocosm lies hell (*an-nar*), arranged in seven layers, where the soul's punishment consists of being far from God, which is considered to be the worst chastisement. More so than Judeo-Christian scriptures, the Koran contains a number of vivid descriptions of both paradise and hell. For instance, in the chapter entitled "The Terror," the Koran says this:

They are brought nigh the Throne, in the Gardens of Delight upon close-wrought couches reclining upon them, set fact to face, immortal youths going round about them with goblets, and ewers, and a cup from a spring and such fruits as they shall choose, and such flesh of fowl as they desire, and wide-eyed houris [servant girls] as the likeness of hidden pearls, a recompense for that they labored.

Equally vivid descriptions of hell can be found throughout the Koran, as in the chapter "The Pilgrimage":

Garments of fire shall be cut, and there shall be poured over their heads boiling water whereby whatsoever is in their bellies and their skins shall be melted; for them await hooked iron rods; as often as they desire in their anguish to come forth from it, they shall be restored into it, and taste the chastisement of the burning.

Islamic theologians, particularly those of the Asharite school, held that if a believer entered hell, God could forgive his sins or nonconformities and remove him, either immediately or after a certain period during which imperfections had been "burned away." The basis for this doctrine is the Hadith,* "He shall make men come out

*Hadith are believed to be the preserved sayings or direct quotations of Mohammed.

of hell after they have been burned and reduced to cinders." In addition to this purgatory of suffering, there is another Muslim limbo—*al-A'raf*, the "heights" or "ramparts," described in a chapter of the Koran by that name—in which those souls reside who do not merit damnation, yet who are unable to enter paradise.

Beyond certain commonalities, the views of Shiites and Sunnis (the two principal Muslim "denominations") on the destiny of the body and the soul differ greatly. Shiites hold that the human being is a spirit, the *ruh* (spiritual breath, which is immortal by nature), which uses the body as instrument. Upon death the spirit, liberated from the body, can rediscover its true nature. The souls of those who believed in God at this point live until the day of resurrection, enjoying the vision of God. On the day of resurrection the bodies of the righteous will join their souls and will enter paradise forever, whereas the unbelievers' souls will suffer until the last day and, once rejoined with their bodies, will suffer eternal punishment.

Sunnis, in contrast, consider the human being as a material compound of body and soul. Upon death, both body and spirit die, spend a certain period in the grave where they undergo a personal judgment by two angels and a divine judge. This personal judgment is followed by a second death which is, however, abrogated for those who died in name of God (i.e., martyrs). Souls are then believed to vanish and to appear again on Judgment Day where they rejoin their original bodies.

Thus we see how the prospects of a final re-establishment of justice in the final judgment plus the restoration of God's covenant promises via the resurrection of the dead ultimately persuaded Judaism to adopt Zoroaster's eschatology. From Judaism, this vision of the endtime spread to Christianity and Islam. However, while Zoroastrianism's apocalyptic scenario may have been a highly influential historical first, this does not mean that all subsequent millennialists simply adopted a Middle Eastern eschatology. Rather, for millenarian movements originating in societies outside of the Western cultural sphere, many of the components of new endtime visions are drawn more or less directly out of a given society's own cultural heritage. This point can be adequately demonstrated through the examination of a few different case studies, which occupy the following chapters.

3

NATIVE AMERICAN DOOMSDAYS

Long ago when the people were given these ceremonies, the changing began, if only in the aging of the yellow gourd rattle or the shrinking of the skin around the eagle's claw, if only in the different voices from generation to generation, singing the chants. You see, in many ways, the ceremonies have always been changing. . . . At one time, the ceremonies as they had been performed were enough for the way the world was then. But after the white people came, elements in this world began to shift; and it became necessary to create new ceremonies. I have made changes in the rituals. The people mistrust this greatly, but only this growth keeps the ceremonies strong. . . . Things which don't shift and grow are dead things.

—Leslie Marmon Silko, *Ceremony*

Although T. S. Kuhn's concept of a "paradigm shift" has been popularized to the point of trivialization, it nevertheless remains a lucid statement of the insight that scientific knowledge progresses by a series of "leaps" rather than by a process of even, continuous development. Roughly comparable shifts of perspective occur in such disciplines as history and religious studies, with the important difference that outside of the natural sciences it is some-what easier to cling to older paradigms of scholarship.

While the industrialized West is not necessarily more ethnocentric than other cultures, we have had the political-economic power to impose our perceptions and prejudices on the rest of the world for the past several centuries. One of these perceptions, the perception of an almost impassable gulf between "modern" cultures and traditional cultures, shaped the academic study of religion in ways that persist to the present day. In religious studies, the distinction between the industrialized and the nonindustrialized world worked itself out as a de facto division of labor between, on the one hand, biblical scholars and church historians who studied the West's Judeo-Christian heritage and, on the other, anthropologists and historians of religion who studied the non-West. This disciplinary division involved contrasting methodologies as well as contrasting religious traditions.

The eclipse of colonialism following World War II provided the milieu in which these taken-for-granted distinctions could begin to be questioned. The United States, which was not a major colonial power in the early twentieth century, did not enter a similar period (i.e., one conducive to radical self-questioning) until after the cultural crisis of the 1960s. The paradigm shift implied by these changes involved, among other things, a "decentering" of the West, although we have yet to experience the full impact of this shift. Religious studies in this country, for example, have, for the most part, maintained the old division of labor between the Judeo-Christian tradition and other traditions. It has only been within the past ten years or so that this situation has begun to change.

A different phase of the decentering process that was initiated in the wake of the sixties was a recognition of the importance of various minorities as well as women in U.S. history. The invisibility of certain minorities in pre-1960s scholarship can only be called amazing. With respect to American Indians, for example, Oscar Handlin's preface to Edmund Morgan's *Puritan Dilemma* begins with the observation that "the emptiness of the New World made it the field for social experiment." In a similar vein, Perry Miller states that his criterion for determining which essays were included in *Errand into the Wilder-*

ness was to collect those which seemed "to add up to a rank of spotlights on the massive narrative of the movement of European culture into the vacant wilderness of America." Contemporary researchers no longer refer to the "vacant emptiness" of precolonial America, but the attitude behind such scholarly blindness still persists in many corners of academia.

One of the principal characteristics attributed to the religions of nonindustrialized cultures is that they are static cultural forms without a discernable history. This trait helped to legitimate the traditional division of labor between scholars who studied the religions of white males and scholars who studied everyone else. The view that smaller, tribal traditions were—when left undisturbed by outsiders—largely unchanging persisted in the face of much disconfirming evidence. The principal resistance to acknowledging the implications of such evidence came from the West's civilized-savage ideology—an ideology that required a static, regressive counterimage (i.e., primitive savages) for the West's self-congratulatory self-image as dynamic and progressive. A more contemporary view is that such religions are flexible traditions, quite capable of adapting to social and environmental changes. There are, nevertheless, limits to a culture's adaptability, as when the intrusion of colonialists radically disrupts the lifestyle of a tribal society.

The religious life of a traditional culture is built around the most pressing concerns of the group, such as its economic concerns (e.g., a hunting society will typically have hunting myths and rituals). Thus, a conquest situation in which a defeated people's economic base is shattered and radically reoriented (e.g., hunters who are forced to become farmers) can quite suddenly make irrelevant significant segments of a traditional religion. Conquest also transforms the contact situation itself into one of the more pressing concerns of the conquered group.

Such a state of affairs can lead to several different outcomes. If the intruding society is open to assimilation, one possible scenario is that the conquered group will abandon its traditions in favor of the conqueror's traditions. In the case of American Indians, Euro-American society, although professing an ideology of assimilation, was never really open to accepting Native Americans as equals. After tribal groups such as the Cherokee, for example, had adopted Anglo-American culture in the early nineteenth century, they were rewarded with forced removal to western territories.

With the possibility of full assimilation closed off and the alternative of violent warfare suicidal (particularly after the War of 1812, the last historical juncture at which there was a reasonable chance of turning the tide of conquest), defeated tribes had few options beyond getting by as best they could within the limitations imposed by the United States government. Bare existence is not, however, enough to fulfill a human community. Lacking a spiritual vision that could imaginatively transform their situation into a condition with ultimate meaning, postconquest life tended to be characterized by all of the various traits that one usually associates with demoralized social groups, such as alcoholism and a high suicide rate. While the religions of their ancestors might still have been relevant to many aspects of life, the received tradition did not address their oppressed state. And while Christianity contains many elements that speak to oppressed peoples, it was often rejected because of its association with the conquerors.

Situations such as these constitute ideal environments for the emergence of "new" religions in the form of millenarian movements—also termed messianic movements, nativistic movements, crisis cults, doomsday cults, and so forth. Characteristically, these movements begin with the religious experience of a single "prophet." While there was a fair amount of variability among the religious visions of different American Indian prophets, the central tendency of the new revelations was to speak to those aspects of the new environment that traditional religions did not address. Often these revelations provided divine sanctions for new lifestyles (e.g., the legitimation of male farming in communities that had customarily assigned farming activities to females). New religious visions also tended to address the presence of Euro-Americans in some manner (as in the well-known case of the Ghost Dance). At the level of ritual, the usual effect of prophet religions was to encourage religious practices—often modified versions of traditional dances and rituals—within groups that had partially or completely abandoned community ceremonials, thus providing Native Americans with religio-social activities that helped to preserve group identity.

On the whole, contemporary North Americans are unaware of these prophet religions beyond the so-called Ghost Dance of 1890 (originating with the Paiute prophet Wovoka), a movement that left a significant "trace" in the historical record because of the many tribes affected and because of the Ghost Dancers massacred at Wounded Knee. To convey some sense of how extensive the phenomenon of Native American new religions is, it might be useful simply to list a few of the more important Indian prophets: Neolin (whose religious revelation inspired Pontiac's Rebellion), Handsome Lake (an Iroquois of the late eighteenth and early nineteenth centuries whose religion survives to this day), Tenskwatawa (whose vision of nativistic pan-Indianism lay behind his and his brother Tecumseh's efforts to halt the Euro-American advance), Smohalla (who is said to have been partially responsible for Chief Joseph's stand against Euro-American intrusion), and John Slocum (who founded the Indian Shaker Church over a century ago). Some other Indian prophets were Kenekuk, Main Poc, Josiah Francis, Wodziwob, Jake Hunt, Kolaskin, Isatal, and John Wilson. Even this list is not exhaustive, especially if one takes into consideration the various individuals who adapted the Ghost Dances of 1870 and 1890 to the needs of particular tribal groups.

Native American prophets were usually dissolute (e.g., alcoholic) individuals prior to their visions, and were thus people who had experienced the demoralized state of their group in a concrete, personal way. Prophets were also often drawn from the ranks of shamans, religious functionaries who naturally tended to cast problems in spiritual terms. Typically, these prophets seemed to "die" during their initial contact with the god who gave them their mission, so much so that sometimes—as in the cases of Tenskwatawa and John Slocum—the tribal group actually began preparing their funeral before they revived.

The pattern of the prophetic "call" replicated the pattern of the shamanic call fairly faithfully, although the content of the two visions diverged considerably. The new revelations were more or less syncretic, with even the most nativistic movements adopting at least some elements of Euro-American culture. With remarkable consistency, the new revelations were emphatically moralistic, condemning in strong terms alcoholism, sexual promiscuity, lying, stealing, and so forth. To give this condemnation "teeth," the prophecies warned that a terrible punishment (most often in the form of post-mortem residence in some sort of hell) would be meted out to individuals who failed to mend their ways. The new visions were remarkably similar on this point because the demoralized social conditions that they sought to redress were remarkably similar.

It is not until one examines the position that their revelations took on the topic of the non-Indian presence that Native American prophets begin to diverge significantly from one another. On the one hand, a prophet like Kenekuk led his people to become adjusted to the new lifestyle imposed on them by Euro-American society. For instance, as in the case of other new religious leaders like Handsome Lake, the Kickapoo prophet taught that men should farm in a community where farming had been regarded as women's work. Prophets like Tenskwatawa, on the other hand, encouraged their followers to reject the culture of the intruders, and even to take up arms against Anglo-Americans.

These divergent types of revelation correspond with the analysis of Lanternari, an Italian scholar of religion who groups American Indian messianic movements into two major categories, depending on their attitude toward Euro-Americans—hostile (e.g., Neolin and Tenskwatawa) or adaptive (e.g., Handsome Lake and John Slocum). These two types, to continue to follow Lanternari's discussion, arise at two different phases of Native American history. Hostile movements arise in the first stage, and look back to a recovery of precontact conditions. Adaptive movements, which arise in the second stage, proceed to construct new worlds of meaning that accept the contemporaneous situation, including the ongoing Euro-American presence, as a given.

These categories are useful, although, for our present purposes, they need to be modified so as to include a third category that will distinguish movements that were simultaneously hostile and adaptive. In other words, a war revelation such as Tenskwatawa's was hostile without being adaptive. However, a movement like the Ghost Dance, which Lanternari classifies as hostile, in effect led many tribes to become more adjusted to their situation. Some of the potentially adaptive aspects of Wovoka's teachings are evident in certain passages of the so-called Messiah Letter recorded by James Mooney; for example, "Do not refuse to work for the whites and do not make any trouble with them."

In fact, had it not been for the stupidity of a few key U.S. officials in the Dakotas, the only significant violence resulting from the Ghost Dance—the Wounded Knee Massacre—could easily have been avoided.* Thus modified, Lanternari's classification allows us to explain why a certain subset of Native American prophet movements did not survive: Simply put, movements built around war visions (hostile, nonadaptive movements) were defeated on the battlefield. So that the reader can acquire a clearer sense of this phenomenon, it might be useful to outline representative movements for each of these three categories.

THE SHAWNEE PROPHET'S INDIAN ARMAGEDDON

At first they took it for a great bird, but they soon found it to be a monstrous canoe filled with the very people who had got the knowledge which belonged to the Shawnees. After these white people had landed, they were not content with having the knowledge which belonged to the Shawnees, but they usurped their land also. They pretended, indeed, to have purchased these lands but the very goods they gave for them were more the property of the Indians than of the white people, because the knowledge which enabled them to manufacture these goods actually belonged to the Shawnees. But these things will soon end. The Master of Life is about to restore to the Shawnees their knowledge and their rights and he will trample the Long Knives under his feet.

–R. David Edmunds, *The Shawnee Prophet*, p. 38

---

*By stupid I mean that the government officials thought the Ghost Dancers were preparing an armed revolt, in the ordinary, worldly sense. In actuality, there was no real threat of a serious revolt.

Such was the gist of the conversation in 1803 when a Shawnee delegation explained their vision of the immediate future to American officials. This is clearly an apocalyptic scenario, similar to many of the others we have examined, in which God (in this case, the Shawnee Master of Life) was about to intervene on the side of a people unjustly oppressed. Here we see clearly the central promise that makes apocalyptic thinking so attractive to conquered peoples: Unable to defeat their oppressors by purely military means, the tables are to be turned by the power of divine intervention.

The scenario outlined above would become the fundamental understanding underlying the first pan-Indian religious movement. This movement, like the later and more famous Ghost Dance, originated with the visions of a single prophet among a people demoralized by the intrusion of Euro-Americans. The religious alliances forged by Tenskwatawa, the Shawnee prophet, formed the basis for the military triumphs of Tecumseh, whose activities eventually overshadowed those of Tenskwatawa, his younger brother. As a consequence, few nonspecialists are aware that Tecumseh's followers were initially motivated by a religious vision of a final confrontation in which Native Americans would defeat Euro-Americans, drive them out of North America, and restore American Indians to their former glory. This emergent eschatology was based on traditional mythology, and can best be approached in terms of Shawnee creation myths.

The dominant type of creation myth among the aboriginal peoples of North America is of the earth-diver variety in which a divine being (usually an animal) dives into water to bring up the first particles of earth. The Shawnees, by way of contrast, are one of the few tribes possessing a creation account in which the high god (often referred to as the "Master of Life") creates the world by imposing order on a primordial chaos. Because the original chaos is watery (the Shawnee term for the primordial condition seems to be related to other kinds of words that refer to watery expanses), these two types of creation share certain points in common. In both kinds of stories water is an ambivalent symbol simultaneously representing creative potency as well as the threat of chaos.

After creation is complete, the Creator warns the first people that "even I myself do not know how long this place where you live will survive. And the reason I do not know is this: The world will survive as long as you interpret correctly the way I created you" (cited in Voegelin and Yegerlehner, p. 57). "Interpreting the way" means, for the Shawnee people, adhering to the "laws"—a specific body of oral literature that sets forth the proper relationships that should be followed among human beings as well as between humans and the nonhuman world—which were spoken by the Master of Life in the beginning. The Creator's words cited above indicate that wholesale abandonment of these laws would constitute abandonment of order and return to chaos.

In common with related tribal groups, Shawnee mythology includes a migration narrative in which a large body of water is crossed. This myth has traditionally been viewed by scholars as a "cultural memory" of the migration from Asia to North America. In some versions of the tale, the original people abandon a barren and inhospitable place for a better land across the ocean. But, whatever the motivation for crossing, the great expanse of water is almost always seen as a barrier which must be overcome by magical means. In at least one version, "a great wind and a deep darkness prevailed, and the Great Serpent commenced hissing in the depths of the ocean" during the crossing. The "Great Serpent" referred to here is a marine monster who, like his parallels in other mythologies across the world, concretely embodies the negative, disordering aspect of the primordial waters.

After successfully negotiating the initial stage of the journey, but prior to reaching their eventual resting place, a party of warriors is drowned by a large turtle who is acting as agent for the hostile sea snake. In retaliation, Shawnee shamans slay the serpent and cut it into small pieces. Because of the snake's potency, these fragments do not decay. The tribe collects the pieces with the intention of later using them for beneficent purposes such as healing. As a manifestation of the ambivalent power of the primordial energy, the serpent's power can be used for good or for ill. Although the original motivation behind gathering together the fragments is benevolent, Shawnee witches would later base their malevolent spells on the power of bundles made from these serpent parts.

As part of their migration myth, the Shawnees eventually reached the "heart" of the new continent, an area where the Master of Life had originally intended for them to live. In historical times, the Shawnees were still wanderers who could be found living in different parts of eastern North America during different periods of time. By the middle of the eighteenth century, the great bulk of the Shawnee nation was living in Ohio. Recognizing the threat that settlers posed both to their lands and to their traditional lifestyle, the Shawnees allied themselves first with the French (during the French and Indian War) and later with the British (during the Revolution) to oppose the advances of land-hungry colonists. After the Treaty of Paris ended the Revolutionary War, the Shawnees, in league with other tribes, fought on until decisively defeated at the Battle of Fallen Timbers. They eventually (1795) signed the Treaty of Greenville, an unfavorable agreement in which the tribe gave up most of its homeland in exchange for some trade goods and annuities.

In the wake of defeat, some bands moved further west. Other Shawnees, under the leadership of Black Hoof, attempted to adapt to changed conditions by turning to agriculture. The majority rejected acculturation, continued to follow the hunt as best they could, and clung to memories of a romanticized past. Many tribesmen eventually slid into demoralized, dissolute lifestyles, consuming increasing amounts of alcohol and occasionally venting their frustration in acts of intratribal and intrafamilial violence.

During this period of time Tenskwatawa, the Shawnee prophet, was a less than stunningly successful medicine man for a small village located in eastern Indiana. Tenskwatawa (literally "The Open Door") was one of three male triplets born in early 1775; his more famous brother, Tecumseh, was seven years older. Tenskwatawa's father died at the Battle of Point Pleasant prior to his birth, and, after his mother abandoned him while he was still a small child, he was raised by his older sister Tecumpease, her husband Black Fish, and other Shawnee. While still a child, he lost an eye playing with a bow and arrows. Perhaps as a consequence of this unfortunate childhood, he grew up a boastful alcoholic, acquiring the derogatory nickname Lalawethika ("noisemaker" or "rattle"). As a young man, he took a wife and fathered several children.

In many ways, Tenskwatawa personally embodied the demoralized state of his people. In early 1805, in the wake of an epidemic of some European disease on which the healer's ministrations had little impact, he unexpectedly fell into a coma-like state that the Shawnees interpreted as death. However, before the funeral arrangements could be completed, he revived, to the amazement of his tribesmen. Considerably more amazing were the revelations he had received during his deathlike trance.

Tenskwatawa had been permitted to view heaven, "a rich, fertile country, abounding in game, fish, pleasant hunting grounds, and fine corn fields" (Edmunds, p. 33). But he had also witnessed sinful Shawnee spirits being tortured according to the degree of their wickedness, with drunkards (one of Tenskwatawa's principal vices) being forced to swallow molten lead. Overwhelmed by the power of his vision, Tenskwatawa abandoned his old ways. More revelations followed in succeeding months, revelations that eventually added up to a coherent new vision of religion and society.

Although the new revelation departed from tradition on some points (for example, notions of heavenly and hellish realms were probably not indigenous), its central thrust was a nativistic exhortation to abandon Euro-American ways for the lifestyle of earlier generations. Tenskwatawa successfully extended his religion to other tribes, particularly the Kickapoos, Winnebagos, Sacs, and Miamis. According to Thomas Jefferson's account, the Master of Life instructed Tenskwatawa

> to make known to the Indians that they were created by him distinct from the whites, of different natures, for different purposes, and . . . that they must return from all the ways of the whites to the habits and opinions of their forefathers; they must not eat the flesh of hog, of bullocks, of sheep, etc., the deer and the buffalo having been created for their food; they must not make bread of wheat, but of Indian corn; they must not wear linen nor woolen, but dress like their fathers, in the skins and furs of animals; [and] they must not drink ardent spirits. (Klinek, p. 53)

This revelation called tribesmen back to the lifestyle and the princi-ples (i.e., the laws of Shawnee tradition) prescribed by the Creator. As they had been warned "in the beginning," the abandonment of tradition had brought on social chaos. Although their current degra-dation involved the adoption of Euro-American ways, earlier devia-tions had been responsible for their military defeats. A nontraditional twist to the new revelation was that the forces of chaos were now identified with Euro-Americans.

In another revelation, the Master of Life went so far as to declare that the invaders from the east were "not my children, but the chil-dren of the Evil Spirit. They grew from the scum of the great Water when it was troubled by the Evil Spirit. And the froth was driven into the Woods by a strong east wind. They are numerous, but I hate them. They are unjust. They have taken away your lands, which were not made for them" (Edmunds, p. 38).

Although the inclusion of Euro-Americans was new, in many other ways these teachings fit well into traditional understandings. The Great Serpent was the closest being the Shawnees had to a devil, so that the identification of this snake as the source of their con-querors was a reasonable association: The Serpent was avenging itself for the defeat it had suffered at the hands of the Shawnee people many thousands of years ago.

In a sense, the sea snake was still alive in the form of the various fragments of its flesh used as power-sources in witchcraft. In fact, prior to the Creator's revelations through Tenskwatawa, some Shawnees had already been attributing their degraded state to the machinations of the Evil One through the agency of Indian sorcerers. These associations came together when Tenskwatawa and his fol-lowers began to kill witches.

The new revelation included a redemptive scenario in which Euro-Americans would be defeated and the fortunes of Native Amer-icans restored. The promise of restored greatness had overwhelming appeal, and the prophet's message spread quickly to other tribes. Zealous converts among the Delaware (an Algonquian tribe whose mythology had many parallels to that of the Shawnee) seized fellow tribesmen suspected of witchcraft—who, predictably, turned out to be those Delaware most opposed to the new movement–and requested that Tenskwatawa journey to their village and use his supernatural power to identify witches.

The first prisoner to be condemned by the prophet was Anne Charity, a convert to Christianity who had adopted Euro-American manners and dress. She was suspended over a large campfire and tortured until she confessed that she was indeed a witch, and that she had given her evil medicine bundle to her grandson. After burning the old woman to death, the grandson was apprehended and brought before the assembly. Rightly fearing for his life, the young man admitted to having borrowed the medicine bundle, but claimed that he had returned it to his grandmother after having used it only once, for the innocuous purpose of flying through the air. The grandson was released, but his confession served to confirm the suspicions of widespread witchcraft held by the prophet and his followers. Other individuals who had converted to Christianity or who otherwise had some kind of close association with Euro-Americans were then tortured and burned.

While the new movement experienced its share of ups and downs, the promise of restored greatness was overwhelmingly appealing. Consequently, the religious leadership of the prophet remained strong until Tenskwatawa's prophecy of victory failed at the battle of Tippecanoe on November 7, 1811. Although from a purely military angle the battle was indecisive, Tenskwatawa's status as a leader was irreparably damaged. The hopes that Tenskwatawa's vision addressed were then transferred to the more secular efforts of his brother Tecumseh to unite the tribes in opposition to Euro-Americans.

Following the Battle of the Thames in 1813, Tenskwatawa fled to Canada where he remained for a decade. He returned to the United States after agreeing to lead the remaining Shawnees out of the midwest to Kansas. Subsequently, in and around 1828, tribal bands founded villages along the Kansas River. There, in 1832, the celebrated western artist George Catlin painted a portrait of Tenskwatawa. The prophet died in November 1836 in what is now Kansas City.

Unlike Christian eschatology, the endtime scenario of the Shawnee was never fixed in a single written account. Rather, it was

a flexible narrative that developed over time in response to new historical circumstances. Prior to Euro-American contact, the endtime
was a comparatively vague idea–should the Shawnee nation ever
abandon the Creator's principles, the world would end. Because the
world emerged out of a watery chaos, the Shawnee may have held
the view that the creation would dissolve back into the waters at the
end of time.

The tribe's confrontation with Euro-American colonists influenced the Shawnee to rethink and extend their mythology to cover
the contact situation. The closest beings to evil entities in their tradition were witches and the marine serpent. Even before Tenskwatawa's
vision, the Shawnee had begun to view Euro-Americans in terms of
these negative beings: Colonists were children of the Evil Spirit (i.e.,
the Great Serpent), and Native Americans who converted to Anglo
ways were witches. In the face of this multifaceted threat, the prophet
preached an Armageddon between Native Americans and Euro-
Americans, and, as a new millennium, a return to tradition. While not
as fully developed as the Christian version of the eschaton, this apocalyptic scenario seemed to offer a comprehensible explanation of the
unhappy situation in which the Shawnee found themselves. Like most
traditional apocalyptic thinking worldwide, it promised a happy
ending–the ultimate appeal of doomsday prophecies.

HANDSOME LAKE,
PROPHET OF ACCOMMODATION

*And so the Iroquois stagnated, bartering their self-respect for
trivial concessions from the Americans, drinking heavily when they
had the chance, and quarreling among themselves. Into this moral
chaos, Handsome Lake's revelations of the word of God sped like
a golden arrow, dispelling darkness and gloom. Heavenly messengers, he said, had told him that unless he and his fellows became
new men, they were doomed to be destroyed in an apocalyptic
world destruction.*

–Anthony F. C. Wallace,
Religion: An Anthropological View

In the same way that Tenskwatawa almost perfectly exemplifies the "war prophet," the Iroquois prophet Handsome Lake exemplifies the "peace prophet." The parallels between these two men are striking. Like Tenskwatawa, Handsome Lake was somewhat of a healer (an herbalist, at the very least) and an alcoholic who encountered the Creator during a death-vision. He was also given a vision of heaven and hell, and, in time, instructions for a new religious pattern that selectively revived and rejected parts of the religious tradition of the Iroquois. Like Tenskwatawa, Handsome Lake also preached a strong moral code and instituted formal confessions (his first vision in 1799 focused on the moral reclamation of the Iroquois).

Unlike the Shawnee, however, Handsome Lake did not condemn Euro-Americans as children of the Evil Spirit. The Iroquois Prophet did not even condemn Christianity. Rather, Handsome Lake's visions made it clear that in the same way in which his revelations were directed to Native Americans, Christianity was an appropriate religion for Euro-Americans. During one of his spirit journeys, for instance, the Iroquois prophet met Jesus, with whom he discussed the relative success of their respective missions.

Handsome Lake's teachings included all of the essential ingredients necessary to preserve the Iroquois as a people in the face of Euro-American encroachment. In addition to the points already mentioned, an important tenet of the new faith was the preservation of the tribal land base, while simultaneously maintaining peaceful relations with their non-Indian neighbors. In the words of scholar Anthony F. C. Wallace, who wrote the classic study of Handsome Lake,

> He told the Iroquois to adopt the white man's mode of agriculture, which included a man's working the fields (hitherto a woman's role); he advised that some learn to read and write English; he counseled them to emphasize the integrity of the married couple and its household, rather than the old maternal lineage. In sum, his code was a blueprint of a culture that would be socially and technologically more effective in the new circumstances of reservation life than the old culture could ever have been.

Handsome Lake's religion was so successful that it has survived to the present day.

As members of the same general culture–the cultural sphere anthropologists refer to as the Eastern Woodlands–traditional Iroquois society was not radically different from Shawnee society. In particular, the Iroquois were no less warlike than the Shawnee. They also possessed roughly similar conceptions of witchcraft. Both had suffered defeat at the hands of land-hungry Anglo-American colonials. It is even clear that both Tenskwatawa and Handsome Lake initially experienced comparable visions. Why then, one might ask, did the Shawnee prophet end up following the path of war while Handsome Lake become the prophet of accommodation?

The answer to this question is not simple. For one thing, the Shawnee prophet and the Iroquois prophet faced different historical circumstances. More significantly, for the purposes of our present discussion, the Iroquois possessed an unusual ideological resource in the form of mythologized folklore about Deganawidah (he who thinks), the legendary founder of the Iroquois confederacy. Deganawidah, a Huron who, scholars hypothesize, lived in the fifteenth century, brought peace to the Iroquois people.

Despite a common language and culture, in Deganawidah's day the Iroquois were split into five separate and mutually warring tribes–the Mohawk, the Onondaga, the Seneca, the Oneida, and the Cayuga. Their customs of warfare were brutal, sanctioning the killing of women and children as well as ritual cannibalism. Much of the ongoing conflict involved vendettas in which warriors attacked their neighbors for no other reason than to avenge the deaths of fellow tribesmen–who in turn had to be avenged, thus perpetuating an endless cycle of violence.

Deganawidah, an outcast from his own tribe, wandered into the Iroquois killing fields preaching a message of peace–a vision of unity that would one day be called the Great Law of Peace. According to legend, one of Deganawidah's early converts was the Mohawk Hiawatha. Hiawatha's entire family, a wife and seven daughters, had been murdered by the Onondaga war chief Ododarhoh. Out of his mind with grief, Hiawatha had degenerated into an animalistic recluse who spent his days ambushing and eating hapless travelers.

Coming upon Hiawatha's lodge in the woods, Deganawidah is said to have climbed up onto the roof and peered down the smoke hole. In the midst of preparing a human carcass for dinner, at that precise moment Hiawatha glanced at Deganawidah's reflection in the water of the cooking pot, and mistook it for his own. The reflected image was so full of purity and kindness that Hiawatha was struck by the thought, "This is not the face of a cannibal." The force of emotion evoked by this simple thought was such that his humane side was able to break through the clouds of vengeful anger that had enveloped him ever since the brutal deaths of his family. Hiawatha immediately resolved to abandon his cannibalism. In that very moment he took his pot some distance away from his lodge and cast out its contents.

Returning, he was greeted by Deganawidah, who shared his vision of peace with Hiawatha. His heart already opened by his resolution to abandon cannibalism, and overwhelmed by the boldness of Deganawidah's vision, Hiawatha was immediately transformed into the Huron prophet's right-hand man. At the end of his discourse, Deganawidah addressed his new disciple:

My junior brother, we now shall make our laws and when all are made we shall call the organization we have formed The Great Peace. It shall be the power to abolish war and robbery between brothers and bring peace and quietness. (Peterson, p. 69)

Gradually, over the course of five years of diplomacy, these two men brought the five Iroquois tribes into a confederacy. The Onondaga were the last to join, after the prophet touched the heart of the evil Ododarhoh, the murderer of Hiawatha's family, and Ododarhoh declared himself Deganawidah's disciple. After firmly establishing The Great Peace among the five nations, it is said that Deganawidah disappeared, paddling westward into the setting sun. What happened to the prophet after leaving the Iroquois is unknown.

Like other visionaries, Deganawidah made prophecies of the future, such as the following:

> Deganawidah told the people that in the future they would face a time of great suffering. They would come to distrust their leaders and the principles of peace of the League. A great white serpent would then come upon the Iroquois, and, for a time, would intermingle with them and be accepted as a friend. The serpent would, however, eventually become so powerful that it would attempt to destroy them, choking the life out the of people until all hope seemed to be lost. . . . Then they should gather in the land of the hilly country, beneath the branches of an elm tree. They should burn tobacco and call upon Deganawidah by name when they are facing their darkest hours—and he will return. (Cited in Peterson, pp. 77–78)

This prophecy, a prediction of the second coming of the peacemaker as a millenarian figure who will restore the league in the wake of an assault by a "white serpent," was undoubtedly evoked in the minds of at least a few fellow Iroquois during Handsome Lake's ministry. Although Handsome Lake did not claim the mantle of Deganawidah, the impact of his teachings was to renew the Iroquois people and to restore the league that the Huron prophet had established centuries earlier.

Hence, whether or not the five tribes viewed Handsome Lake as the peacemaker returned, Deganawidah had bequeathed an ideological and spiritual resource to the Iroquois people that enabled them to renew themselves and renew their culture out of the despairing and demoralized conditions that faced them at the end of the eighteenth century. In particular, the Huron prophet had taught the Iroquois people the power of forgiveness and the power of peace, and it was the tradition of these teachings that enabled them to forgive Anglo-Americans and learn to live with them in peace.

WOVOKA'S PACIFIST APOCALYPSE

When I was in the other world with the Old Man, I saw all the people who have died. But they were not sad. They were happy while engaged in their old-time occupations and dancing, gam-

bling, and playing ball. It was a pleasant land, level, without rocks or mountains, green all the time, and rich with an abundance of game and fish. Everyone was forever young.

After showing me all of heaven, God told me to go back to earth and tell his people you must be good and love one another, have no quarreling, and live in peace with the whites; that you must work, and not lie or steal; and that you must put an end to the practice of war.

If you faithfully obey your instructions from on high, you will at last be reunited with your friends in a renewed world where there would be no more death or sickness or old age. First, though, the earth must die. Indians should not be afraid, however. For it will come alive again, just like the sun died and came alive again [during the eclipse]. In the hour of tribulation, a tremendous earthquake will shake the ground. Indians must gather on high ground. A mighty flood shall follow. The water and mud will sweep the white race and all Indian skeptics away to their death. Then the dead Indian ancestors will return, as will the vanished buffalo and other game, and everything on earth will once again be an Indian paradise.

–Scott Peterson, *Native American Prophecies*, p. 99

The Ghost Dance represents an intermediate category between the movements of Tenskwatawa and Handsome Lake–hostile, yet adaptive. The Paiute prophet Wovoka (also called Jack Wilson), unlike either Tenskwatawa or Handsome Lake, was not dissolute. However, like the earlier prophets, Wovoka was a healing shaman who experienced his revelation in a death-vision during which God gave him strongly ethical teachings, although the usual pattern of heavenly and hellish realms was missing. Instead, Wovoka received a revelation of a millennium in which the earth would be renewed and the spirits of the dead would return. The millennium would be preceded by a general catastrophe that would destroy Euro-Americans and their material culture. This would be a cosmic rather than a military-political catastrophe. Consequently, Native Americans were instructed to keep the peace and wait.

Beyond remaining at peace and following Wovoka's ethical injunctions, American Indians were periodically to perform what

Euro-Americans came to call the Ghost Dance. An extended account from a contemporary Anglo-American observer of a Sioux Ghost Dance follows:

[The shirts and dresses of the Ghost Dancers were covered with] figures of birds, bows and arrows, sun, moon, and stars, and everything they saw in nature. . . . A number had stuffed birds, squirrel heads, etc., tied in their long hair. The faces of all were painted red with a black half-moon on the forehead or on one cheek.

One stood directly behind another, each with his hands on his neighbor's shoulders. After walking about a few times, chanting, "Father, I come," they stopped marching, but remained in the circle, and set up the most fearful, heart-piercing wails I ever heard—crying, moaning, groaning, and shrieking out their grief, and naming over their departed friends and relatives, at the same time taking up handfuls of dust at their feet, washing their hands in it, and throwing it over their heads. Finally, they raised their eyes to heaven, their hands clasped high above their heads, and stood straight and perfectly still, invoking the power of the Great Spirit to allow them to see and talk with their people who had died. . . .

And now the most intense excitement began. They would go as fast as they could, their hands moving from side to side, their bodies swaying, their arms, with hands gripped tightly in their neighbors', swinging back and forth with all their might. The ground had been worked and worn by many feet, until the fine, flour-like dust lay light and loose and to the depth of two or three inches. The wind, which had increased, would sometimes take it up, enveloping the dancers and hiding them from view. In the ring were men, women, and children; the strong and the robust, the weak, consumptive, and those near to death's door. They believed those who were sick would be cured by joining in the dancing and losing consciousness. From the beginning they chanted, to a monotonous tune, the words, "Father, I come; Mother, I come; Brother, I come; Father, give us back our arrows."

All of which they would repeat over and over again until first one then another would break from the ring and stagger away and fall down. . . . No one ever disturbed those who fell or took any notice of them except to keep the crowd away.

They kept up dancing until fully 100 persons were lying unconscious. Then they stopped and seated themselves in a circle, and as each one recovered from his trance he was brought to the center of the ring to relate his experience. (Cited in Peterson, pp. 114–15)

Eventually some participants fell down into a trance during which they received revelations, usually from departed relatives. Performing the dance would hasten the advent of the new age—the millennium was coming, but doing the dance would make it arrive sooner.

Wovoka's revelation spoke powerfully to his contemporaries, and the dance was taken up by a wide variety of different tribes, such as the Shoshoni, Arapaho, Crow, Cheyenne, Pawnee, Kiowa, Comanche, and Sioux. As one might anticipate, relatively stable tribal groups that had adjusted successfully to changed conditions were least inclined to accept the new teaching. The widespread excitement generated by Wovoka's vision declined rapidly in the wake of the Wounded Knee massacre (December 29, 1890), so that the effective lifespan of the Ghost Dance as a mass movement was no more than a few years. The prophet himself died many years later, on September 20, 1932. Quite independently of the prophet, however, the Ghost Dance continued to be practiced. For example, as late as the 1950s the dance was still being performed by the Shoshonis in something like its original form. Perhaps the most important adaptive responses were in tribal groups that partially adopted the Ghost Dance as a medium for reviving selected aspects of their traditional religion.

The above discussion brings us to the issue of the unstable, ephemeral nature that has traditionally been attributed to "nonmainstream" religious movements. While American Indian movements belong in a somewhat different category from groups like the Unification Church, they have shared the imputed characterization of being ephemeral phenomena. It is thus relevant to the larger issue at hand to question the conventional wisdom about Native American messianic movements.

To begin with, one should immediately note that no scholar with a reasonably broad knowledge of American Indian prophets would accept the attribution of instability as being a generally applicable trait. The movements initiated by Handsome Lake, Kenekuk, and

John Slocum—all founded over a hundred years ago—survive to the present day. Also, certain offshoots of the Ghost Dance, such as the Maru Cult, as well as the Native American Church, are still very much alive.

The impression of ephemerality appears to be the result of superficial acquaintance with the Ghost Dance of 1890, the one American Indian messiah movement with which there is widespread familiarity. There is a general awareness that the Ghost Dance led to a brief period of intense millenarian expectancy among Native Americans, an expectancy that rapidly diminished in the wake of Wounded Knee. However, most people are not aware that the Ghost Dance continued to be practiced, especially in tribes where elements of the Dance became blended with the group's traditional religion. Even among academics, religion scholars without a background in Native American studies often have no acquaintance with American Indian prophet religions beyond the short segment on the Ghost Dance of 1890 in *Black Elk Speaks* (see Neihardt 1961), a reading that reinforces the impression of prophet religions as ephemeral phenomena that flare up and then die.

The picture presented by this narrow base of information dovetails nicely with the "common sense" view of messianic movements, which is that when predicted events do not occur, participants lose faith and the movement collapses. However, as Festinger et al.'s classic study *When Prophecy Fails* argued, the failure of prophecy can, in certain circumstances, actually have the opposite effect of increasing one's faith. One might also recall that, if we accept the testimony of the synoptic gospels, Jesus predicted an imminent apocalypse that never occurred: "This generation will not pass away before all these things take place" (Mark 13:30). Despite this failed prophecy, the Christian Church went on to become one of the biggest "success stories" of all time.

The case of Christianity should also cause us to question the bit of conventional wisdom that views the death of the founding prophet as a crisis that usually leads more or less immediately to the death of the prophet's movement. This "common sense" notion has almost no empirical foundation. The evidence supplied by the history of Native American prophet religions only further serves to undercut the conventional wisdom on this point. If we set aside the nonadaptive visions of the war prophets, the majority of American Indian movements found in the ethnographic literature—almost all of which were initiated in the nineteenth century—either persist in some form to the present day, or at least persisted well after the deaths of their founders. Beyond these ongoing "success stories," we can find other demonstrations of the point that the demise of a prophet religion is rarely correlated with the founder's death.

For example, as far as can be determined, Wodziwob, the initiator of the Ghost Dance of 1870, lived well into the twentieth century, although his movement among the Paiute collapsed within a few years of its founding. There is also the very unusual case of the prophet Kolaskin, whose religion persisted not only after his death, but prior to his death it had continued to exist even after the prophet himself abandoned the movement.

Beyond the ethnocentric attitude that leads one to perceive "eccentric" visions of the world as by nature unstable, a key factor in causing academics to attribute emphemerality to messianic movements is a mistaken theoretical perspective that portrays the personal charisma of the founder as the "glue" holding together alternative views of reality. Such a perspective misconstrues the role of charisma. In the first place, no matter how charismatic the prophet, his or her message must somehow address the concerns of the community in a satisfactory manner if he is to convince more than a handful of close associates. In other words, a contagious new vision has more going for it than merely the personality of the revealer.

In the second place, although the prophet's charisma may be necessary in giving life to the vision during the nascent stages of the new movement, the actual adoption of an emergent religion by a human community recruits the forces of social consensus to the side of the new revelation—forces that tend to maintain the alternative vision of reality independently of the charisma of the founder. To think of this in terms of the sociology of knowledge, the plausibility of a particular worldview and its accompanying lifestyle is maintained by the ongoing "conversation" that takes place among the members of a particular community. If an entire community is converted to a new vision of reality, as Native American tribes frequently were, the possibility of encountering dissonance as a result of interaction with nonbelieving conversation partners is largely eliminated.

Because social consensus is the real "glue" that maintains the plausibility of any given worldview, potential sources of crisis in the life of a religious movement lie in the area of breakdowns of social consensus, not in the passing away of the founder. Thus as long as a new religion continues satisfactorily to address the concerns of the community, the prophet's death will not induce a crisis of faith.

4

RESCRIPTING ARMAGEDDON
Could Biblical Scholars Have Prevented the Waco Holocaust?

Thus says the Lord concerning the king of Assyria: He shall not come into this city, or come before it with a shield, or cast up a siege mound against it. . . . For I will defend this city to save it, for my own sake and for the sake of my servant David.

(Isaiah 37:33–35)

Hearts were pounding in tense expectancy when three National Guard helicopters swooped over the ridgeline and converged on Mt. Carmel, the compound near Waco, Texas, that housed a religious sect known as the Branch Davidians. Gunfire was exchanged, and the Davidians incurred several casualties. Not long afterwards, two pick-up trucks pulling canvas-covered livestock trailers rushed up the driveway and stopped in front of the building, positioning themselves between reporters and Mt. Carmel.

Bureau of Alcohol, Tobacco and Firearms (ATF) agents in dark blue uniforms jumped out of the trucks, tossing concussion grenades and screaming "Come out!" The firefight then began in earnest. Thousands of bullets filled the air, crashing through the buildings and vehicles, and throwing up geysers of dirt as they furiously buried themselves in the Texas earth. It happened quickly, like the crashing of a tidal wave over a sleepy coastal village. A man who had been scraping rust off of the community water tower–the ATF subsequently dubbed it a "watchtower"–died as he turned his head to see what was the commotion was all about. A woman who had stayed in bed nursing a cold was struck and killed by bullets before she could even jump up to find out what was happening. Another man in the lunch room eating a late breakfast of French toast was gunned down by unseen assailants who were firing blindly into the thin wooden walls of Mt. Carmel. The children, screaming in fear, hid themselves under beds and any other available cover as the undirected fusillade of bullets whizzed through the air. Leader David Koresh's two-year old daughter died immediately from the ATF's irresponsible gunfire.

> And the angel of the Lord went forth, and slew . . . in the camp of the Assyrians; and when men arose early in the morning, behold, these were all dead bodies. (Isaiah 37:36)

The Branch Davidians quickly called 911 for help. The details of this conversation reveal a community startled by the violence of the assault. At one point Koresh, speaking to the Waco police, shouted in anguish, "You killed some of my children!" "There is a bunch of us dead and a bunch of you guys dead now–that's your fault!" At other points in the conversation, Koresh made such assertions as, "We told you we wanted to talk!" "Now we are willing and we've been willing all this time to sit down with anybody!" These assertions align well with the attitude of cooperation the Davidians had displayed in the past, and call into question the necessity for a dramatic, quasimilitary assault.

Despite public statements to the contrary, agents fired indiscriminately into walls and windows, a shooting style pejoratively referred to as "spray and pray" in law enforcement circles. The attack plan failed to foresee the possibility that the assault team crossing the roof from south to north would be in the line of gunfire from agents firing from behind vehicles located on the front (west) side of the building complex. Also, helicopter gunfire was misdirected so that it went completely through the building, impacting among agents on the ground. The failure to take this cross-fire situation into account was compounded by the special bullets utilized by agents, the 9mm Cyclone. This bullet, available only to law enforcement, is a hollow steel cylinder, designed to slice through body armor like a "flying cookie cutter," in the words of one writer (Pate 1993). To increase its power to pierce through armor and other obstacles, the powder in the shell propels the bullet to exceedingly high, supersonic velocities. These deep penetration bullets could only have increased the possibility of agents shooting each other as they assaulted different parts of the complex. Thus, despite heated ATF denials, many—perhaps even the majority—of agency casualties were sustained as a result of "friendly fire."

Outside the building complex, a bullet shattered the windshield of one of the press vehicles. Another flattened a tire. KWTX cameraman Dan Mulloney later told the *Dallas Morning News* that "The first five minutes was just a job. Then we started seeing people get hit and we heard bullets hitting around us. I figured I was going to get shot. I started thinking of my kids. . . ." KWTX reporter John McLemore further related that "People were being hit. You could hear people screaming in agony." One agent shouted at McLemore: "Hey! TV man! Call for an ambulance!" McLemore got up and rushed some yards across open ground, leaping into his jeep and grabbing his radio as a round hit the door. Other bullets made sickening metallic sounds as they slammed into the side of his vehicle. "I got scared," he recalled (Pate 1993).

The worst ATF casualties occurred when a team of agents went for the gun locker located in one of the upper rooms. Video footage from this dramatic episode showing an agent on the roof dodging bullets fired through an adjacent wall appeared on the news the same day, and was reshown over and over again in subsequent weeks, not unlike the video footage of the beating of Rodney King that was aired every time the case was mentioned. Three agents were wounded and three killed in this tragically botched phase of the operation. Had the raid truly been a surprise, this move would have effectively prevented the Davidians from arming themselves. Without a backup plan for a nonsurprise scenario, however, the agents charged blindly forward with this phase of the attack, and were massacred as a result.

Soon after the failed raid, rumors—based in part on news video footage—circulated to the effect that the exchange of gunfire did not

begin until after an agent, Conway C. LeBleu, fell off a ladder, accidentally shot himself in the foot, and started yelling "I'm hit! I'm hit!"
His pistol discharged while still in the holster. Despite this wound,
LeBleu continued to carry out his assigned part of the raid, eventually
meeting death with Agents McKeehan and Williams. While his self-
inflicted wound may not have actually initiated the fire fight, the image
of having such a flawed, unprofessional raid begin with an agent
shooting himself in the foot has a certain strange appeal, which may
explain why the story was repeated over and over again in the media.

Toward the end of the raid, a lone Davidian repeatedly called for
"peace" as he appeared in a lower story doorway. Each time, he was
answered with a hail of gunfire. The ATF did not see fit to end the
assault until they were almost completely out of ammunition. Only
at that point did they call for a cease fire, which the religious community readily granted. The Davidians further allowed the ATF to
remove wounded agents, even assisting them in this task. These acts
of reasonableness and kindness, coming from a community that had
been violently assaulted, were quickly forgotten. Both the agency and
the media, motivated by different but convergent agendas, proceeded immediately to demonize the Davidians as evil fanatics.

FROM MEDIA CIRCUS TO HOLOCAUST

*The media were content to cover the Waco situation like a football
game, counting the score in bodies and rehashing the plays. It's sad
to see American reporters and editors playing cheerleader for Big
Brother.*
—Chas S. Clifton, letter to the editor, *Time* (May 24, 1993)

Less than a week after the ATF attack on the Branch Davidian community, the Rev. Mike Evans, who in 1986 had published a popular
book about the end of the world, publicly pronounced that David
Koresh was possessed by demons. The Waco confrontation had
already begun to settle into the routine of an uneventful standoff, and
the media were searching around for colorful news—hence the decision to feature a story on the Texas evangelist. "Satan is alive and well

on planet earth," claimed Evans in the words of a popular book title. "The spirit that is in Koresh and his followers needs to be exorcised" (Lewis, 1998a, p. 28).

He generously offered his services to the authorities: "If it would save innocent lives, I would be willing to go in there one on one with him and cast that demon out." While he said that he "would prefer going in there and laying hands on him and rebuking the demons in him," Brother Evans also noted that the next best thing to a personal exorcism would be to repeat a prayer through a loudspeaker, "rebuking the demon spirits in Koresh and commanding them to come out in the name of Jesus. Turn it up so loud that Koresh will not have a moment of rest 24 hours a day" (Lewis, 1998a, p. 28).

Perhaps taking their cue from Evans, it was not long afterwards that the FBI initiated an harassment campaign against Mt. Carmel. However, rather than attempting to exorcise Koresh, the FBI seemed intent on feeding his demon. Instead of prayers, authorities broadcast, among other sound tracks, Nancy Sinatra music (admittedly pretty bad stuff, but for *real* harassment they should have tried Barry Manilow), the sound of a dentist's drill (talk about cruel and unusual punishment!), and the cries of rabbits being tortured to death. (One wonders what kind of audio library stocks rabbit murder sounds—or were the fuzzy cottontails slain at the behest of the FBI and custom-taped for the occasion?) It is difficult to understand what this audio assault and the accompanying light show—spotlights were swept across the compound all night, every night—could have accomplished, except to increase the level of paranoia among the Davidians.

While Reverend Evans had recommended casting out demons, and while the FBI tried to provoke Koresh's inner devils, the media took a somewhat different approach and proceeded to demonize the Davidian leader. In addition to the usual generic accusations about evil "cult" leaders and the ad nauseam comparisons with Jim Jones,* reporters searched far and wide for "dirt" about David Koresh and

---

*In 1978, in Jonestown, an American settlement in Guyana, South America, cult leader Jim Jones killed a U.S. congressman investigating the sect and then convinced his 900 followers to commit mass suicide.

dutifully repeated every slanderous remark, however disreputable the source. Clearly the intention was to appeal to readers/viewers with sensationalism rather than to produce a balanced picture of the Branch Davidians.

More generally, the journalistic penchant for sensationalism has been a decisive factor in promoting the stereotype of "evil cults" to the larger society. The mass media are not, of course, motivated primarily by the quest for truth, although some reporters have more integrity than others. Instead, the mainstream media are driven by market forces and by the necessity of competing with other newspapers, TV news shows, and so forth.

This is not to say that reporters necessarily lie or fabricate their stories. Rather, in the case of New Religious Movements (NRMs), news people tend to accentuate those facets of "cults" that seem to be strange, exploitative, dangerous, totalitarian, sensational, and the like because such portrayals titillate consumers of news. This kind of reporting contributes to the perpetuation of the cult stereotype. In the words of British sociologist James Beckford,

> Journalists need no other reason for writing about any particular NRM except that it is counted as a cult. This categorization is sufficient to justify a story, especially if the story illustrates many of the other components which conventionally make up the "cult" category. This puts pressure on journalists to find more and more evidence which conforms with the categorical image of cults and therefore confirms the idea that a NRM is newsworthy to the extent that it does match the category. It is no part of conventional journalistic practice to look for stories about NRMs which do *not* conform to the category of cult. (p. 146)

Another important factor is the marked tendency of the mass media to report on a phenomenon only when it results in conflicts and problems. To again cite from Beckford's important paper, "The Media and New Religious Movements,"

> NRMs are only newsworthy when a problem occurs. Scandals, atrocities, spectacular failures, "tug-of-love" stories, defections, ex-

posés, outrageous conduct–these are the main criteria of NRMs' newsworthiness. . . . And, of course, the unspectacular, non-sensational NRMs are permanently invisible in journalists' accounts. (pp. 144–45)

The different media vary somewhat in their tendency to produce unbalanced reports. "TV tabloids" such as *20/20* and *Hard Copy* that have to compete with prime time TV programming tend to be the most unbalanced. Rather than attempting to produce programs that examine the complex ramifications of issues, news shows usually present melodramas in which guys in white hats are shown locked in conflict with guys in black hats. On the opposite extreme are the major newspapers, such as the *Los Angeles Times* and the *Washington Post*, which tend to do the best job of attempting to present balanced articles on controversial subjects. Such "balance," however, usually only means finding the space for opposing views. The journalist appears to be objective when her or his story is two-sided rather than one-sided. The news magazines such as *Time* and *Newsweek* tend to fall somewhere in between.

One of the more unusual aspects of the Waco standoff was the decision of NBC to create a "docudrama" about the Branch Davidians and the events leading up to the original ATF assault *before* the siege ended. The title of this made-for-TV movie, "Ambush in Waco," seemed to evoke images from the quasimythical past of frontier Texas, when sinister savages ambushed noble lawmen. Television, as we have already mentioned, is the least suitable medium for coming to grips with complex moral issues. In the case of "Ambush in Waco," the ATF agents were dressed in white hats and David Koresh in a black hat. It was, as might be expected, a shallow, rambling production built around a disconnected framework of accusations leveled against Koresh. The ATF was completely whitewashed as a group of noble-minded public servants–not a single question was raised about the propriety of the ATF's actions. The filming of "Ambush" was still in process when the FBI attacked Mt. Carmel. Appealing to the public hunger for sensationalism and violence, the docudrama was a smashing success.

The collapse of the distinction between dramatic time and real time in this and other productions represents a disturbing trend. One

82   DOOMSDAY PROPHECIES

can well imagine the creation of a "quickie" docudrama on a sensationalistic murder in which the murder suspect is convicted on TV–but who later turns out to be innocent. It has become increasingly clear that something like this was the case with the Davidians (i.e., a TV conviction), but the "evidence"–as presented in "Ambush in Waco"–has helped to blind the public to the possibility that Koresh and company could have been innocent. Instead, "Ambush" merely reinforced the news media's demonization of the Branch Davidians, and helped to make the final holocaust of Mt. Carmel more acceptable to Americans.

In an important 1993 article on the docudrama trend, "From Headline to Prime Time" (published in *TV Guide*), David Shaw observes that "Fact based movies are suddenly the Hula-Hoop, the skateboard, the Nintendo of the '90s." He further points out that most such movies are based on disasters, and notes that "the instant dramatization of real tragedy has become a kind of video fast food, drama McNuggets." Shaw's conclusion is worth citing at length:

> Using the powerful and intimate medium of television to pander to the viewer's base instincts is not new, but this rush to do so is the latest step down a very dangerous road. Where will it all end? Will the next David Koresh be able to sit in his compound and watch his own dramatized death on television–and maybe figure out how to kill the cops instead? . . . Will producers decide that, rather than risk waiting until dramatic events actually take place before they begin costly bidding wars for the dramatic rights of the players, they should open negotiations with soldiers of fortune, jilted lovers, and putative terrorists *before* they do their dastardly deeds . . . perhaps even suggesting a traumatic twist or two in the ultimate execution to jack up the asking price?

THE BOTTOM-FEEDERS OF LAW ENFORCEMENT

Prior to Feb. 27, 1993, the followers of David Koresh were citizens that to my knowledge had caused no problems of any kind in

their community. On Feb. 28, 1993, following what appeared to
be a staged for TV assault by BATF on the compound they were
living in, they all became heinous criminals.
                                        –Rep. Harold Volkmer, D-Mo.,
                                        from the *Congressional Record*

The "revenuers" of cartoon fame who traded shots with Snuffy Smith
and Li'l Abner in real life were agents of the Bureau of Alcohol,
Tobacco, and Firearms (ATF), a branch of the U.S. Treasury Department. The least well-trained and least professional of all federal cops
(Pate 1993), a North Carolina lawyer once described them as
"bottom-feeders in the evolutionary scale of Federal law enforcement." The rationale for the continued existence of the ATF as a distinct entity has often been called into question, and the agency had
to defend itself against the Reagan administration's attempts to abolish the agency (former President Reagan went so far as to describe
the ATF as a "rogue agency") and transfer its functions to the Customs Service and the Secret Service.

Perhaps as a holdover from the days when its primary enforcement activity was busting up stills in rural Appalachia, the ATF has a
marked propensity for breaking down doors and roughing up suspects. (According to James Pate, even other law enforcement agencies describe ATF agents as "cowboys.") Quite recently, the ATF has
been investigated for discriminating against minorities in its hiring
and promotional practices. The agency has also been accused of
turning a blind eye to sexual harassment charges within its ranks. As
reported in *U.S. News and World Report*, the prospect of overcoming
this tarnished image probably "influenced the decision to proceed
with the high-profile raid" of the Branch Davidian community outside of Waco, Texas.

It has also been suggested that ATF began searching for such a
high-profile operation soon after it became apparent that Bill Clinton
would become the next president of the United States. President
Clinton had been broadcasting a strong anti-gun message, and certain ATF officials perceived an opportunity to expand the scope and
powers of their agency within the new president's anti-gun agenda.

The Waco attack, if this suggestion is correct, was designed to attract positive attention to the ATF in a highly publicized raid. The raid was apparently planned with an eye to the Senate Appropriations Sub-committee on Treasury, Postal Service, and General Government that was slated to meet in early March 1993.

Another factor playing into the Branch Davidian fiasco was the ATF's well-deserved reputation for initiating dramatic raids on the basis of ill-founded rumors. The Johnnie Lawmaster incident is a case in point. This is an interesting incident, worth recounting for the light it throws on the ATF assault on the Branch Davidians.

On December 16, 1991–the first day of the third century of the Bill of Rights–agents from the Bureau of Alcohol, Tobacco, and Firearms forced their way into the Tulsa, Oklahoma, house of Johnnie Lawmaster. The ATF was acting on a *rumor* that Lawmaster had illegally modified a semiautomatic rifle to fire in full automatic mode. Although he would have been happy to have let them in, the ATF broke into Lawmaster's house, kicked down the door and cut the locks off his gun safe. Federal agents chose to show up while Law-master was away from home, and used his absence as a pretext to ransack the premises.

Despite the fact that he had never been guilty of anything more serious than a traffic violation, ATF and local police assaulted Law-master's home with a total of sixty law enforcement officers. Accord-ing to an account published in the *American Hunter,*

> They cordoned off the street; took station with weapons drawn in the back yard; used a battering ram to break through the front door; kicked in the back door; broke into his gun safe; threw per-sonal papers around the house; spilled boxes of ammunition on the floor; broke into a small, locked box that contained precious coins; and stood on a table to peer through the ceiling tiles, breaking the table in the process. Then, they left. The doors were closed but not latched, much less locked. The ammo and guns were left unse-cured. (Cited in Lewis 1994)

As Lawmaster later remarked, "Anybody could have waltzed in there and stolen everything I own. A child could have taken a gun. The guns, the safe—everything was open and laying around" (cited in Lewis, p. 89).

When he returned home after the raid, Lawmaster felt he had walked into a nightmare. He was still standing around in shock when the gas, electric, and water companies showed up to turn everything off. They informed Lawmaster that they had been told to shut things down. He then discovered a brief note: "Nothing found–ATF." In Lawmaster's words, "They didn't make any attempt to notify me. I've lived in Tulsa all my life and never got more than a traffic ticket. How come they can't look that up, realize I've been law-abiding my whole life, then come to the door when I'm home? They didn't leave someone here to watch over my private property. They didn't even come by to explain what happened. They just raided my home, ransacked it, left it wide open and left" (cited in Lewis 1994, p. 89).

The parallels between the Lawmaster case and the assault on the Branch Davidians are both illuminating and disturbing. Lawmaster's case, however, was only the most recent in a long series of abusive raids on the homes of law-abiding citizens. Considering what happened to Kenyon Ballew some twenty years earlier, Lawmaster should regard himself as fortunate that he was away from home when the ATF arrived.

On June 7, 1971, Kenyon F. Ballew, a former U.S. Air Force policeman, was dozing in the bathtub of his Silver Spring, Maryland, home. He was awakened by the sounds of his wife screaming and the front door being broken down. Neither fully clothed nor fully awake, Ballew jumped out of the tub and grabbed the first weapon he could lay his hands on—an antique 1847 cap-and-ball revolver. Rushing out into the hall to defend his family, he was cut down by a barrage of gunfire. One of the bullets lodged in his brain, destroying most of the tissues that controlled his right arm and leg. A total of four bullets hit him, several after he had already fallen to the floor unconscious. He was permanently crippled (Lewis 1994, pp. 89–90).

ATF agents, acting on a *rumor* (thirdhand information from an anonymous tipster) that Ballew had created live grenades out of empty grenade shells (similar to the rumor about the Branch Davidians), chose to burst into a law-abiding citizen's home instead of politely coming to the door with a search warrant and peaceably examining the premises. If the intruders had even as much as yelled "police," Ballew did not hear them. In a show of bravado, one of the agents even fired bullets into the ceiling as he stepped into the apartment—a stunt worthy of a B-grade movie actor. None of the grenade shells contained explosives, and Ballew was not charged. He was, however, left a penniless cripple, getting by as best as he could on welfare. Although he sought retribution, none was made.

Rep. Gilbert Gude, in whose district Ballew was shot, later urged a thorough investigation. His ringing indictment of the ATF, as recorded in the *Congressional Record*, included statements such as the following:

> I am thoroughly appalled by this revelation of the reckless, brutal, and inept methods employed by the Alcohol, Tobacco, and Firearms Division . . . in executing search warrants in private homes. This kind of storm-trooper exercise may have been commendable in Nazi Germany, but it must be made unmistakably clear to the ATFD that it is intolerable here. . . . In my opinion, the manner in which this search was conducted was not only unreasonable, it was high-handed and incredibly stupid, if not criminal.

In words that seem prophetic in light of what later happened at the Branch Davidian community, Gude went on to say that,

> When police are permitted to barge into people's homes . . . they are just inviting violent resistance. The present deplorable tactics of the ATFD demonstrate nothing less than a callous disregard for the probable and predictable consequences.

COOPERATIVE CULTISTS VS. RIVAL CULT LEADER

David Koresh's community—Mt. Carmel—was rarely a problem to their neighbors or to the residents of Waco. The only incident of note was that in 1987 Koresh and seven followers were involved in a shoot-out with George Roden, a rival "cult" leader. Koresh had been invited to Mt. Carmel by Roden as part of a rather bizarre challenge, taken from the story of Christ's resurrection of Lazarus, to resurrect a corpse (George was later incarcerated in an insane asylum; Kopel and Blackman, p. 42, n. 42). Suspecting foul play, Koresh and seven associates showed up armed—his right under a Texas law that allows one to seek out an adversary, and to do so armed if one feels the threat to be serious enough. Koresh's people prevailed over Roden without casualties, but the shoot-out could not be overlooked by the authorities.

The local sheriff, Jack Harwell, phoned Vernon Howell (who did not legally change his name to David Koresh until 1990), and informed him that, well, charges were pending from the shoot-out and that he would have to be placed under arrest and give up his weapons. Howell acknowledged that, yes, it was a serious incident, and promised full cooperation. Two law officers were then dispatched to Mt. Carmel where they arrested Howell and the seven associates and confiscated their weapons. (ATF officials could have learned some lessons in etiquette, not to mention proper law enforcement procedure, from the McLennan County Sheriff's Department.) The Davidians were eventually acquitted on charges of attempted murder.

The prosecutor in the case, then District Attorney Vic Feazell, recalled that the Davidians had cooperated completely with law enforcement officials, and condemned the 1993 ATF assault on Mt. Carmel as totally unnecessary: "We treated them like human beings [after the shoot-out], rather than storm-trooping the place. They were extremely polite" and cooperative. Feazell further condemned the ATF raid as "a vulgar display of power on the part of the feds. . . . If they'd called and talked to them, the Davidians would've given them what they wanted." Within a few days after the ATF raid, he offered to help mediate the crisis. In words that, retrospectively, seem prophetic, Feazell expressed his doubts about the final outcome of the siege:

> The feds are preparing to kill them. That way they can bury their mistakes. And they won't have attorneys looking over what they

did later at a trial. I'd represent these boys for free if they'd surrender without bloodshed. But I'm afraid I'm going to wake up and
see headlines that say they all died. It's sad for the Davidians. And
it's sad for our government.

Given the Davidians' history, which reflects an obvious desire on the
part of the community to cooperate with the authorities, locals felt no
fear of the Branch Davidians. Rather than arising from local concerns, the intrusion of federal agents was the product of forces oper-
ating outside the sociopolitical ecosystem of McLennan County. The
February 28, 1993, raid was the end result of efforts by three groups
of outsiders—the ATF, the anticult movement, and rival "cult"
leaders—who all opportunistically portrayed the Davidians as "dangerous cultists" for self-serving reasons.

According to authors David Kopel and Paul Blackman, one of the
candidates for the person most responsible for initiating the Davidian
tragedy is Marc Breault of Melbourne, Australia. Portrayed by the
media as a former member crusading to make the world aware of
Koresh's atrocities, surviving Davidians paint a very different picture
of Breault's motivations. Breault, it turns out, was a convert to the
Branch Davidians who decided that he was a better prophet than
David Koresh, and started his own group—sort of a branch of the
Branch Davidians (later, he disingenuously claimed that he had
formed his own group for the sole purpose of rescuing people from
Koresh's clutches). The problem, however, was that, to Breault's considerable chagrin, the Davidians failed to be convinced that he had
"out-propheted" Koresh, and, as a consequence, he attracted few followers. This disappointment awakened Breault's demon of revenge,
and he began a concerted campaign to bring down his rival.

Breault sent innumerable letters to various U.S. government
agencies alleging everything from child sacrifice to the accusation
that the Branch Davidians were a violent, apocalyptic cult ready
either to massacre every citizen of Waco or to re-enact Jonestown at
the drop of a hat. Finding himself brushed aside on the absurd charge
of child sacrifice, he soon moderated his allegations to sex with
underage females—an accusation that, while still sensationalistic, was

easier for authorities to swallow. As for the horrific charge of massacring the citizenry of Waco, this was soon moderated to simpler charges of illegally modifying weapons to fire in full-automatic mode and manufacturing live hand grenades. His accusations in combination with the accusations of other disgruntled former members of the group were the driving force behind the Child Protective Service investigations of the Mt. Carmel children–investigations that invariably exonerated the Davidians. Breault's baseless allegations, minus child sacrifice, were reprinted as gospel truth in the March 15, 1993, issue of *People* magazine. Breault's prolonged efforts to invoke the repressive power of the U.S. government finally paid off when the ATF accepted his trumped up accusations about Koresh and company illegally modifying firearms.

KIDNAPPERS, INC.

A comparatively minor, yet still important player in the Waco killing fields was the anticult movement. In the early 1970s, opposition to religious innovation organized itself around deprogrammers–individuals who forcibly and often violently abducted individuals from nontraditional religions. "Cult" members were snatched off the street and locked up in houses or motel rooms, where they were assaulted until their religious faith was destroyed. Despite claims that deprogramming is a therapeutic intervention that breaks through "cult" members' "hypnotic trance" and forces them to think again, it is clear to objective observers that deprogrammers are little more than marketers of fear, preying on parents upset by the religious choices of their adult children.

Deprogramming, controlled entirely by independent entrepreneurs, could never have developed into a viable profession without the simultaneous development of secular "cult watchdog groups." These organizations, despite vigorous public denials to the contrary, regularly refer concerned parents to deprogrammers. At the national gatherings of the old Cult Awareness Network (CAN; formerly the Citizens Freedom Foundation, or CFF), for example, one always found a host of deprogrammers actively marketing their services to the concerned parents in attendance. Deprogrammers, in turn, allegedly kicked back a certain percentage of their "take" to CAN. John Myles Sweeney, former national director of CAN/CFF, described this arrangement in the following words:

> Because of the large amount of money they make due to referrals received from CFF members, deprogrammers usually kick back money to the CFF member who gave the referral.... The kick backs would either be in cash or would be hidden in the form of a tax-deductible "donation" to the CFF.

One of the results of the financial alliance between anticult groups and deprogrammers is that anticult groups have acquired a vested interest in promoting the worst possible stereotypes of non-traditional religions. In other words, if one is making a handsome profit referring worried parents to deprogrammers, it makes no sense to inform parents that the religion their child has joined is compara-tively benign. Instead, one tends to paint such religions in the exag-gerated colors of fear and fanaticism, hinting darkly that, unless their child is "rescued" immediately, he or she could end up as a lobo-tomized robot, suffering permanent psychological damage.

Similarly, it makes little sense to propagate a balanced view of alternative religions to the press. If one profits from the fear sur-rounding "cult" groups, then one takes every opportunity to spread frightening rumors, however ill-founded. It is, in fact, the two-decade-long interaction between the anticult movement and the media that has been responsible for the widespread view that all "cults" are dan-gerous organizations, this despite the fact that comparatively few such groups constitute a genuine threat, either to themselves or to society. The general atmosphere of distrust toward minority religions con-tributed significantly to public support for the ATF raid against Mt. Carmel, and probably even explains why the ATF picked a group like the Davidians for their dramatic public raid.

While there were comparatively few direct connections between the ATF and the anticult movement that contributed to the Waco fiasco, they were significant. In particular, the testimony of deprogrammed former Davidians was used to support the contention that Koresh had to be served a search warrant (the reports of deprogrammees about their former religious group, however, are notoriously suspect). Also important was the advisory role that a man named Rick Ross played with the ATF prior to the attack.

Before the blood had even dried in the fields surrounding Mt. Carmel, Ross was busy promoting himself to the media on the basis of his role as advisor to the ATF. What were the qualifications that allowed this person to have the ear of the ATF? Ross, it turns out, had "deprogrammed" several Branch Davidians. What was his background and training? It certainly was not counseling; it was crime. After completing an apprenticeship in petty crime, he graduated to the more lucrative career of deprogrammer. And as someone who makes his living kidnapping "cult" members for money, Ross clearly has a vested interest in portraying nontraditional religions in the worst possible light. For example, in his forward to Tim Madigan's *See No Evil: Blind Devotion and Bloodshed in David Koresh's Holy Way*, Ross paints a picture of the evils of all nontraditional religions in the boldest possible colors:

> America must take a long, hard look at Vernon Howell, later known to the world as David Koresh, because among cult leaders, he is not atypical. It seems they are all the same. As I travel the country and delve into different destructive cults, I meet the same cult leader over and over again. Only the names are different. They are self-obsessed, egomaniacal, sociopathic and heartless individuals with no regard whatsoever for their followers. They seek only their personal aggrandizement, financial well-being and physical pleasure. Such leaders exercise total control over their followers. The personalities of those adherents have been dismantled by systematic brainwashing to the point where the leader's desires become their own. Cult victims and fanatical followers of radical sects are deceived, lied to, manipulated and ultimately exploited. (p. x)

From this statement, it is easy to see how the ATF's distorted impressions of the Branch Davidians could easily have been created by misinformation received from Ross and others of his ilk.

LIES, HALF-TRUTHS, AND STUPIDITY

*I regret to say it, but there are those on the street who believe that
the ATF's objective on the morning of 28 February was to impress
the new secretary of the Treasury Department, to pave part of the
way for a larger annual budget.*

                                                    –Col. Charlie Beckwith

The ATF was, however, no innocent pawn of plotting rival cult leaders
and scheming anticultists. Indeed, the ATF was primarily a victim of its
own leaders' greed and stupidity, who fed the misinformation provided
by Breault, Ross, and other rogues into their own scheme to promote
the agency. It has already been mentioned that the overriding motivation for the February 28 attack appears to have been the desire to attract
favorable publicity to the ATF, as well as to attract increased funding.
The Davidians were, however, such a poor choice for the raid that
agency officials had to manufacture evidence to support a warrant–the
Branch Davidians were, in other words, *framed* by the ATF. Initially
hidden from public view, cries of cover-up eventually forced the ATF
to release the original warrant and its supporting affidavit. The misinformation contained in the affidavit documents a fantastic abuse of
power exercised by ATF officials in their frame up of the Branch Davidians (for one of many sources, see Kopel and Blackman, chapter 2).

A close examination of the affidavit, nominally authored by Davy
Aguilera, a relatively inexperienced special agent, reveals that it failed
to establish the "probable cause" necessary to justify a search warrant.
Certain assertions in the Aguilera report are false. For example, in an
unsettling commentary published in the *Washington Times* (June 1,
1993), Thomas Fiddleman and David Kopel point out that

> Some parts of the affidavit were plainly false. For example, Agent
> Aguilera told the federal magistrate that Mr. Koresh had possession
> of a "clandestine" firearms publication. The "clandestine" publica-
> tion was *Shotgun News*, a national newspaper that carries want-ads
> by gun retailers and wholesalers. The newspaper is sold at news-
> stands all over the country, and to tens of thousands of subscribers.

With a circulation of more than 150,000, it's no more clandestine than the *New Republic.*

Certain other parts of the affidavit misrepresented the situation by excluding key information. Fiddleman and Kopel, for instance, point out that

> Mr. Aguilera asserted that a neighbor heard machine-gun fire, but Mr. Aguilera failed to tell the magistrate that the same neighbor had previously reported the noise to the sheriff, who investigated the noise. The sheriff found Mr. Koresh had a lawful item called a "hell fire device" which simulates the sound of machine-gun fire but does not turn a regular gun into a machine gun.

Other information in this document reflects an ignorance about firearms that Aguilera and the U.S. Magistrate, Judge Dennis G. Green, apparently shared. For example, the affidavit noted that Koresh had obtained the "upper and lower receivers" (a receiver contains the inner mechanism of a firearm) of an AK-47 rifle—an observation that implies the Davidians were modifying the inner workings so the AK would fire in full automatic mode. This observation is, however, inaccurate, because the AK-47, as well as its legal, semiautomatic versions (the type of firearms possessed by the Davidians) have a solid receiver that cannot be broken into upper and lower halves.

Perhaps the most peculiar section of this strange and twisted document was the report of a conversation of Agent Carlos Torres with Joyce Sparks of the Texas Department of Human Services. Sparks was the official who investigated the Davidians on charges of child abuse. Fiddleman and Kopel describe how, during her second visit to Mt. Carmel on April 6, 1992, she had a conversation with David Koresh in which, according to Aguilera,

> Koresh told her that he was the "Messenger" from God, that the world was coming to an end, and that when he "reveals" himself the riots in Los Angeles would pale in comparison to what was going to happen in Waco, Texas. Koresh stated that it would be a "military type operation" and that all the "non-believers" would have to suffer.

This information was widely repeated by the media, helping to shape the public image of Koresh as a violent, dangerous fanatic. The L.A. riots did not, however, begin until April 30–twenty-four days following the supposed conversation between Sparks and the Davidian leader. Clearly, either Koresh had *truly* prophetic gifts, or someone fabricated the conversation for the purpose of further demonizing the Davidians. In either case, neither Judge Green nor Aguilera noticed this peculiar discrepancy.

Many other discrepancies and bits of odd, irrelevant information pepper the document. On pages fourteen and fifteen, for example, Aguilera asserts that Koresh stated to an ATF undercover agent that he "did not pay [federal] taxes or local taxes because he felt he did not have to." However, this assertion flies in the face of the statement on page three of the affidavit that "the taxes owed on the Mt. Carmel Center have been paid by Howell's [Koresh's] group." Again, neither Green nor Aguilera noticed the discrepancy.

Aguilera also often repeats the accusations about Koresh being a child molester who beat the children excessively. At points, he seems to go on and on about this, as well as about various sundry sexual accusations. As an example of the latter, on page eleven of the affidavit he relates the following:

> Both interviews with [former member] Poia Vaega revealed a false imprisonment for a term of three and one half months . . . and physical and sexual abuse of one of Mrs. Vaega's sisters, Doreen Saipaia. . . . The physical and sexual abuse was done by Vernon Wayne Howell and Stanley Sylvia. . . . According to Mrs. Vaega, all the girls and women at the compound were exclusively reserved for Howell.

The problem with repeating these kinds of accusations is that they are totally irrelevant to the case at hand. ATF's responsibility lies in the enforcement of firearms laws; the other matters mentioned in the affidavit are the responsibility of the state. To repeat these unsubstantiated rumors merely to stress to the judge that "we're dealing with evil people" shows either a lack of understanding or a lack of professionalism.

MORE LIES, HALF-TRUTHS, AND STUPIDITY

It is only when one examines BATF's actions subsequent to their ill-fated assault that the clearest picture comes into focus of just how terribly inept and treacherous the agency truly is. Willikers! BATF's attempt at a cover-up was so bad as to make their initial actions look almost professional by comparison.

—Dean Speir

In a useful commentary, "Wither BATF in Future" (*Gun Week*, June 11, 1993), Dean Speir offers a few insights into the ATF's bungled cover-up of the agency's lies and ineptitude. ATF spokesperson David Troy, who had initially stood beside FBI spokespeople in joint press briefings, disappeared from these briefings after six weeks because the FBI had become embarrassed by his presence. According to Speir,

> Troy (BATF's "minister of propaganda," one [reporter] called him) had changed his stories so many times that he had lost all credibility with the assembled press crews. ("He's a pathological liar," was an assessment made of Troy by two independent sources on the Lone Star scene.)

Beyond the affidavit supporting the search warrant, ATF's misinformation campaign was most blatant in the agency's response to the accusation that they had acquired National Guard helicopters under false pretenses. The only legal way the ATF could have obtained the use of these aircraft was if they had claimed that the Branch Davidians were involved in illegal drug trafficking. Aguilera's affidavit, however, contains no mention of the important issue of illegal drugs, although it does mention comparatively minor bits of information, such as the comment of one young boy that he wanted to own a gun when he grew up. Also, according to Speir,

> twice during the first week of the siege, Troy, in direct response to questions posed by *Soldier of Fortune*'s Jim Pate, denied that illegal

drugs played any part in the government's interest in the soon-to-be-late David Koresh and his followers.

The Texas governor's office, however, saw fit to complain about ATF's deception. Rather than offer apologies on this point, the agency responded by attempting to cover their earlier lie to the governor's office with a new lie to the press:

> Troy immediately went before the TV cameras to say that "... a prior infrared overflight had revealed the presence of a 'meth lab' " in the compound. Not only was that an outright lie, but it was a stupid one. ... A confidential source inside the U.S. Drug Enforcement Administration expressed incredulity that Troy would prevaricate so clumsily. (Speir 1993)

On March 29, 1993, an ATF source told *Soldier of Fortune* magazine that the "meth lab" ploy "was made up out of whole cloth . . . a complete fabrication" to avoid further criticism (Pate 1993).

The ATF responded to every criticism leveled against it with lame excuses and more disinformation. The agency's botched cover-up made Richard Nixon's Watergate look slick by comparison. While these awkward falsehoods would fill a book, for our present purposes we can restrict our examination to one more point in the ATF disinformation campaign—the lies about David Koresh's activities during the weeks leading up to February 28, 1993.

One of the most frequently asked questions about the initial ATF attack has been "Why didn't agents simply pick up Koresh while he was downtown having a beer, rather than assaulting Mt. Carmel with a dangerous frontal attack?" The stated or unstated implication behind such a pointed question is that the agency was more concerned about staging a dramatic raid for the media than with the smooth running of the wheels of justice or with the safety of their agents. ATF's immediate response to this question was that Mt. Carmel had been under constant surveillance for over two months prior to the raid, that Koresh had not been outside the community for over five weeks, and, further, that he was not expected to leave Mt. Carmel anytime soon. This, however, was another fabrication.

David Koresh, it was subsequently discovered, had been seen all around Waco by innumerable people, as recently as the week or two before the attack. The *Waco Tribune-Herald,* for example, noted that Koresh had been in town as recently as February 22–six days prior to the assault–at an auto repair shop. Koresh was also a regular at the Chelsea Street Pub in Waco, which he routinely visited once a week. The manager, Brent Moore, was familiar with the Davidian prophet, who, he noted, always carried a cellular phone, and had ordered bean-and-cheese nachos and iced tea during his last visit to the pub.

Paul Fatta, a Davidian who had been outside the community during the raid, said that in recent weeks he, Koresh, and others had been

> jogging down the road, almost three miles. . . . Five guys in tennis shoes jogging in shorts. I want to know why, at that time, if they wanted him to come peacefully or serve the warrant why wasn't it done then? We were off the property several times.

The agency was forced to confess that, contrary to their earlier assertions, they had *not* monitored Mt. Carmel on an around-the-clock basis, and thus really had no idea as to David Koresh's comings and goings. This falsehood, while seemingly minor, is a key to understanding the February 28 raid: The ATF really had no interest in finding a peaceful resolution; instead, they wanted to stage a made-for-TV assault on a group of people they could characterize as gun-crazy religious fanatics.

ATTACK OF THE KEYSTONE COPS

On February 27, 1993, Sharon Wheeler, a secretary working for the Bureau of Alcohol, Tobacco, and Firearms in Dallas, called various news media, some from as far away as Oklahoma: Would they be interested in reporting a weapons raid against a local "cult"? (Wheeler later denied being this specific; rather, she claimed, she had just informed them that "something big" was going to happen.) The ATF initially denied contacting the media–more clumsy prevarication (Kopel and Blackman, p. 48). Uncovered by the congressional committee investigating the Waco fiasco, the phone calls were but one manifestation of the increasingly ghoulish pact between media and law enforcement: You give me free publicity; I'll give you newsworthy violence. This ill-considered bid for the media spotlight, sanctioned and initiated by senior ATF officials, set the stage for the tragic fiasco at the Mt. Carmel headquarters of the Branch Davidian Seventh Day Adventists.

The Davidians learned of the raid at least forty-five minutes—some sources say two hours—beforehand. When news of the tip-off became public, the ATF immediately fingered the media as the responsible party. If this attribution is correct, it means the agency, which contacted the press the preceding day, has only itself to blame for the deaths of its agents. There are, however, many other possibilities. In the first place, the Davidians were wise to the undercover informant, Agent Robert Rodriguez, who lived in a shack near Mt. Carmel, but who also wore new clothing and drove a late model automobile (Kopel and Blackman, p. 122, n. 169). Rodriguez heard Koresh exclaiming that the ATF and the National Guard were "coming to get him" some two hours before the attack. Koresh later claimed he knew something was amiss when the agent bolted from the community on Sunday morning. Rodriguez immediately contacted his superiors, advising them that the Davidians were wise to their raid, and that it should be called off. Perhaps in order to avoid disappointing the reporters who had gathered to see the show, this advice was ignored.

The many ATF agents clad in body armor and gun gear who were suspiciously milling around in motel lobbies throughout Waco earlier Sunday morning might also have been the source of the tip-off. This situation prompted Col. Charlie Beckwith, retired founder of the U.S. Army's elite Delta Force unit, to remark that "The ATF might just as well run a flag up telling everyone something was about to happen." Beckwith's analysis of the ATF attack also called attention to the "gross error of judgement" involved in the selection of the time for the assault: "Successful assault operations are conducted during the hours of darkness or a few minutes before first light." One can only surmise that the agency selected full daylight because of their overriding concern that the raid be recorded by TV cameramen (Oliver, p. 75).

Yet another possibility were the walkie-talkie conversations between ATF agents that the agency failed to screen from civilian monitoring. There were also at least eleven reporters on the scene prior to the arrival of the assault team. Given this gross neglect of basic security matters, it is no surprise that the Davidians found out ahead of time (Kopel and Blackman, pp. 96ff). What *is* shocking is that ATF officials ordered their agents in even after they discovered that Koresh and company knew they were coming.

On this point, the ATF also denied knowing that they had lost the element of surprise, but, once again, this denial was a lie. Surviving Branch Davidians assert that the raid began when the helicopters controlling the mission fired on Mt. Carmel. In response, a few shots were fired back from the community. The ATF officers in the air, Ted Royster and Phil Chojnacki, then ordered the ground troops in without informing them that the helicopters had already taken fire (Kopel and Blackman 1997).

One of the Branch Davidians I interviewed after the raid had been with Koresh for over ten years. An important piece of the puzzle supplied by this Davidian was the explanation for the large store of guns and ammunition at Mt. Carmel: One of Koresh's followers, Paul Fatta, was a gun dealer, and his merchandise was stored in the community. Also, contrary to the NBC docudrama, "Ambush at Waco," most community members were *not* trained to use weapons–the interviewee had fired a gun twice in the ten years he was with David Koresh. The ATF knew all of this–they keep records on guns, especially those owned as stock by dealers–which is why they felt safe to go ahead and attack Mt. Carmel even after they knew they had lost the element of surprise. Some of the young men, however, took guns from Fatta's stock (Fatta was at a gun show on the morning of the raid) and prepared to fight off attackers.

Ninety-one heavily armed ATF agents drove up to Mt. Carmel–almost as many agents as community members. They were hidden in cattle trailers–like lambs to the slaughter–but the Davidians knew who their visitors were. The agency claimed that the Davidians fired first. However, given ATF's track record of one falsehood after another, as well as Koresh's history of peaceful cooperation with law enforcement officials, his assertion that he just opened the door and was shot at seems far more believable than the agency account. To a religious group nourished on apocalyptic images from the Book of Revelation, the assault must have seemed like the first skirmish in Armageddon.

While ATF has repeatedly asserted that they had been practicing the assault for months, at least some of the agents involved were not briefed until the preceding day, and were never told that they would be facing high power, assault-type weapons. Incredibly, the ATF did not even bring a doctor to treat wounded agents–a standard practice of more professional agencies like the FBI (Pate 1993). These inept, keystone cop antics of the ATF are difficult to understand unless we suppose that agency officials simply assumed that the Davidians would give up at the first sign of a superior force–a fatal assumption that would have been immediately rejected by anyone who had researched survivalist religious groups. The stupidity of the attack was exceeded only by the stupidity of the explanation ATF spokespersons offered for the attack's failure: "We had an excellent plan and we practiced it for months. Everything would have been fine, except we were outgunned" (Richardson, p. 181).

What? If the ATF was serving a search warrant to a heavily armed "cult" believed to have automatic weapons and perhaps even hand grenades, why were they surprised by the Davidians' powerful gunfire? Especially after they had lost the element of surprise, why did ATF agents charge in with their guns blazing? If Mt. Carmel was such a dangerous place, why didn't they just lay siege to it from the very beginning rather than sacrificing the lives of their agents? The reason given to the public was that, in the words of one ATF official,

> Either they were going to come out and attack the citizens of Waco or do a Jonestown, which was why an operation was staged that placed our agents between a rock and a hard place. Our information was that was how bad it was.

The mythic imaginations of the Davidians were shaped by biblical narratives, but what about the ATF? The imaginative fantasies of ATF officials seem to have been programmed by late-night action-adventure movies. Their fatal decision to invite the media to what should have been a private party appears to have been an attempt to cast themselves in the role of the rescuing heroes—kind of a real-life *Rambo IV*. Clearly the ATF saw itself as staging a rescue operation—rescuing not only hostages, but also ATF's status as an independent agency—a cause noble enough to legitimate an aggressive assault. Their reasoning was comparable to Sylvester Stallone's, who once defended his character John Rambo from charges of being a violent aggressor by asserting that Rambo was a reluctant warrior:

> He's dragged into these things kicking and screaming. When he does get into a combative situation it's never against the enemy directly. It's always trying to rescue somebody.

ATF officials' defense of their actions followed a similar logic, although one must ask the pointed question whether the "logic" fit the situation.

The pretext for the ATF raid was that the Branch Davidians were illegally modifying their firearms to fire in full automatic mode. The gunfire recorded by TV cameras on the day of the assault, however, was that of *completely legal*, semiautomatic assault rifles. There is thus room to question both the ATF's tactics as well as the information on which the ATF chose to act. The Waco raid may have been another Johnnie Lawmaster fiasco—an expensive, time-consuming raid undertaken against someone who was not actually violating the law. Given the thoroughness of the final, fiery holocaust, we will probably never know if Koresh and company were actually violating federal gun laws. However dubious the victory, the ATF was not above celebrating its grim final triumph by raising its flag over the ashes of the Davidian community. One reporter reacted with the comment, "I don't think any flag should be raised over the bodies of dead children" (cited in Lewis 1994, p. 99).

One of the numerous disturbing aspects of this whole affair is that scholars of alternative religions—many of whom have devoted their careers to the study of such religions—were not consulted, either prior to the initial raid of the Davidian community or during the siege. Law enforcement officials persisted in regarding the Branch Davidians as a criminal organization parading under the guise of religion. Thus, to their mind, no specialized knowledge of the dynamics of a *religious* group was required. Had the ATF consulted and followed the advice of mainstream academic experts, the Waco tragedy could have been avoided. In the aftermath of the ATF attack, two academics—James A. Tabor and J. Phillip Arnold—heroically attempted to prevent further bloodshed by the application of their hard-earned knowledge of biblical apocalypticism. Had the FBI listened to them, the final tragedy might never have occurred. Tabor and Arnold began their efforts to influence the course of events soon after the initial ATF raid.

ONE ATTEMPT TO AVERT DISASTER*

At 7:25 P.M. on Sunday, February 28, 1993, James Tabor, professor of Religious Studies at the University of North Carolina, Charlotte, was enjoying a quiet evening at home. His attention was suddenly riveted to an unfamiliar voice, edged with an appealing intensity, coming over CNN on the television in the next room. Anchorman David French had someone on a phone hookup who was quoting biblical passages in a steady stream. A photo of a young man with glasses and long wavy hair which was later to become familiar around the world was on the TV screen against a backdrop of a map of Texas with a place marked "Mt. Carmel" near Waco. Regular CNN programming had been interrupted. It was obvious that some emergency situation was unfolding.

Professor Tabor had not yet heard of the ATF raid which resulted in a two-hour gun battle with the Branch Davidians. For the moment Tabor's attention was drawn to two things which fascinated him. The

*This section depends significantly on the work of James Tabor (1994).

young man from Texas called himself David Koresh, and he was talking about the "seven seals"* of the Book of Revelation. A biblical scholar, Tabor knew that "Koresh" was the Hebrew name for Cyrus, the ancient Persian king who destroyed the Babylonian empire in 539 B.C.E. He was intrigued that anyone would have such a last name. Also, he was quite familiar with the mysterious seven seals in the last book of the Bible and how they unfolded in an apocalyptic sequence leading to the Judgment Day and the "end of the world."

Like any good newsperson, CNN anchorman French kept trying to get Koresh to talk about the morning raid, how many had been killed or wounded from his group, and whether he planned to surrender. Koresh admitted he was wounded badly, that his two-year-old daughter had been killed, and some others were killed and wounded from his group. But it was clear that he mainly wanted to quote scriptures, mostly from the Book of Revelation. He said he was the lamb, chosen to open the seven seals. He challenged religious leaders and biblical scholars from around the world to come to Texas and engage in debate with him on the Bible, and particularly to try and match his understanding in unlocking the mystery of the seven seals.

The phone conversation on CNN continued for about forty-five minutes. Tabor was utterly taken with the whole scene. Here in the year 1993 this young Cyrus, would-be challenger of modern Babylon, was actually delving into the details of the Book of Revelation during prime time, over a worldwide television network. Tabor pulled out a Bible and turned to Isaiah 45, where he recalled the ancient Persian king Cyrus was addressed by God himself:

> Thus says the LORD to his anointed, to Cyrus [Koresh],
> whose right hand I have grasped to subdue nations before him
> and strip kings of their robes, to open doors before him. (45:1)

Here Cyrus is actually called "messiah," that is, one who is anointed. The Greek translation of this Hebrew word, *mashiach*, is "Christos," from which we get our term "Christ." So, one could accurately say

---

*The seven seals will be discussed in detail shortly.

that this ancient Persian king was called Christ. David Koresh also claimed to be such a "Christ." This biblical terminology led to endless confusion and miscommunication between the secular media and the FBI on the one hand and the followers of Koresh who lived and breathed these ancient texts on the other. It was widely but incorrectly reported, even by the most responsible media, that David Koresh claimed to be Jesus Christ, or even God himself. This confusion resulted from a lack of understanding of the biblical use of the term "anointed." In biblical times both the high priests and the kings of Israel were anointed in a ceremony in which oil was poured over the head and beard (see Ps. 133). In other words, in this general sense of the term the Bible speaks of many "christs" or messiahs, not one. The word refers to one who is especially selected by God for a mission, as was the Persian king Cyrus.

It was in this sense that David Koresh took the label "Christ" or messiah. He believed he was the chosen one who was to open the seven seals of the Book of Revelation and bring on the downfall of "Babylon." The early Christians were quite fond of the same kind of coded language. They routinely referred to the Roman empire as "Babylon." The letter of 1 Peter closes with such a reference: "She who is at Babylon [i.e., Rome], who is likewise chosen, sends you greetings" (1 Pet. 5:13). The Book of Revelation is essentially a cryptic account of the destruction of "Babylon," which was understood to be Rome (Rev. 19). Tabor was later to learn that the children of the Branch Davidians routinely referred to the FBI and any other "outsiders" as Babylonians.

Over the next few days, as the FBI took control of the siege of the Mt. Carmel complex from the ATF, it became clear that neither the officials in charge nor the media who were sensationally reporting the sexual escapades of David Koresh (he practiced polygamy) had a clue about the biblical world which this group inhabited. Their entire frame of reference came from the Bible, especially from the Book of Revelation and the ancient Hebrew prophets. Tabor realized that in order to deal with David Koresh, and to have any chance for a peaceful resolution of the Waco situation, one would have to understand and make use of these biblical texts. In other words, one would need to enter into the apocalyptic world of David Koresh and his dedicated followers. It was obvious that the Branch Davidians were willing to die for what they believed, and they would not surrender under threat of force. He decided to contact the FBI and offer his services.

Tabor first called his friend Dr. Phillip Arnold, director of Reunion Institute in Houston, Texas. Arnold was also a specialist in biblical studies, and the two men shared a special interest in ancient and modern forms of *apocalypticism,* a term that comes from the Greek word *apocalypsis,* which means "to uncover, to reveal." The Book of Revelation is often called the Apocalypse. An apocalyptic group is one that believes that the end of history is near and that the signs and secrets of the final scenario have been revealed to them. The followers of Jesus are properly understood as an apocalyptic movement within ancient Judaism, as was the group that produced the Dead Sea Scrolls. Since the third century B.C.E. many such groups, first Jewish and later Christian, have proclaimed the imminent end of the world on the basis of their understanding of biblical prophetic texts. Arnold agreed with Tabor that it was urgent and vital that someone who understood the biblical texts become involved in the situation in Waco.

The first FBI agent they contacted admitted that they were hopelessly confused when David Koresh went into one of his lengthy expositions of scripture, which occurred regularly in their daily telephone negotiations. The one point made repeatedly and consistently in later interviews with survivors of the Waco tragedy was that the source of members' attraction to Koresh was his knowledge of the scriptures, particularly the Book of Revelation. The FBI does not routinely pack Bibles when facing what they categorize as a hostage situation. The FBI agent contacted by Arnold and Tabor told them how the FBI had been frantically reading through the Book of Revelation in the Gideon Bibles in their hotel rooms. This image struck the two scholars as almost comical, but at the same time frightening. The agent also told them they found the Book of Revelation, and David Koresh's extended biblical monologues, wholly incomprehensible. He asked, "What is this about the seven seals?" Tabor and Arnold began to explain this reference mentioned in the Book of

Revelation to a mysterious scroll that was sealed with wax stamps (the seven seals) and could only be opened by a figure variously referred to as the lamb, the anointed one (i.e., Christ), or the "Branch of David." David Koresh claimed to be this person, sent to the world before the end of the age and empowered to finally open this scroll. He interpreted the seven seals of the Book of Revelation by using certain key chapters from the Book of Psalms, which he took to be the enigmatic "key of David" mentioned in Revelation 3:7. Psalms 40 and 45–the latter of which describes a rider on the white horse who goes forth with a bow to conquer–were especially important to his self-understanding. Koresh connected these to the meaning of the first seal. He understood himself to be that rider, a so-called sinful messiah who was written of in a scroll:

> Then I said, "Here I am; *in the scroll of the book it is written of me.* I delight to do your will, O my God; your law is within my heart. . . . For evils have encompassed me without number; *my iniquities have overtaken me, until I cannot see; they are more than the hairs of my head,* and my heart fails me." (Ps. 40:7–8, 12, emphasis added)

Psalm 45, which he understood to refer to the same figure, namely himself, speaks of a mighty king, anointed by Yahweh, who rides victoriously, marrying princesses and bearing many sons who will rule the earth (4–7, 10–16). This psalm explains why Koresh felt he was supposed to father children with the former wives of his male followers. He was the Branch of David who was to build up a dynasty that would someday rule the world from Jerusalem (Jer. 23:3–5). Koresh argued that these and many other passages, which were applied to Jesus Christ by mainstream Christianity, simply could not refer to the earlier "Messiah." Jesus was said to be without sin, he never married and bore children, and the Branch of David is to be raised up only at the endtime, when the Jewish people return to the land. Koresh insisted that if the scriptures be true, a latter-day messiah must appear, fulfilling the details of these prophecies.

Over the next few weeks Arnold and Tabor spent many hours in technical and lengthy discussions with Livingston Fagan, an articulate member of the Branch Davidians who had been sent out of the compound by David Koresh as a spokesperson and was being held in jail. With their knowledge of the prophetic texts of the Bible, and especially the Book of Revelation, Tabor and Arnold slowly began to attain some understanding of David Koresh's interpretation.

It became obvious to the two scholars that the Branch Davidian group understood itself to be actually living through the events of the seven seals, found primarily in chapter 6 of the Book of Revelation. They became persuaded that the Davidians understood themselves to be "in the fifth seal." The text reads

> When he opened the fifth seal, I saw under the altar the souls of those who had been slaughtered for the word of God and for the testimony they had given; they cried out with a loud voice, "Sovereign Lord, holy and true, *how long will it be* before you judge and avenge our blood on the inhabitants of the earth?" They were each given a white robe and told to wait a *little season*, until the number would be complete both of their fellow servants and of their brothers who were *soon to be killed* as they themselves had been killed. (Rev. 6:9–11, emphasis added)

Arnold and Tabor discussed the chilling implications of these verses with the FBI. For the Koresh group the Book of Revelation was like a script, setting forth in vivid detail what would transpire, and instructing them as to what they should do. The reason they refused to come out of their compound was that they felt God was telling them in these verses to wait "a little season." But the verse goes on to predict that they, like the others in the February 28 ATF raid, would then be killed. David Koresh once told the federal agents, "I knew you were coming before you knew you were coming." On the morning of the initial raid Koresh had said to ATF undercover agent Robert Rodriguez, who was spying on the group, "What thou doest, do quickly" (John 13:27). Koresh had been studying the Bible with Rodriguez for weeks, even though he had figured out Rodriguez was working for the ATF, and now considered him a Judas figure, one who had been given an opportunity to know the truth but rejected it and then went on to betray the messiah. It was as if the entire situation in Waco was locked into a predetermined pattern, set forth in a book written around 96 C.E., during the reign of the Roman emperor Domitian. What worried Tabor and Arnold was the very real possibility of a self-fulfilling prophecy. If the Koresh group found itself living "in the fifth seal," did that mean it was inevitable that the remaining eighty-seven men, women, and children in the Mt. Carmel compound must also die? Might they not provoke a violent end to things simply because they felt it was the predetermined will of God, moving things along to the sixth seal, which was the great Judgment Day of God? The scholars were fascinated by the way in which the literal words of this text dominated the entire situation. David Koresh insisted to the FBI that God had told him to "wait" an unspecified time, and the FBI constantly pushed him, asking, "How long?" not understanding that the entire drama was being played out according to a biblical script.

Through hours of conversations with one another and consultation with Davidian Livingston Fagan, Tabor and Arnold slowly began to map out the apocalyptic scenario or "script" that David Koresh and his followers were expecting. The academics were absolutely convinced that Koresh would never surrender from pressure or harassment. Given his understanding of himself as the messenger, or "anointed one" who had been given the secret of the seven seals, he would only act as he felt God was leading him. And the text of the Book of Revelation was his primary guide. According to his reading of the seven seals, five had now been fulfilled and God was telling him to wait. Given such a view, he simply would not come out and surrender as the FBI demanded. To Koresh and his followers, such a move, before the proper time, would have been inconceivable. They would have seen it as disobedience to God. Slowly Arnold and Tabor formulated a plan to approach Koresh with an alternative scenario, seeking to meet him within his own interpretive world.

Their first step was a radio broadcast over KGBS, the Dallas radio station that Koresh and his followers tuned to each morning on their battery-operated transistor radios (the FBI had shut off the compound's electricity). It was April 1, thirty-three days since the siege had begun. The talk show host, Ron Engelman, who had been critical of the federal authorities since the February 28 ATF raid, allowed Tabor and Arnold full use of air time to begin a dialogue with Koresh. Dick DeGuerin, Koresh's attorney who had been meeting with him for the past four days, was clued into the plan. He assured Arnold and Tabor that Koresh and his followers would be listening to the discussion. What the scholars presented, in give-and-take dialogue form, was a rather technical discussion of an alternative interpretation of the Book of Revelation that they thought Koresh might accept. As academics, they were not presenting this interpretation as their own personal view. Rather, their approach was hypothetical–given Koresh's general worldview and the interpretation he was following of the seven seals, what about an alternative understanding? Three days later, on Sunday, April 4, DeGuerin also took a cassette tape of the discussion of the Book of Revelation into the Mt. Carmel compound so that Koresh and his followers would have it to listen to and study. Passover, an eight-day holiday and one of the holiest feasts of the Jewish year which the Branch Davidians also observed, was approaching. Koresh had announced that following the Passover festival he would announce his plan for surrender.

On Wednesday, April 14, just five days before the fire that consumed the compound, David Koresh released a letter through his lawyer. It was to be his last. He said that at long last his wait was over; that he had been instructed by God to write an exposition detailing the secrets of the seven seals of Revelation:

> I am presently being permitted to document in structured form the decoded messages of the seven seals. Upon the completion of this task, I will be freed of my waiting period. I hope to finish this as soon as possible and stand before man and answer any and all questions regarding my activities. . . . I have been praying for so long for this opportunity to put the Seals in written form. Speaking the truth seems to have very little effect on man. I have been shown that as soon as I am given over to the hands of man, I will be made a spectacle of and people will not be concerned about the truth of God, but just the bizarrity of me in the flesh. I want the people of this gener-

ation to be saved. I am working night and day to complete my final work of writing out these seals. I thank my Father, He has finally granted me this chance to do this. It will bring new light and hope for many and they won't have to deal with me the person. As soon as I can see that people like Jim Tabor and Phil Arnold have a copy, I will come out and then you can do your thing with this beast. (Tabor, p. 19)

Arnold and Tabor were elated. They felt they had been successful at last. In their tapes to David Koresh they had argued this very point. They had tried to convince him that he was not necessarily "in the fifth seal" of Revelation, chapter 6, which would mandate the death of the group. They also argued that the "little season" mentioned in Revelation 6:11 could be an extended period. It was logically correlated with the "delay" mentioned in Revelation 7:1–3, which they maintained, given such a literal interpretation, could last several years. Further, on the basis of chapter 10 they had stressed the idea of a message written in a "little book" that would be given to the world (Rev. 10:11). The two scholars had pointed out to Koresh that although he had appeared on the covers of *Time, Newsweek,* and *People* magazines all in the same week, and was being mentioned hourly on CNN and daily on the network news reports, no one had a clue as to his message. They told him that most people had the idea that he was an insane sex pervert who molested children and claimed to be Jesus Christ, or even God. Koresh apparently accepted their arguments. Once Koresh released his letter, Tabor and Arnold, along with the attorneys, were absolutely convinced, based on the dynamics of apocalypticism, that Koresh would come out and that this writing of the seven seals, in his mind, was the answer from God he had been talking about for the past six weeks. Apocalypticism always operates in a complex play between the fixed text or "script," the shifting circumstances of outside events, and the imaginative casting of the interpreter. Arnold and Tabor had not been trying to manipulate Koresh, but they honestly believed that given his literalist view of the text, there were other viable alternatives.

The FBI had a different reaction. Following Passover week they stepped up their pressure tactics, demanding once and for all that Koresh and his people surrender. They took this latest move on Koresh's part as one more in a long series of delay tactics. In their daily press briefings over the next few days they belittled Koresh as a grade school drop-out who would hardly be capable of writing a book. They said he was a manipulating madman who thought he was God and who interpreted the Bible through the barrel of a gun. He was mockingly pictured as the cartoon character Lucy, who always "moves the football" at the last moment. Nonetheless they did allow writing supplies to be delivered to the Mt. Carmel compound on Sunday evening, April 18, the very evening before the tear gas assault.

Despite this show of "goodwill," the authorities had clearly lost all patience. At 5:50 A.M. Monday morning they called the compound and informed the group that if they did not surrender the place would be gassed. What took place in the Mt. Carmel compound from that point on is uncertain. One survivor of the April 19 blaze set by the FBI that consumed the compound had spoken to Tabor and told him that the last time he saw David Koresh was about 5 A.M. that morning. Koresh had come down from his room looking very tired. He said he had been working most of the night on his manuscript on the seven seals.

When the FBI began their tear gas assault that Monday morning Koresh must have been profoundly disappointed and confused. He had become convinced that God not only was going to graciously allow him to write this most important explanation of the seven seals for the world, but that this was part of the apocalyptic script. In a split second, as the buildings shook, the walls were punched with holes, and the tear gas was injected, he must have thought to himself, "Well, I guess I was right all along. We are in the fifth seal after all, and we must die like the others." It is obvious that one does not write a manuscript if the walls of one's home are being broken down. The actions of the FBI forced Koresh to revise his apocalyptic understanding. Any fulfillment of Revelation 10:11–"And I was told, 'You must again prophesy about many peoples and nations. . . .' "–which he had become convinced would now take place, became impossible. There was not a chance in the world that Koresh or his followers would "come out and surrender to proper authority" as the FBI loud-speakers urged them that morning. To them the only proper authority was God, not the forces of the wicked Babylonians. In their minds, based on Revelation 6:11, they saw their deaths as a necessary martyrdom, a self-sacrifice that would lead to the final collapse of the enemy and the coming of Jesus Christ.

Like the famous biblical scene at ancient Mt. Carmel, the contest between the forces of good and evil is decided by a burnt offering (1 Kings 18). For Koresh's followers, the fifth seal has been fulfilled and all that remains is the sudden revelation of the "Great Day of God's Wrath," associated with the sixth seal (Rev. 6:12–17). Modern Babylon has been weighed in the balance and found wanting; her final collapse is imminent.

There is a final bit of historical irony in the Waco tragedy. The defenders of Masada* had also died at precisely the same time of year, a few days after Passover in the year 73 C.E. after a lengthy siege by the Roman military forces. Like Koresh they were serious students of the prophecies of Daniel, the text upon which the Book of Revelation is mainly based. Daniel 11:33 says that in the final battle the remnant of God's true people would die "by sword and by flame." Koresh knew about Masada. In his communications with Tabor and Arnold he also said he was familiar with the newly released Dead Sea Scrolls and had been following the debates surrounding them.† It is worth noting that one of the most disputed texts, in one possible translation, speaks of a "Branch of David" being wounded and killed by the authorities. David Koresh, born Vernon Howell, died, like the Jesus he claimed to emulate, at age thirty-three, around the time of Passover.

There is not the slightest doubt in Arnold's and Tabor's minds that David Koresh would have surrendered peacefully when he finished his manuscript. After the fire some federal agents said they doubted that Koresh was even working on such a project. They took

---

*Jews (zealots) who killed themselves rather than surrender to the Romans.

†The scrolls were originally ascribed to the Essenes. Some people even thought Jesus had belonged to that community. Both of these ideas were disputed, and both are now rejected by most scholars.

his talk about being allowed by God to finally write the interpretation of the seven seals as a ploy to further delay things. We now know this was not the case. Ruth Riddle, one of the survivors of the fire, had a computer disk in the right pocket of her jacket when she emerged from the compound. She had been typing David's hand-written manuscript the day before the fire. On that disk was his exposition of the first seal.

5

HAPPY HOOKERS FOR JESUS

*"Everyone of you girls who spreads out your arms and your legs on
the bed for those men are just like Jesus, exactly like Jesus!"*
                                                    –Father David

Father David, born David Brandt Berg, was the founder of one
of the most controversial Christian missionary movements of
the twentieth century. This movement, The Family–originally known
as the Children of God–has the distinction of having been the target
of the first anti-"cult" organization. Also, the practice of "deprogramming" was developed in direct response to the recruiting success of
the Children of God.

Following their exit from the United States in the mid-1970s, The
Family continued to attract unfavorable attention from the media
and from various government agencies. Their most sensational practice was "Flirty Fishing," a form of witnessing (public preaching that
often borders on harassment) that could and often did involve sexual

---

In addition to those sources specifically cited, the material for this chapter has been
derived from personal research, as well as Melton 1992 and Lewis 1999.

115

sharing. In 1993, on the heels of the holocaust of the Branch Davidian community in Waco, Texas, homes of Family members were raided in several countries on the pretext of alleged child abuse.

The roots of The Family can be traced to Berg's childhood. Virginia Brandt Berg, David's mother, had a considerable influence on her son. She was raised in a Christian home, but eventually became a virtual atheist. However, an accident that left her bedridden for nearly five years led her to a conversion experience. After she was miraculously raised from her deathbed, she spent the rest of her life with her husband in active Christian service as a pastor and evangelist.

David Berg spent his first years traveling with his parents during their evangelical mission. In 1924 they settled in Miami, Florida, which became their home for the next fourteen years. In the late 1930s Virginia Berg returned to her favorite ministry as a traveling evangelist, and her son accompanied her for most of the next ten years.

In early 1942, after a few months of basic training in the U.S. Army, Berg fell sick with double pneumonia and a severely damaged heart. In a near-comatose condition, he promised God that, if he was healed, he would dedicate the rest of his life to full-time Christian service. Shortly afterwards, he experienced a miraculous recovery. Although the doctors recognized that the healing was spectacular, they discharged him from the army when they discovered his heart was enlarged and leaking blood, and they predicted he would live at most only a year or two. He was to spend the next fifty-two years in active Christian ministry.

In 1944, Berg met and married Jane Miller, an active member of the Alliance church in Sherman Oaks, California. In late 1948 he began ministering at a small Christian and Missionary Alliance church in rural Arizona, built a new church for his congregation, and opened it to the Native and Mexican-American population of the community. The white church board members were disappointed at this racial make-up, and in early 1951 he was forced to resign his pastorate.

For the next fifteen years, Berg taught secondary school, held a number of other secular jobs, attended several secular and Christian colleges, opened and ran a small center for missionaries, and traveled the United States booking an evangelical program on radio and television. He also applied for a mission to Southeast Asia. He eventually became more convinced of the ineffectiveness of organized, traditional "Churchianity" and its emphasis on ceremonialism and lavish buildings, as well as its general lack of interest in evangelical outreach. These convictions were later adopted by the Children of God.

In 1962, while facing a serious illness, he desperately asked God if there was a particular message that he was supposed to preach. Berg believed he received a response naming the Book of Jeremiah as the message for modern America. After this episode, however, Berg sensed that he had not yet found God's full calling for his life.

In the mid-1960s, Berg began traveling in evangelistic outreach, and in early 1968 he and his family journeyed to Huntington Beach, California, a beach town that had become a gathering place for thousands of hippies. Here he found his life's calling, and the movement now known as The Family was founded. He began ministering to the youth in a small Christian coffee house, the Light Club, which, within a few months, was full every night. Hundreds of followers became Christians and stopped taking drugs.

Berg's new ministry to the hippies marked his total rupture with mainstream Christian denominations. At Huntington Beach, he became convinced that the time had come for a complete break. His newly saved hippie congregation wanted the raw truth of the Gospel rather than the version that permeated mainstream Christianity. In a talk given in September 1968 at the Light Club, Berg explained that Jesus was a true revolutionary.

During this period, Berg met his second wife, Maria, who in January 1969 was working as a secretary in Tucson, Arizona, when a few members of his "Teens of Christ" visited from California. She returned to Huntington Beach with them and remained Berg's constant companion for twenty-five years, from the spring of 1969 until his death in 1994.

In 1970, the "Teens of Christ," who were likened by a newspaper reporter to "Moses and the Children of God," settled at an abandoned ranch in Texas that had formerly been Fred Jordan's Texas Soul Clinic. There Berg implemented his vision for a true New Testament community. After nearly a year in Texas, David and Maria left for Europe, looking for new regions to evangelize.

During these travels abroad, Berg received a new calling from God. He was told to provide written counsel, teaching, and guidance to his followers. For the balance of his life he remained behind the scenes, constantly teaching and advising, while the Children of God (COG) and later The Family rapidly expanded throughout the world. Berg's writings focused upon the fundamental teachings of the Bible, as well as the mission of his new movement. At the heart of his teaching was the conviction that the love of God, as manifested in the Bible and the person of Jesus, was the solution to every human need, and that the Christian's primary responsibility is to dedicate time, energy, and resources to sharing the Gospel with others.

Among Berg's most controversial beliefs was his adherence to the principle that he called the Law of Love, a principle he applied most shockingly to matters of sex. He claimed that sex was not inherently evil in the eyes of God, and that loving, consensual, heterosexual relations were permissible, as long as no one was hurt or offended.

Father David, as Berg had taken to calling himself, declared that the key to the erroneous teaching on sex was the "false doctrine that sex is sin." In sharp contrast, he emphasized a doctrine of positive sexuality. The Children of God's basic problem would be their establishment of a proper attitude toward sex. From the acceptance of that new perspective, one could then make judgments on proper action and gauge the acceptability of various forms of sexual behavior. Sex, asserted Father David, was "normal, healthful, natural, God-created, God-given, and God-permitted." It should be seen as a normal activity, just like eating, exercising, or sleeping. Problems resulted from having either too much or too little food, exercise, or sleep. In like measure, we needed some sex, and both denial and over indulgence were harmful. Sex was also a healthful physical activity and should be enjoyed just as swimming or hiking. It was as natural as breathing. The world's system corrupted sexuality by making it a matter of law. In addition, the laws concerning acceptable behavior varied widely from place to place since they were dictated by local custom and tradition.

Biblically speaking (and the Children of God was and The Family remains a biblically based group), there were only four forms of sexual behavior forbidden and/or limited by God: fornication, adultery, incest, and sodomy. Fornication included a variety of sexual behavior indulged in outside of marriage. Adultery was illicit sex with a married person. Incest was intercourse with a close relative. Sodomy was male homosexuality. Of these four, there were exceptions to the first three, and bigamy and polygamy were allowed. Jesus seemed to frown upon bigamy and held the monogamous couple as the ideal. Of the four, only male homosexuality was totally condemned. Even lesbianism was not specifically prohibited by the Bible. Father David was most insistent about the acceptability and naturalness of masturbation (which is not discussed in the Bible) and nudity (which is discussed most favorably in the Bible). On the other hand, birth control (including the practice of *coitus interruptus*) and abortion were an abomination to God.

Revolutionary sex provided guidance for the young married couples among the Children. Father David intended to free couples sexually and he invited them to enjoy their life together uninhibited by guilt, false modesty, and unbiblical pronouncements of the System—the mainstream churches and communities. By this time, the discouragement of the use of birth control methods had had a side effect among the married members that had not previously been well thought out: An increasing number of infants were becoming a part of the Family units. By 1973, the question of sex education now demanded some attention. In offering a solution to the problem Father David reached back into his own childhood experiences, some contemporary reading about sexual development, and his most favorable impressions of the Jewish Kibbutz. He suggested that children should be allowed complete sexual freedom, by which he meant that, first, they should be taught that their body was the beautiful creation of God and that the sexual parts were just as good as the rest of their body. They should learn that the pleasurable feeling that emanated from their sexual parts, even during the prepubescent years, were normal and should be enjoyed without threats of punishment or the imposition of guilt. Also, parents should allow the natural curiosity about the different body parts of members of the opposite sex to be satisfied, as long as it did not lead to anything harmful. However, as the children matured, they should be warned of the unlawful or excessive use of their sexual organs.

In advising the COG parents concerning their children, Father David reacted to his own childhood experience of sexual suppression, and sought to free the COG children from suffering in a similar manner. He had come to believe that ignoring and denying the sexual life of children amounted to a form of suppression that led to a sex-obsessed adulthood.

Father David's original writings on sexual ethics were prompted by the realities of colony life. However, at the same time he was writing the early Mo Letters–a kind of movement "newsletter" with "Mo" being short for "Moses"–on sex and marriage, he was developing a new and controversial form of evangelistic outreach that would become an additional factor contributing to his mature statement of the Law of Love.

What would be known as flirty fishing (or FFing) originated in London in 1973. At some point during the year, seeking a little recreation, Father David and his wife, Maria, began attending ballroom dance classes. During one session they noticed all of the lonely people who were also taking the classes. Seizing the moment, they selected people and danced with them. Rather than stopping with the music, they also tried to build relationships as friends and saw the new friendships as arenas in which a witness of faith could be made. Success led them to pursue the idea. Then, in one incident with a man called Arthur, the relationship with Maria moved in a more intimate direction. Father David encouraged her to see what would happen if she allowed their friendship to lead to a sexual relationship. Again the results were positive (Maria was able to convert him), and Father David decided to conduct a more ambitious experiment.

Meanwhile, at the beginning of 1974 Father David shared the results of the early flirty fishing with the movement as a whole in a Mo Letter titled *Flirty Little Fishy*. He urged his female readers to express their abundant love by flirting with lonely men, even to the point of some physical contact (kissing), and allowing the men to fall in love with them. Thus would they establish a context for witnessing God's love for the fish (as the men were called).

At this point nothing had been said to the larger membership about Maria's relationship with Arthur. In March 1974, Maria and Father David moved to Tenerife, a tourist spot in the Canary Islands. Here Berg gathered a group of older, trusted members, mostly females, and quietly launched a more challenging experiment. Accompanied by the men, the women frequented the bars and dance clubs to meet, befriend, and witness to the men they encountered. Subsequently, when the situation suggested it, they would have sex with the men they met in an attempt to set a better context for witnessing. There was some attempt to have men practice flirty fishing, but for much the same reason that the great majority of prostitutes are women, the success of the technique depended upon the women.

While the experiment was proceeding, Father David's thoughts on sexual ethics and theology coalesced in the concept of the Law of Love, and he began to expound the new doctrine to the larger movement. He had, of course, earlier appropriated the idea of a law of love from the Bible and made use of it in his 1973 epistles on sexuality, but he now offered it as the broad new foundation of the Children's code of conduct.

According to Father David, the Children of God constituted the Church of the Last Generation of Humankind, before the apocalypse and the end of time. As such it has been given the same total freedom as the church of the first generation. God had given the Children of God "complete freedom from the bondage of the law" and "complete freedom of life and liberty through love." Rather than being bound by rules, anything was allowed, as long as it was done out of love. The question of the hour was, "Can you handle this new toy (i.e., sex) safely so as to bring joy and pleasure to yourself and others around you without endangering anyone or harming anyone or infringing on anyone else's freedom and others' rights?" If the Children could not handle the freedom, God would take it away.

In accordance with the original statements concerning the Law of Love's practical application to sexual relationships, Father David continued to teach that monogamous marriage was to be the norm.

However, the law held out the possibility of some extramarital sexual activity, though there must be a strong and compelling reason for such activity. To determine if an extramarital sexual contact was correct, the person contemplating such an encounter must first be able to answer in the affirmative a number of questions. For example, does such activity promote the Children's evangelical mission? Is it good for COG? It is good for the individual? Does it assist you or your partner in the service of God? If the answer to all of these questions was yes, the individuals considering an extramarital liaison were to seek and obtain the consent of all concerned parties, including their spouse, those with whom they lived communally, and their immediate leaders.

For Father David, one's motivation was all important. Any extramarital sex must be undertaken for love's sake, in a spirit of self-sacrifice. It should not be the occasion of simply indulging one's lustful urges. Thus, while the Law of Love offered the possibility of legitimate extramarital sex, in fact, the only acceptable occasion for such relations was in the context of flirty fishing. The precise way in which the FFing ministry worked was tied to the Children of God's doctrine of salvation.

Father David understood the atonement in traditional terms, emphasizing Christ's death as a propitiation for the sins of all humanity. But there is also a strong theme within his writings which elevates the exemplary aspect of Christ's death. As "love" is the ethical reference point within the life of the group, The Family/COG look to Christ as the model in this respect. They believe salvation is achieved when people invite Christ to come into their lives. This is done through the simple act of praying to Jesus and asking Him to come in. It is one of the distinctive aspects of The Family's belief that they place great significance on this act of prayer. Even if there is little outward sign of repentance or change in lifestyle, or even if a person cannot say that he experienced anything of any significance following the moment of asking Jesus to come into his heart, the act of asking is regarded as the dividing line between those who "know the Lord" and those who do not. This is what separates a person from being saved and not being saved. It is this act which takes a person from the reign of darkness to the reign of light. When The Family records in their statistics the number of "souls" they have won, this is what they are talking about.

They further emphasize the decisive nature of this act by saying that it is eternal in its effects. They follow the school of thought which says, "once saved always saved." The Children of God do not hold the equivocal position that one can be saved and later lose that salvation. It is this specific perspective that allowed members to take a "one night stand" approach to salvation: Once someone confessed Jesus, he or she was saved. It was unnecessary to recruit her or him into The Family proper (in point of fact, few if any core members were ever recruited in this manner). Hence, no further evangelization was required, and the flirty fisher moved on to locate more "fish." Flirty Fishing was practiced by Family members until 1987, when it was officially discontinued because it was evoking too much external criticism. Also, The Family did not want their children to become involved in missionary sex. Nowhere near the unbridled license it was portrayed to be, the Flirty Fishing ministry would become the basis for widespread allegations of child abuse later leveled at The Family. (Critics asserted that such a loose, sexual group must also be having sex with their own children.)

ESCHATOLOGY*

While much of the attention of the world outside The Family has been directed to their teachings on sexuality, the theological concepts that most influence their lives are those associated with eschatology. At the heart of Father David's vision, and indeed his greatest theological passion, are his revelations concerning the end of the world. This, more than any other aspect of Father David's theology, including his views about sexuality, defines the character of The Family. They believe the world is about to end, and most Family members believe it will take place within a matter of years.

---

*This section relies heavily on the work of David Millikan (1994).

The Family believe this end will occur over a series of stages that begin with a terrible time of persecution on earth known in the Bible as the "Great Tribulation" (Matt. 24:21), followed by the Second Coming of Jesus Christ and the Rapture of the Saved (Matt. 24:29–31), and then the awesome Wrath of God that will culminate in the Battle of Armageddon (Rev. 15–16), to be followed by the thousand-year rule and reign of Christ on earth known as the "Millennium" (Rev. 20:1–6), which ends with the cataclysmic Battle of Gog and Magog (Rev. 20:6–10), and eventually the end of all punishment in Hell and the restoration of all–or nearly all–souls into a heavenly existence either inside the Heavenly City or on the recreated New Earth.

Family members believe that the heart of the Christian message is the need for salvation in Jesus Christ. Outside of this relationship, they do not allow that there is any salvation. And yet, unlike many fundamentalists, Father David is a universalist: He believes that people who never heard the Gospel in this life are not condemned, but are given a chance to receive it in the next life. Even many of those condemned to Hell will finally be released in time, to live outside the Heavenly City on the paradisiacal New Earth described in Revelation 21 and 22. But Father David is not a strict universalist; in his opinion, there are some who will never know salvation.

> I think I'm getting more and more to where I don't know whether you could ever rehabilitate or convert some of those guys, like the Devil and the Antichrist, the False Prophet, Hitler and some of the worst characters in history and the cruelest tyrants and whatnot. I'm beginning to be a little doubtful as to whether there's any hope for some of those guys, they've just gone too far! They can be thankful they're just going to be annihilated and they don't have to be tormented forever. They're going to have been tormented for quite awhile, the Thousand Years of the Millennium and some things like that, so after the Great White Throne Judgement it looks to me like the best thing to do is get rid of the whole bunch that can't be rehabilitated! ("Judah on Pearly Gate & the Doctrine of Annihilation!" D.O. 2142, 02/85, Vol. 17, p. 71)

The Family believes that its members are shortly to enter into the Tribulation, a three-and-a-half-year period when the constraints against the Devil and his Antichrist are removed and evil will expand in ways that are unimaginable to us now. (The Family holds a literal view of the Devil or Satan. Members see him as a formidable and frightening figure utterly devoted to the destruction of God's plan and all who follow Him. The Devil is a fallen angel who is locked in an unrelenting struggle against God and is assisted in his activities by a force of lesser spirits—demons and the souls of people who died in a state of rebellion against Christ.) The Great Tribulation, however, will be followed by the Rapture and the Second Coming of Christ.

Father David took the millennialist beliefs popular in American fundamentalist Christianity with radical seriousness. There is little, if anything, original in his vision. He has done little to advance the descriptions of the Antichrist put forward by early church leader Lactantius in the fourth century and the best-selling *Letter on the Origin and Time of the Antichrist*, written in about 915 C.E. by a man known as Brother Adso. Father David and the members of The Family believe that they will witness the great events that will be the end of the world and these beliefs are of great significance to the way in which they behave in the present.

Father David believes that the Bible can be read as a virtual textbook of the events leading up to the end of the world. He has interpreted the strange prophecies and visions of Daniel and Revelation as spelling out in detail the rise of Russia, the birthplace of the Antichrist, the location of the battle of Armageddon, and the date at which these events will occur. The same verses that Father David interprets as prophecies directed at this present age have been the source of similar speculations from the very beginning of the life of the Church. But Father David believes that he has been called as the last of God's prophets. What he is saying is this:

Everything's going just like the Bible predicted and we've explained to you: It'll all eventually erupt into the Atomic War, from the chaos of which will arise the A.C. [Antichrist] who will temporarily sign a *compromise* with the Jews, Arabs, and Christians to neutralise

Jerusalem and let the Jews rebuild their Temple (Daniel 9:27a). When he has everything under control $3\frac{1}{2}$ years later, he'll break the Covenant, declare himself god, set up his *image* in the Temple area, try to force everyone to worship him, and try to kill all who won't, thereby bringing on the *Great Tribulation*, ended $3\frac{1}{2}$ years later by the *Second Coming of Christ* and Rapture of the Saved, Wrath of God on Earth, and Marriage Feast of Christians with Jesus in the Heavenly City above! (Daniel 9:27b; 11:30–31; Matthew 24:15–31; Revelation 15–19). Then we return with him to conquer and rule the earth for 1000 years of Heaven on Earth like the Garden of Eden, with worldwide peace, no more wars for 1000 years, Satan and his forces bound, the curse removed and *Paradise Regained!* (Revelation 20). (Mo Letters, *Wars and Rumours of War*, p. 45)

The major events of the end times will center on the Middle East. The Antichrist is said to be a man who was born in the Middle East and is presently making his way toward his goal of world domination. Many Family members believe the Antichrist will come from among the Jews. At first he will appear to be an attractive person who is able to bring some order into international affairs. This will occur at a time when people will have become so disillusioned with the degeneration in world affairs that they will gratefully look to him as an antidote to the chaos. He will set up his headquarters in Jerusalem, where he will work relentlessly to create reconciliation between the warring factions of the world, including the world religions. For the first time in history, all the major world religions will recognize his authority and unite under him in one form of worship, based on the Temple in Jerusalem: "For a while it will seem to be absolutely heaven on earth." There will be a large number of Christians who will be fooled by his early appearance. They will think that he is a man of God. Because the Antichrist will encourage the Jews to begin again the sacrifice of animals in the temple, there will be many who will see him as the Messiah. In fact, it will be the Jews who make the first move to proclaim him as divine.

The Antichrist, along with his right-hand man, the False Prophet, will have the power to do miraculous things. He will cause disturbances in the natural order and he will be able to heal people of sickness (Rev. 13:3, 13, 14). But after three and a half years, he will suddenly change. God will pull off the restraints which have kept him in check and evil will be let loose:

> Like a dam being opened or removed a *flood* of *iniquity* is going to circle the World under the reign of the Devil himself in the person of the Antichrist. (*Wars and Rumours of War*)

At this stage the relationship between the Antichrist and the Devil will undergo a decisive change. The distance between them will collapse and Satan will come to possess the Antichrist until he will be the Devil himself. In effect the Devil will incarnate within the person of the Antichrist (Rev. 13:2).

Once the true colors of the Antichrist are revealed he will set about the task of bringing the world under his control. To achieve this end he will use the most sophisticated modern technology. In particular, in the same Mo Letter just quoted, Father David described a central super computer that will differ from other computers in one fundamental respect—it will have a soul, given to it by the Devil:

> I'm convinced that the super computer will actually be *demonically inspired* to where it actually *does* have *demon intelligence,* . . . it will be a real *wonder,* and will really be *worshipped!* (p. 74, emphasis added)

With this computer and other sophisticated devices the Antichrist will take charge of people's lives. He will enforce a financial system which uses an identification number that everyone will have branded on or implanted under their skin. Family members are convinced that the world is rapidly being prepared to receive the "mark of the beast" foretold in Revelation chapter 13, verses 14–18:

> And he [the Antichrist's false prophet] deceiveth them that dwell on the earth by the means of those miracles which he had power to do in the sight of the beast; saying to them that dwell on the earth, that they should make an image to the beast. . . . And he had power to give life unto the image of the beast, that the image of the beast

should both speak, and cause that as many as would not worship the image of the beast should be killed. And he causeth all, both small and great, rich and poor, free and bond, to receive a mark in their right hand, or in their foreheads: And *that no man might buy or sell, save he that had the mark, or the name* of the beast, or the *number* of his name. Here is wisdom. Let him that hath understanding count the number of the beast: for it is the number of a man; and his number is *Six hundred threescore and six* [666]. (emphasis added)

The mark of the beast is one of the most feared dimensions of the endtime. The Family believe this will be achieved through the implementation of a computer chip either in the hand or forehead. Following the trends of the moment, humanity will enter a cashless society:

Men will no longer buy or sell with money as a means of exchange, but with a number, a number which will be given to them *permanently*, without any possibility of counterfeit, change, manipulation or forgery, because it will be branded on each person. (Children of God literature, *Book of the Future*, p. 76)

This will be placed either on the right hand or the forehead, and will be the instrument of the Antichrist's control. With this in place no one will escape his scrutiny. Thus, The Family are very concerned at the use of bar codes and the growth of a cashless financial order, as well as the recent moves in agriculture to permanently place miniature plastic tags bearing identification numbers under the skin of animals. They oppose these moves not only because of their implications for civil liberties, but also because they see it as part of the inexorable progress of the Antichrist. They are alarmed that our societies seem so unaware that they are actually aiding and abetting the progress of the Antichrist by delivering the most powerful tools into his hands.

The control that Satan will exercise over the world through the Antichrist will almost be total. Father David reads Revelation 13:5 to indicate that this control will extend to war and victories over the saints:

And it was given unto him to make war with the saints, and *overcome* them. . . . But these victories will not be decisive: [He] . . . will be

allowed to overcome us *physically,* obviously destroying the or-
ganised temporal power of the Church, he will not and cannot overcome us *spiritually.* . . . (*Book of the Future,* p. 93, emphasis added)

There will, of course, be a great difference between the way in which
The Family survives the Tribulation and the way the mass of Christians in the churches do. The mainline churches will be ill-prepared
for these events. They will not understand what is happening. They
have no stomach for a fight, and in most cases they will simply lie
down and refuse to fight back. But The Family will be equipped with
the Power of God. They will be given a special measure of the power
of the spirit which will not only protect them but will give them the
power to win some victories themselves.

I believe we're going to have a time of greater power even than the
early church, greater manifestations, mightier works, mightier witnessing than has *ever* been done before! (*Book of the Future,* p. 93)

The Tribulation will be a time of terrible persecution for Christians.
Despite the protection God will give through the special powers he
grants, many will succumb to the persecution.

For then shall be great tribulation, such as was not since the beginning of the world to this time, no, nor ever shall be (Matt. 24:21).
And some of them of understanding shall fall, to try them, and to
purge, and to make them white, even to the time of the end (Dan.
11:35). (*Book of the Future*)

It is a sober picture for The Family, and their fortune is a little
ambiguous. Father David is not sure whether most of The Family will
survive or be killed. He is certain that some will succumb and be
martyred, and in his more pessimistic moments he suspects that a
large number of them will be taken. The weight, though, is on the
side of optimism: Father David is certain that God will make a special point of protecting The Family. After all, there must be some
reward for the present years of sacrifice, obedience, and discipline.
The Family will, for example, have learned Scripture by heart in

readiness for the day their Bibles and Mo Letters will be taken. They will have leaders who have the spiritual power to draw on the resources of heaven and protect The Family:

> Certain very powerful men and women of God, like the ancient prophets and prophetesses of old, are going to be the leaders and have these supernatural miraculous powers to protect and defend their flocks and followers and help them to survive to the very end. (Mo Letter, *The Real Victors of the Tribulation*, p. 290)

Such powers are vividly portrayed in Revelation 11, where some of God's final witnesses against the world of the Antichrist call down fire from Heaven, smite the earth with plagues, and so on. Toward the end, when things are at their worst, God will enter the struggle directly by initiating a number of attacks to divert the attention of the Antichrist away from the Christians. God will let loose a range of monsters and plagues that will target the forces of Satan:

> They'll have so much on their hands defending themselves from these monsters and these plagues that they won't have much time to persecute you and me! (*Book of the Future*, p. 97)

(See Revelation 8 and 9 for a description of the trumpets of tribulation that sound at this time, summoning plagues, judgments, and strange monsters to torment the ungodly followers of the Antichrist.) But in the last few days of the Tribulation, the protection of God will be withdrawn even from the saints. In a period of three and a half days before the return of Christ, "[Satan] will finally be allowed to kill them, that the cup of iniquity of the wicked may be filled!"

During this time the Antichrist will align himself with "Ten Kings," with whom he will attack and destroy the mysterious Whore of Babylon, described in Revelation 17 and 18. From the first century until now those interested in apocalypticism have identified the whore as a wide range of figures. Some early Christians believed it to be the Roman Empire; during the Islamic expansion into Europe it was the Moslem religion; in the sixteenth-century Protestant churches believed the Whore to be the Roman Catholic church; and in our century it has variously been identified with Hitler and Stalin, while the Jehovah's Witnesses see it as the traditional churches, in particular the Roman Catholics. Father David believes the Whore is epitomized by the international commercial system, centered on the United States:

> I am convinced that today's capitalistic commercial system, led of course by America, is the epitome of the Great Whore of Revelation, and is in fact its ultimate fulfillment! (*Book of the Future*, p. 120)

Father David insists that Bible passages such as Revelation 18:3 are fulfilled in the United States:

> For all nations have drunk of the wine of the wrath of her [the Whore's] fornication, and the kings of the earth have committed fornication with her, and the merchants of the earth are waxed rich through the abundance of her delicacies.

During the time after the Rapture, when there will be rewards and feasting in Heaven for the saved, the fifteenth and sixteenth chapters of Revelation portray an earth that will feel the full fury of God's anger. Only the unsaved will remain and God's wrath will have no reason for restraint. The Seven Vials of Wrath described in these chapters of Revelation will be let loose. God will send plagues and disasters into the world in the same way he did in the time of Moses and the recalcitrant Pharaoh. The first of these vials of wrath will cause a sudden spread of terrible suppurating sores—like skin cancer—on the bodies of those who have accepted the mark of the beast. Then the sea will turn to blood and the creatures remaining after the earlier fury of God will all be killed. The sea will be left stinking and dead. The third vial will see the rivers and lakes and streams of the world suffer the same fate as the sea. They, too, will fill with blood so that all life within them will suffocate. There will be no fresh water left to drink, only blood. Fourth, God will intensify the heat from the sun seven times. The searing heat will shrivel life so that nothing will be able to move in the open and survive. Fifth will come permanent darkness:

[They will be] left to their sufferings and torments, their tortures and their plagues, licking their sores, drinking blood, scorched with fire and now finally in darkness!–Groping around in such thick darkness they can't even find their way!–How horrible! (*Book of the Future*, p. 176)

The sixth vial of wrath will see the Euphrates River dried up to make way for the kings of the world to gather for the final battle. (Of course, one has to wonder how anything at all would be possible in a situation where everything was in darkness, where there was no water, no electricity, no food, and no communications.) It is the end of all forms of civilization:

[It means the] destruction of so-called modern civilization and return to savagery and return to native type living in the wilderness or on the farm. (Mo Letter, *The Oil Shortage!*, p. 7072)

Somehow, the forces of the world will respond to the call of Satan and come together in the valley of Jezreel in Israel, the site of the Battle of Armageddon.

The seventh vial sees the arrival of Jesus and the warrior saints, who will stream out of Heaven mounted on white horses and dressed in beautiful, sparkling, white robes. But before they arrive a hail of fire will be poured out of heaven, accompanied by thunder and lightning. The final act before the battle will be a devastating global earthquake of such magnitude that all the world's cities will be reduced to rubble:

One great final earthquake is going to destroy all the hell-houses of Satanic power called cities, those horrible cancers on the body politic of man, those cesspools of iniquity in which man prides himself–his cities. God's gonna throw them all to the ground! (*The Oil Shortage!*, p. 180)

The carnage of this event is impossible to imagine. It is a vision of unrelenting destruction. Father David sees these passages from Revelation in literal terms. A Christ-rejecting world is reduced to a hideous inferno of total darkness, populated by people without food or water who are suffering from painful cancerous sores and who are ultimately defenseless against the weapons of war God brings against them. The surface of the earth will pile high with the rotting corpses of the Antichrist's hordes, so God will bring in his "garbage men." Drawing on the images of Ezekiel and John, Father David talks of scavenger birds like vultures and buzzards invited by God to feast off the flesh of the millions of dead (Ezek. 39:17–20; Rev. 19:17–18).

There is a powerful and unmistakable note of apocalyptic retribution in Father David's interpretation of these biblical visions and prophecies. He looks for vindication and even revenge in the next life, because of the indignities and lack of respect that Christians have suffered in this life. The Battle of Armageddon is the moment The Family will be able finally to settle some old scores:

> . . . all the enemies we've had, we're going to get our revenge in that day. We're going to get vengeance in that day against our enemies! It's going to be a *righteous* vengeance!–They're going to get what they *deserve* and *we're* going to give it to 'm! (*Book of the Future*, p. 186, emphasis added)

Father David defends himself against the charge that he is being uncharitable or un-Christian by pointing to the Book of Revelation, which tells us that the souls of the Christian martyrs in Heaven cry out for vengeance in a similar manner:

> And when He had opened the fifth seal, I saw under the altar the souls of them that were slain for the Word of God, and for the testimony which they held: And they cried with a loud voice, saying, How long, O Lord, holy and true, dost Thou not *judge and avenge our blood* on them that dwell on the earth (Rev. 6:9–11)? (*Book of the Future*, emphasis added)

The Battle of Armageddon will be the final and greatest act of carnage before the Millennium. There will be blood flowing from the slaughter over a distance of 200 miles. In some places the blood will

rise to the height of a horse's bridle (Rev. 14:20), and the millions of
rotting corpses will fill the air with a suffocating putrid stench. Father
David quotes from Ezekiel 39, indicating it will take seven years to
dispose of the destroyed weaponry (verse 9), and that grave diggers
will take seven months to dispose of the corpses (verses 11 to 13). By
the end they will be putting "little signs or markers" over what
remains of the bodies exposed to the hot sun and the vultures.

> And the passengers that pass through the land, when any seeth a
> man's bone, then shall he set up a sign by it, till the buriers have
> buried it in the valley of Hamongog (Ezek. 39:15). (*Book of the Future*)

Clearly Satan will be exposed as the instigator of the entire
episode. He and his minion the Antichrist will be decisively defeated.
A group comprised of the real recalcitrants and haters of God will be
thrown into hell and chained for a thousand years to "a bottomless
pit" located within the bowels of the earth (Rev. 20:1–3). During this
time Satan will remain there without influence on the earth. But he is
not finished, for in the last years of the Millennium God will once
again pull off his constraints and let him loose to stir up the final confrontation at the battle of Gog and Magog (Rev. 20:7–9). In the meantime, out of the devastation of the Battle of Armageddon, some
people will survive. With considerable understatement Father David
says of them "they must be pretty tough or they must live a pretty
charmed life." These are the people whom Jesus and his helpers are
going to rule for the next thousand years. And this is the time for
which The Family waits. It is the reward and the vindication. It happens in the same cities and before the same people who were their
detractors and persecutors in the past. Their real spiritual powers will
be obvious, and they will rule with authority:

> We are going to rule and reign and teach and train, to show how the
> World *should* have been run and to be an example to the Universe
> of what kind of government man *could* have had it he had only
> obeyed the Lord. (*Book of the Future*, p. 197, emphasis in original)

Again, the Bible is quoted:

> And he that overcometh, and keepeth My works unto the end, to
> him will I give power over the nations: And he shall rule them with
> a rod of iron; as the vessels of a potter shall they be broken to
> shivers: even as I received of My Father. (Rev. 2:25–27)

The Millennium is about giving people another chance at salvation. It is also about justifying God's anger and the annihilation of the
unsaved. If God acts with such fury, there must be a counterbal-
ancing display of his mercy and grace. After the horrors of the Battle
of Armageddon, God steps back to show he still has the best interests
of the world at heart. He draws together the shattered remains of the
earth and provides the possibility for peace:

> The Lord will set up His kingdom here on Earth for a thousand
> years to try to salvage what He can and who He can and give them
> another chance or perhaps their first chance. (*Book of the Future*,
> p. 198)

Once again the note of vindication emerges. Father David is angry at
the way he and his people have been treated by the world. He has had
to hide and creep around like a criminal. He has seen The Family vil-
ified and attacked and abused. And he has been given no respect or
honor in this life. He has been mocked and treated by the world as a
fool and a criminal. The Millennium will finally put that right, and his
tormentors will be forced to respect The Family's authority:

> We will no longer be the poor, persecuted, hounded few of the poor
> bedeviled sects or cults or whatever they want to call us. . . . We are
> going to rule the Earth with Jesus Christ over our God-damned ene-
> mies who have tormented us and persecuted us and hounded us
> from country to country throughout the Earth . . . so don't worry,
> we're going to have a country to call our own one of these days,
> thank the Lord! (*Book of the Future*, p. 201)

The character of life in the Millennium will in many ways be like the best of what we know now. But there will, of course, be some fundamental differences. The first will be the change in the bodies of the saved. They will be given spiritual bodies that will not age or become sick (Phil. 3:21), so The Family and all of the rest who have been saved through the ages will not die. Those who are not saved will go on as usual, but because the curse will be lifted from the Earth, like the Old Testament characters before the flood, they will live for more than 900 years. But they will still be subject to many of the limitations that we know in this present life.

The first task in the Millennium will be cleaning up the carnage and wreckage of Armageddon. As mentioned earlier, the prophet Ezekiel says it will take seven months to bury the dead and seven years to destroy the instruments of war. It will be a formidable task, but with the organizational directions from the Lord and the added powers given to the saints in their supernatural bodies, it will be done and the earth will be restored to the state of paradise. The eighth chapter of the Book of Romans talks about the expectation with which the earth waits for the moment of liberation from the effects of sin. It is like a woman in the pains of childbirth–it groans as it waits to be released from the bonds of mortality. The Millennium is when liberation happens. Father David draws a utopian picture of the whole of nature blossoming in the joy of paradise. The birds will stop singing in a minor key, the animals will all become herbivores, and people will become vegetarian. This, Father David believes, was the state of people before the Great Flood. The removal of sin will mean that the earth will be able to flourish without the evil things like weeds, thistles, thorns and flies. There will be no cars. On the seas there will only be sail boats. There will be much less disease and for the people who are not saved, life will go on but in more pleasant circumstances. They will marry, have children, and go about their business.

The resurrected saved of all ages are going to rule the world with a "rod of iron." There will still be some sin left in the world, so they will force people to be good. The resurrected will have to teach them about the ways of the Lord, and they will be forced to listen and obey. People will be required to confess their sins and put things right with the world around them. The style of government will be strictly authoritarian:

> They will all be *compelled* and *forced* to obey whether they like it or not–Absolutely no democracy, absolutely no freedom of man, or wicked man!–No more wicked democracies with wicked majorities voting for wicked governments and wicked rulers in a wicked world– but a complete totalitarian *dictatorship* of the *righteous* with Jesus Christ as Dictator. (*Book of the Future*, p. 219, emphasis in original)

Father David clearly relishes the prospect of these years in control for he emphasizes over and over the role The Family as those who run the show. He has given a description of the sort of powers they will have to allow them to assert their authority. He speculates that it may involve a capacity to immobilize people, or perhaps just cause them to go blind:

> We'll just *look* at them or *think* or point our finger at them or whatever we want to do! And they won't be able to touch us or do a thing!–*We* will be the power and the government in control! (Mo Letter, *Here and Now for There and Then*, p. 1092)

He also sees some parallels with what he has seen in *Star Trek*:

> . . . where they freeze when they point their finger at 'm or they disappear or they wind up in a different place or something–that's actually going to happen, we'll have such powers! That's one reason I enjoy "Star Trek," I think that guy was almost inspired! (*Here and Now*, p. 1092, emphasis in original)

It must be emphasized that this description reflects a widely held belief within large sections of Christianity. A number of large, conservative, theological seminaries teach this view of the endtimes as standard theology. It is, for example, the generally held view of the Southern Baptists, the largest denomination in the United States. The Jehovah's Witnesses hold a similar eschatology. There are numerous other groups who would be in complete sympathy with this vision of the endtimes; they would differ only in the details.

This raises an interesting issue concerning the nature of reward and the doctrine of "works." The literature of The Family is keen to make a distinction between salvation by "grace" and salvation by "works." They make it clear that salvation is not earned, or in any way contributed to by the actions of humankind. They see it as an act of divine grace, unmerited and undeserved. But they go to some lengths to indicate that there are various levels at which one can enjoy the benefits of salvation. So salvation itself is not at stake, but the level at which it may be enjoyed is. They see support for this in various places in the Bible. The most pointed is Matthew 5:19, which reads,

> Anyone who breaks one of the least of these commandments and teaches others to do the same will be called least in the Kingdom of Heaven, but whoever practices and teaches these commands will be called great in the Kingdom of Heaven.

The Family interprets this as a series of rewards for righteousness: "The Lord is keeping books on everyone, but it's hard in this life to know who is going to get what." It is hard to avoid the feeling that this view of reward has a salutary effect on the behavior of Family members.

It must be understood that The Family have a palpable sense of the Millennium and Heaven. They see these as physical realities in which they will be present in the resurrected body. In fact, at one of The Family's major training facilities in Japan, there is an elaborate model of the Heavenly City held in a pyramid building on a hill above the training center. The Family has a self-conscious commitment to the Christian teaching concerning the "resurrection of the body." They see Heaven as a physical "place," indeed a city, somewhere above the earth. Their descriptions of the New Jerusalem, based on St. John's vision in Revelation 21 and 22, have allowed The Family to produce detailed maps, including descriptions of various structures, the layout of streets, and the nature of the materials used. According to their interpretation, the city is shaped like a pyramid 1,500 miles high, 1,500 miles wide, and covering an area of 2.25 million square miles.

PERSECUTION

Many of The Family's detractors, through envy and ignorance, construed flirty fishing as prostitution, open and casual sex, and hence evil, and rushed to label the Children of God a "sex cult." Furthermore, their critics claimed that with such open sexual practices, they must be sexually abusing their own children. The Family's actual policy in such matters, however, calls for immediate expulsion of an adult who has sex with a minor. Some of those expelled for this reason are among the most fervent antagonists of The Family today.

During the formative years of the group, many incidents occurred that the current followers of Father David would prefer not to have happened. For example, as the Children of God grew, some authority had to be delegated to others within the various communes, and some of those in positions of power became abusive in the exercise of their authority. The Family's detractors found it easy to attribute many of these deviations to the Children of God as a whole and to Father David in particular.

Reports of serious misconduct by many of the established leaders caused Father David to dismiss over 300 of them and declare the general dissolution of the movement. The Children of God as an organizational entity ceased to exist in February 1978. Some of the leaders who lost power—including Father David's own daughter, Deborah (Linda) Davis and her husband, Bill Davis—subsequently launched a bitter campaign against Father David.

A third of the total members at the time of dissolution (2,600) decided to return to secular lives or remain independent missionaries with no further ties to Father David. The members who remained chose to form a new fellowship of autonomous communities called "The Family of Love," later shortened to "The Family," with Father David as their prophet and spiritual head. Most of the dismissed leaders and the majority of the members who left in 1978 bear no ill will toward The Family today.

The sexual aspects of The Family began to change and evolve. In March 1983, sexual relationships between members living in different communities were stopped. A bit later, in December 1984, sexual relations with new members of less than six months was made an excommunicable offense. With the rising threat of AIDS, all flirty fishing was officially banned in September 1987.

With the evolution of The Family's sexual policies, many materials that reflected previous sexual experiments, such as "dance videos" portraying female members in various stages of undress dancing to music, were ordered removed from all remaining Family communities. However, a small number of such videos were overlooked in trunks at a storage facility near The Family's home in Manila, Philippines.

In October 1992, two former members posing as current members on a mission from Family headquarters made an illegal incursion into a Family community in Manila. According to arrest warrants in the Philippines, they stole $25,000 cash and several trunks containing video- and audiotape masters valued at $3 million. While there, the thieves tried to forcibly "deprogram" members of The Family. They were subsequently arrested, but fled with the stolen property before trial. Warrants were issued for their arrest by the Philippine government.

The stolen videos depicting members of the defunct Children of God were edited so as to support the detractors' slanted views, and then disseminated to the international news media. The sensational media hype that followed precipitated witch hunts against The Family.

In November 1993, Family members in southern California began to be harassed by hostile ex-members. After The Family obtained restraining orders against them, reports of child abuse were made against The Family. Some of these reports were received through "anonymous phone tips." Not satisfied with making false reports to a single agency, the detractors made several false reports to numerous local government agencies. From May 6 through June 10, 1993, local officials, including the Sheriff's Office, the Department of Children's Services, the Department of Health, building inspectors, the Environmental Services Department, and even the City Council, descended on Family homes.

According to The Family, the investigating agencies began antagonistically, but soon became less hostile and even friendly after they discovered the allegations to be untrue. There are, however, lingering doubts and questions about the accusers. Documents given to Los Angeles officials show that two of the detractors were wanted criminals, one using an alias. According to documents given to the FBI by The Family, these two individuals had been involved in the fraud and theft by fraud that followed the thefts in the Philippines.

Why were such people allowed to get away with making false reports of nonexistent crimes? To knowingly make a false report of a crime is in itself a criminal act. Why were the Philippine warrants not recognized? Why has the FBI not acted on the obvious interstate/international transportation of stolen property? To date, these questions have not been answered.

The United States and the Philippines were not the only countries in which detractors chose to attack The Family. In Spain, two ex-members in cooperation with CROAS and "ProJuventud" (two vehement Spanish anticult groups in Spain) and the Barcelona Bishop's Conference goaded the Catalonian police into action against The Family with spurious charges of child abuse. The Catalonian police carried out a twenty-four-hour surveillance of The Family in Barcelona with hidden cameras and tapped phone lines for four months before their July 8, 1990, raid. Based on this surveillance, they should have known that there was no truth in the allegations.

Fifty Catalonian police smashed into the Barcelona Family home, dragging out ten adults and twenty-two children, aged eleven months to fourteen years. The adults were soon released, but the children were kept in institutions for the next eleven months. During the illegal imprisonment of these terrified children, they were plagued by phony psychiatrists who attempted to break the children's faith and submitted phony psychiatric reports against the children and their parents.

While the children were illegally incarcerated, they were often neglected and/or mistreated by social workers, which resulted in numerous serious injuries. Non-Family Spanish citizens who were neighbors that supported and/or were friendly with The Family were visited by the police, who attempted to intimidate them. However, this tactic failed and the friends showed up and testified for The Family in the Spanish courts.

A final hearing in the civil case to remove the children from their parents on grounds of child abuse was held on May 22, 1992. The presiding judge, Adolfo Fernando Oubiña, described the actions by the Catalonian government as "reminiscent of the Spanish Inquisitions" (a comparison not lightly made in Spain), and compared their incarceration with the "concentration camps of those former empires that ceased to be when human dignity brought down the Berlin Wall."

The judge further noted the lengths the detractors were willing to go, declaring that The Family was an "attacked group." He further decried the so-called care the children received while in state custody, saying,

> They were put in the hands of a group of psychologists who, in a language the children did not understand, psychoanalyzed them for prolonged periods, and issued reports cast in esoteric language designed rather to justify the operation (the seizure of the children by the authorities) than to describe any intellectual anomalies, which are completely nonexistent. (Cited in Lewis and Melton, 1994, p. 143)

In June the Catalonian district attorney, Teresa Lema, seeing the civil case disintegrating about her, pressed for a criminal case against The Family. She accused them of such crimes that, had they actually been convicted, would have resulted in collective sentences of two hundred years in prison for the ten Family adults. But in this criminal case, the judge wrote a strongly worded forty-two-page verdict which, as in the civil case, cleared The Family of any wrongdoing.

The Family has not been free from oppression in England, either, where, in January 1991, they were accused of child abuse and pornography. Police, acting on information provided by the cult-watch groups Cult Information Center (CIC) and Family Action Information Center (FAIR), and armed with search warrants, raided two Family communities looking for "sex literature." Naturally, the press had been informed of the "nasty sex-cult" and were tagging along to get their titillating stories.

At one home, a police sergeant kicked in a glass panel of the front door to enter. When members of the community attempted to call their lawyer, the officer ripped out the phone. The officer was later reprimanded for his actions. No one was arrested, and none of the children were removed.

The homes were searched for more than six hours, but no evidence of child abuse was uncovered, nor was any pornography. The children were examined for abuse and were found to be in perfect health. The officials apologized for the raid, and said they must have been given "misinformation." (No kidding!) However, charges of providing false information were never subsequently filed against those responsible.

Family communities in Norway, Australia, France, Argentina, and other places have all been subjected to similar Gestapo-like searches, prompted by allegations of child abuse and sexual abuse by Family detractors. Mistreatment of members, including children, by the authorities, was widespread, but charges in all the cases were determined to be unfounded (Lewis and Melton 1994).

Many crimes have been committed, not *by* The Family but *against* The Family—crimes by alliances of bigots, aided by corrupt police and government officials, perpetuated and fueled by tabloid media and yellow journalism. The human rights violations against The Family by Argentine officials during a September 1, 1993, raid—including children and adults alike being terrorized by police wielding assault rifles as well as unsanitary medical exams performed on the children to check for signs of abuse—provide the grossest example of violations against a religious community in the modern era, exceeded only by the extermination of the Branch Davidians in Waco, Texas, earlier the same year. How many more massacres of falsely accused men, women, and children have to occur before this travesty is brought to a halt?

Colleague examining a special meditation device worn by an AUM Shinrikyo member. The visual impact of such strange meditation "helmets" had the effect of reinforcing the impression that AUM disciples are "brainwashed cultists." (Photo from author's personal collection.)

Lord Maitreya, the apocalyptic future Buddha. (Photo courtesy of Omotokyo.)

Father David. (Photo courtesy of World Services.)

Young members of The Family reenacting the type of protest activity that characterized the early days of the Children of God. (Photo courtesy of World Services.)

Eighteenth-century "alien." (Image courtesy of the American Religion Collection.)

HUMANS:

▶ DO YOU KNOW WHAT CHRIST **REALLY** CAME TO TELL US?

▶ DO YOU BELIEVE IN FLYING SAUCERS?

▶ ARE YOU READY TO TAKE YOUR PHYSICAL BODY TO THE NEXT EVOLUTIONARY KINGDOM?

THIS METAMORPHIC PROCESS WILL BE DISCUSSED AT A MEETING:

Tuesday Dec. 9   7:00 P.M.
at: American Legion Hall
      behind Post Office
in: Cottonwood, Arizona

Early Heaven's Gate flyer. (Courtesy Robert Balch.)

A gathering of people attending a Raelian "Course of Awakening." The Raelians are one of the few contemporary UFO religions to encourage open sexual expression. (Photo courtesy of the Raelian Movement.)

JZ Knight, prominent New Age channel, channeling "Ramtha." (Photo courtesy of the Ramtha School of Enlightenment.)

6

LOST IN SPACE
UFO Doomsdays

*Puerto Vallarta, Mexico–A Mexican gardener is living in fear
because the space alien that beat him to a pulp and tried to mate
with his weed eater returned to his house–and raped his electric
broom! . . .*

*"I though I'd seen the last of him until [recently when] some-
body ransacked my house while I was at work. . . . The next
morning I heard gasping and grunting noises coming from my
closet and when I opened the door I found the alien on top of my
electric broom." He called the police, "but by the time they arrived
the alien was gone and my electric broom was twisted like a
corkscrew. I know it was the same space alien. You never forget a
face like that."*

This story appeared in the *Weekly World News* of April 16, 1991,
under the title, "A Space Alien Raped My ELECTRIC
BROOM." Tabloid aliens are a staple of supermarket reading matter.
The extraterrestrials who grace the pages of the *Weekly World News*,
the *National Enquirer*, the *National Tattler*, and the like are usually fascinating beings who are neither particularly hostile nor kindly beings
and have come to Earth to warn or to help humanity in some
manner. As examples of the latter, one can simply list stories whose

145

titles indicate "humanitarian" themes: "UFO Aliens Kidnapped Me. . . . Now I Can Heal with Miracle Powers," "UFOs Warn of Atomic Disaster," and "UFO Drops Christmas Food to Starving Ethiopians."

Less frequently, but still on a regular basis, one comes across negative narratives featuring hostile aliens, such as "UFO Vampires May be Murdering Fishermen," or the story quoted above, "A Space Alien Raped My ELECTRIC BROOM." These contrasting images reflect our ambivalence in the face of the unknown: On the one hand we find the alien fascinating, and on the other fearful. Either side of this attraction-aversion response leads the human imagination into apocalyptic, doomsday themes.

On the attraction side, for example, one often comes across films and literature that portray the "Space Brothers" as working to rescue humanity–either by forcibly preventing a nuclear Armageddon or by taking select members of the human race to another planet to preserve the species. Psychologist Carl Jung referred to this portrayal of ufonauts (flying saucer pilots) by the term "technological angels." The idea of positive, helpful extraterrestrials has been a common theme of much science fiction, from *Superman* (who, it will be remembered, was from another planet) to the friendly alien of Steven Spielberg's *E.T.*

Jung postulated a drive toward self-realization and self-integration that he referred to as the individuation process. The goal of this process was represented by the *Self* archetype, an archetype characterized by wholeness and completeness. One of the concrete symbols of this archetype is a circle, and Jung referred to various forms of the circle as mandalas. According to Jung, mandala symbols emerge in dreams when the individual is seeking harmony and wholeness, which frequently occurs during periods of crisis and insecurity. Jung interpreted the phenomenon of flying saucers–which often appear in the form of circular disks–as mandala symbols, reflecting the human mind's desire for stability in a confused world.

Another line of thought regarding religious interpretations of the UFO phenomenon is that the Western tradition's marked tendency to imagine God as somehow residing in the sky gives us a predisposition to view unusual *flying* objects as well as beings from outer space in spiritual terms. In other words, the god of the Bible is, in a certain sense, an extraterrestrial being. Not all spiritual beings are, however, beneficent. A more negative interpretation of UFOs is evident in recent claims of alien abductions.

If in the earlier literature flying saucers were technological angels, in abductee literature ufonauts are technological demons. Abductees, most of whom appear to have been genuinely traumatized by their experience, report being treated coldly and inhumanely by their alien captors—much like animals are treated when captured, tagged, and released by human zoologists. During their brief captivity, frightened abductees also often report having been tortured, usually in the form of a painful examination. If such reports are to be taken seriously, it appears that many alien scientists involved in kidnapping human beings are proctologists.

A careful reading of abduction narratives indicates that the patterns alleged to have been discovered by abduction investigators often have religious overtones or similarities with more traditional types of religious experience—similarities often ignored by UFO researchers. Hypnosis, which is generally used to explore the abduction experience, allows access to a subconscious level of an individual's psyche. This enables the hypnotic subject to recall repressed memories of actual events, but also makes it possible to derive "memories" of things which never happened.

As Jung argued, the subconscious is a storehouse of religious ideas and symbols. Such symbols can become exteriorized (projected so as to appear as a "real" external object) through anxiety or stress. Thus, the crypto-religious imagery brought out by hypnosis—in this case torment by demonic beings, which is an initiatory motif—could be a confabulation, a "mis-remembering" by the subject's subconscious, perhaps worked into a UFO narrative in an effort to please the hypnotist. More literal demonologies have been proffered by conservative Christian observers of the UFO scene, many of whom view ufonauts as demons in disguise.

Inverted images of "friendly aliens" are reflected in the many portrayals of hostile aliens found in film and literature. The ugly, octopus-like extraterrestrials of H. G. Wells's imagination have their counterparts in innumerable invasion narratives, from straight horror movies like *The Blob* (which dropped to earth inside a meteorite) to such recent offerings as the box office record-breaker *Independence Day* and the short-lived TV series *Dark Skies*. While friendly aliens appear to be projections of our hopes of being rescued from doomsday, hostile aliens seem to embody our worst fears of the apocalypse.

THE UFO CONTACTEE MOVEMENT

In 1946 the phrases "flying saucers," "unidentified flying objects," and "contactees" did not exist in anyone's vocabulary, though sightings of unusual aerial phenomena had been reported for at least the previous century and a half. Charles Fort's *The Book of the Damned* (1919), the first book on what would be called UFOs, had linked such oddities to visitors from space. Fort even speculated, perhaps facetiously, that certain individuals were in contact with the UFOs' pilots. If so, no one owned up to it until the evening of October 9, 1946, when an object flew over San Diego.

It appeared as a long, bullet-shaped structure with large wings which looked to witnesses like a giant bat's. Those who saw it said it was dark except for two red lights along the side. Visible for an hour and a half and moving at speeds varying from slow to very fast, it periodically swept a searchlight along the ground.

Not until the following summer, following private pilot Kenneth Arnold's widely publicized June 24, 1947, encounter with nine shiny discs over Mount Rainier, Washington, would things like this get to be called flying saucers. Even in 1946, however, San Diegans did not have to be told that this object was something decidedly out of the ordinary.

Just how out of the ordinary, however, was left to local medium Mark Probert to say. Probert had been channeling (conveying) messages from a variety of discarnates who discoursed at stultifying length on cosmic philosophical issues for the recently formed San Diego-based Borderland Sciences Research Associates (BSRA), directed by occult theorist N. Meade Layne.

As it happened, Probert was among the many San Diegans who, their eyes raised skyward in anticipation of a meteor shower, observed the passage of the mysterious structure. While it was still in view, Probert phoned Layne, who urged his associate to attempt telepathic communication with the craft's presumed occupants. The attempt succeeded, Probert would assert, telling a newspaper reporter

> The strange machine is called the Kareeta. . . . It is attracted at this time because the earth is emitting a column of light which makes it easier of approach. The machine is powered by people possessing a very advanced knowledge of anti-gravity forces. It has 10,000 parts, a small but very powerful motor operating by electricity, and moving the wings, and an outer structure of light balsam wood, coated with an alloy. The people are nonaggressive and have been trying to contact the earth for many years. They have very light bodies. They fear to land, but would be willing to meet a committee of scientists at an isolated spot, or on a mountain top. (Cited in Clark 1997, p. 204)

So Probert would distinguish himself as the first of what soon would be called "contactees." Not at first a term of endearment, in time it became merely descriptive, a way of characterizing the worldwide host of human beings who would profess to believe themselves to be recipients of messages with friendly extraterrestrials looking out for our best interests.

The heretofore scattered contactee subculture coalesced into a movement in January 1952, when aircraft mechanic George W. Van Tassel initiated a series of public gatherings in the high desert country of southern California. Van Tassel channeled elaborate messages from starship ("ventla") commanders, soon introducing the first metaphysical superstar of the flying-saucer age, Ashtar, "commandant quadra sector, patrol section Schare, all projections, all waves"– an extraterrestrial/interdimensional being who even today communes with a small army of mediums and automatic writers.

On November 20, 1952, George Adamski entered occult history through his claimed meeting with Orthon, a golden-haired Venusian, near Desert Center, California. In no time at all others were alleging physical encounters with benevolently intentioned "Space Brothers," here to rescue the human race from imminent nuclear war. As if to up the ante, contactees soon recounted rides in flying saucers into outer space or to neighboring planets.

One figure who quickly rose to prominence in the new movement, occultist and maverick anthropologist George Hunt Williamson, first heard from extraterrestrials in mid-1952, when a Martian named Nah-9 psychically warned him and his associates that malevolent space people were conspiring with evil earthlings to wreak havoc. As the messages grew ever more ominous, a frightened Williamson wrote a friend in Guatemala that "time is *very, very short!* . . . Disaster will come before Dec. 1st, this year! So only a few weeks remain!" He went on:

> We have been told that a man will contact us soon, when all is in readiness! And there will be a landing in this vicinity by special ship direct from Mars within two or three weeks from now! . . . The landing will be near here. (Clark 1997, p. 205)

Williamson was able to pull himself together enough to be in Desert Center on November 20, when he served as one of the six "witnesses"–albeit at some considerable distance–to the epochal Adamski/Orthon rendezvous.

Most contactees believe that the Space Brothers are representatives of a galaxy-wide civilization, here to guide humanity. Many believe there will be some physical cataclysm on Earth, during which many will die, and the survivors will be rescued by the Space Brothers; this appears to be an interpretation influenced by concepts derived from the Revelation to John in the Christian Bible.

Contactees differ from abductees in being essentially volunteers, with a positive attitude toward the extraterrestrials they communicate with, and usually with a strong background in metaphysical religion. Abductees, in contrast, believe themselves to have been victims of a kidnapping by humanoid aliens that was at best traumatic. They do not tend to have religious beliefs different from those of the general population. Ufologists tend to regard abductees as part of UFO phenomena as such, but contactees as part of a religious movement based on a theology about UFO phenomena. Whitley Strieber's books, beginning with *Communion,* attempted to persuade the public that the humanoids also have benevolent intentions. Strieber was not very successful in doing so, although his books have generated a following of their own.

Contactees are often thought to be typified by George Adamski, who claimed to have had rides in flying saucers. Aside from a few devoted followers, most people consider Adamski to have been a fraud. Current contactees, in contrast, rarely claim physical contact. Far more often, their contact is mental, via the medium of channeling, automatic writing, visions, dreams, and voices heard in the mind. Some of these mental phenomena can be symptoms of mental illness, but among contactees they appear to be aspects of spiritual experience, as they might be in any other religious movement.

In 1960, John Alva Keel reported on the growing number of "silent contactees," that is, members of a growing religious movement; he believed they were dealing with "ultraterrestrials," beings intent on harming them, a notion quickly taken up by the Christian right wing. In the 1970s, Brad Steiger's writings chronicled the growing phenomenon of channeling, and began offering new interpretations of its significance. The 1970s also saw the emergence of the idea of extraterrestrials being reincarnated as earthlings, either at birth or as "walk-ins"—that is, alien humans who take over a human body when the ordinary human personality is about to depart (i.e., die). This latter experience has been described by many contactees; it may be a way of relating a conversion experience. In any event, religious scholars have been observing the growth of the contactee movement since the 1970s as a new type of metaphysical religion.

In 1980 R. Leo Sprinkle, a psychologist, organized the first Rocky Mountain Conference on UFO Investigation in Laramie, Wyoming; it has been an annual event ever since, usually with entirely new attendees. It is not a gathering of ufologists, but of contactees, who thus become a support group for one another, sharing and validating their similar experiences. Sprinkle and other psychologists have also used this as an opportunity to investigate the psychological makeup of contactees, who turn out to be no different from the general population in any significant way.

A complete list of contactees who channel messages from the Space Brothers would be extensive. Among the more prominent are Michael and Aurora El-Legion of Malibu, California, who receive messages from Space Brothers known as the Ashtar Command. It is sometimes not clear whether the intelligences whom clairvoyants channel are Space Brothers or not; as a result, the boundaries of the contactee movement are sometimes difficult to define.

Truman Bethurum also joined the swelling contactee ranks with his own tale of friendly space people. He met them one night in July 1952, he said, while employed as a heavy-equipment operator in the Nevada desert. A between-shifts nap was interrupted by eight little men with "Latin" features. They guided him to a nearby flying saucer and its captain, "a gorgeous woman, shorter than any of the men, neatly attired, and also having a Latin appearance: coal black hair and olive complexion. She appeared to be about 42 years old." Her name, she told him, was Aura Rhanes (Clark 1997, p. 205). She and the crew of the "scow" (spaceship) hailed from the planet Clarion, a world never visible to us because it is always on the other side of the moon. As Bethurum would learn in subsequent contacts, Clarion is an idyllic world devoid of conflict or disease. Clarionites had come here out of concern that human beings might blow up their planet in a nuclear war.

In August 1953 the first major contactee gathering, the Interplanetary Spacecraft Convention, brought more than 10,000 space communicants, true believers, and curiosity-seekers to Van Tassel's property at Giant Rock, between Lucerne Valley and Twenty-Nine Palms, California. The Giant Rock meetings, which were held every year through 1977, provided a forum in which contactees could exchange information and ideas. In the process they borrowed names and concepts from one another, even as the meaning and context changed from telling to telling. Though contactees agreed on a general view of the cosmos, no two of them described a precisely similar one.

Believers either ignored these disparities or dismissed them as meaningless, much to the exasperation of skeptics. One skeptic, ufologist Isabel L. Davis, wrote in the November 1957 edition of the science-fiction magazine *Fantastic Universe*:

> Where was Clarion . . . during the night of August 23–24, 1954? On that night, Adamski claims, he was shown both sides of the Moon by Ramu of Saturn, through an instrument on the Venusian carrier ship. . . . As the ship goes around from the familiar toward the unfamiliar side, ahead of it in the sky should have been Captain Aura Rhanes' Clarion. But neither Ramu nor Adamski mention[s] it. Adamski certainly knew about Clarion—for Bethurum had visited Palomar Gardens [Adamski's residence] during the summer of 1953, and Adamski had then accepted Bethurum's story. But with a whole planet missing from where it should be, Adamski is neither surprised nor curious.

The claims of these metaphysically oriented contactees were only slightly more surrealistic than other kinds of close-encounter claims. For example, in the wee hours of March 28, 1967, David Morris was on his way home in Monroe Falls, Ohio, from a graveyard shift at an electrical plant when his attention was distracted by a glowing, cone-like UFO in a wheat field. Glancing back at the foggy highway, he discerned four or five glowing, unearthly "midgets" walking on the road, seemingly unaware of his car. Slamming on the brakes, Morris hit one of the short beings with his right front bumper, and saw a thumbless hand suddenly jut upward and then down again. Coming to a stop some ten feet beyond, he instinctively started to get out and try to help the victim when he realized the strangeness of his situation. Glancing backwards as he sped away, he saw a group of the beings standing around as if they were circling a body. The next morning, Morris found dents on the right front side of his car.

Some half-dozen years earlier, Joe Simonton, a fifty-four-year-old plumber from Eagle River, Wisconsin, looked out his kitchen window one morning to find a bright chrome, disk-shaped vehicle (like two saucers back to back) with no windows parked in his driveway. Curious and unafraid, he went out to meet the short man in the saucer's doorway who was holding an empty jug and silently gesturing for some water. After filling the jug and handing it back to the man, Simonton noticed two other men dressed in black suits in the saucer near control panels. One was cooking pancakes. Simonton's efforts to strike up a conversation resulted in the cook handing over four hot pancakes. Shortly afterward, the saucer abruptly flew away.

Many ordinary contactees made no claims of profound revelations. The close encounter of E. Carl Higdon Jr. with "men" who took him to their home planet began with a simple hunting outing. On Friday, October 25, 1974, this resident of Rawlins, Wyoming, had an elk in his sights when he realized his bullet had fallen to the ground just fifty feet from him as if it had hit some invisible object. When he investigated, he saw a very tall humanoid figure with no chin, ears, or brows under a tree wearing a black coverall. The figure offered Higdon some pills and a ride back to his home planet 163,000 light miles away. Higdon accepted. They traveled via a cubicle that was small but held three humanoids and five elks. There, Higdon and the figure named "Ausso One" floated over to a mushroomlike tower before Higdon heard the verdict that he wasn't "any good for what they needed," and he was returned to Earth.

One of the more celebrated of early close encounters seems to have involved nothing more serious than an alien one-night stand. On the evening of October 14, 1957, Braziliam Villas-Boas was plowing when he saw a blindingly bright object hovering 300 feet above the end of the field. When he tried to approach it, it evaded him and then disappeared. The next night, at 1 A.M., he saw a big red egg-shaped object which accelerated toward him until it was 160 feet above his head, shining as bright as daylight. Villas-Boas watched the object land. He described it as an elongated egg with three metal bars sticking out of it. Above the egg, something rotated rapidly. As the object descended, three legs extended from its underside to support it on the ground. Villas-Boas started to flee but felt someone grab his arm. He turned around to see a small figure, which he shoved to the ground. Three others then grabbed him, lifted him off the ground and carried him to the machine. There was a door in the object which opened from top to bottom, forming an entry ramp with a ladder on the end. Despite his struggles, Villas-Boas found himself inside a room with metal walls.

The figures communicated with each other through growling sounds. They were covered from head to toe with clothing. Even their eyes were partially obscured with glasses. The helmets they wore gave the appearance that their heads were twice the size of human heads. Three tubes ran between their helmets and their suits, which were made of a striped gray material. The figures grabbed Villas-Boas and undressed him without hurting him or tearing his clothes. They spread a thick, odorless liquid all over his body and then took a blood sample from under his chin.

The figures then left him alone for a while. A gray smoke emanating from metal tubes in the ceiling made Villas-Boas violently ill and he vomited. Then a nude woman entered the room. She had whitish blond hair, a wide face, pointed chin, and big blue eyes. She and Villas-Boas had intercourse twice. The woman left the room, a man returned with Villas-Boas's clothes, and he was given a tour of the ship. He was then ushered out and watched as it flew off at around 5:30 A.M.

Some contactees have gone so far as to actually form religions based on messages they received from extraterrestrials. The Cosmic Circle of Fellowship, for instance, was formed in Chicago in 1954 by William A. Ferguson. Ferguson was a mail carrier who learned the techniques of absolute relaxation and became adept at relaxing his body, mind, and conscious spirit. In 1937, Ferguson wrote *Relax First* and then began to teach relaxation techniques to others.

On July 9, 1938, while lying in a state of absolute relaxation, Ferguson's body was charged with energy and he was carried away to what he called the Seventh Dimension. He stayed there two hours and his soul became "illuminated." When he returned to normal waking consciousness, he found that his physical body was no longer where he had left it and he could not be seen nor heard by his wife and his friend. He placed his noncorporeal being back where his body and been and soon regained physical, three-dimensional form.

One week later, Ferguson was carried away to the "center of creation" and experienced the "Sixth Dimension." He saw creation in action: Rays of pure intelligent energy of all forms and colors were flowing throughout a cube of "pure universal substance."

In 1947, a being named Khauga (also identified as the Spirit of Truth, the angel who gave the Book of Revelation to St. John and a perfected being from the Holy Triune) took Ferguson on a trip to Mars. Upon his return, family and friends could not see or hear Ferguson until he went into the next room, lay on a cot and was rematerialized. He delivered a message that the Martians were sending an expedition to earth. Within a few months, many UFOs were reported and several people claimed to have made personal contacts with their inhabitants.

About this time, Ferguson began to form a group primarily focused on cosmic healing techniques, especially the "clarified water device" which Ferguson learned to build from Khauga. This device, thought to impart healing properties to water, got Ferguson in trouble with the American Medical Association. In 1947 he was convicted of fraud in relation to the claims he made regarding the clarified water device and served a year in prison.

In 1954 Ferguson was taken aboard a Venusian spacecraft where he learned that spacecraft normally function in four dimensions and are therefore invisible to us, but they can also function in three dimensions. When they disappear suddenly, they have merely changed back into the fourth dimension. The same year Ferguson joined with Edward A. Surine and Edna I. Valverde to form the Cosmic Circle of Fellowship. The group incorporated in the State of Illinois in 1955. In 1958 Ferguson started traveling around the country, founding circles in other cities, including Washington, Philadelphia, New York, and San Francisco. Since Ferguson's death in 1967, the Chicago group has continued to publish his writings.

Perhaps the most exotic UFO religion is the Raelian Movement. Rael, born Claude Vorilhon in 1946, a French race-car driver and journalist, was the founder of this movement. When he began his charismatic career, he was married and a father, although he subsequently separated from his wife. He founded the Raelian movement in 1973, as a result of his alleged encounter with space aliens during a walking tour of the Clermont-Ferrand volcanic mountain range in France. He subsequently wrote two books, in 1974 and 1975, that were published in English in one volume as *Space Aliens Took Me to Their Planet: The Most Important Revelation in the History of Mankind* (1978).

Rael described the aliens of his encounter as small human-shaped beings with pale green skin and almond eyes. He claimed that these aliens entrusted him with a "message" concerning humans' true identity. According to this message, human beings were "implanted" on Earth by superior extraterrestrial scientists, the "Elohim," who created man from DNA in their laboratories. Rael's doctrine claiming that a renegade group of aliens gave early humans knowledge that was forbidden by the other extraterrestrials echoes the story of Prometheus, who, according to Greek mythology, stole fire from the gods for the benefit of humankind.

Rael asserted that Elohim society is composed of 90,000 quasi-immortal men and women who can unite sexually among themselves as they wish, although they are not allowed to have children, and undergo a small sterilization operation. (The society continues its existence through cloning.) Rael also claimed to be "the last of forty prophets" whose mission was to warn humankind that since 1945 and Hiroshima we have entered the "Age of Apocalypse." During this period humankind has the choice of destroying itself with nuclear weapons or making the leap into planetary consciousness, which can qualify man to inherit the scientific knowledge of his space forefathers. Science will thus enable 4 percent of the human species in the future to clone themselves and travel through space, populating virgin planets in their own image.

Rael denies the existence of God or the soul. He claims that the only hope of immortality is represented by a regeneration through science. In order to achieve immortality, members of his movement participate in four annual festivals, during which the Elohim is believed to fly overhead and register their DNA codes on machines. During this initiation ritual, which is called "the transmission of the cellular plan," new initiates sign a contract permitting a mortician to cut out a piece of bone in their forehead–believed to be the third eye–which is then stored in ice awaiting the descent of the Elohim.

New initiates are also supposed to send a letter of apostasy to the church in which they were baptized.

The Raelians, that is, those who have acknowledged the Elohim as their fathers by taking the steps of initiation and making funeral arrangements, count 20,000 members worldwide, and are distributed mainly throughout France, Japan, and Quebec. They publish books and lecture in order to unite Christians, Jews, and Muslims in a "demythologized" interpretation of Scripture as the true history of a space colonization. Those who work for the organization are known as the Structure. Their goals consist of spreading the message to mankind and building an embassy in Jerusalem by the year 2025 in order to receive the Elohim. They are required to avoid pressure tactics and evangelizing. Those who do not avoid evangelizing are excommunicated from the movement for seven years, which is the time it takes to replace all their body cells.

The Raelian movement can be considered millenarian in that it focuses in preparing for the descent of the UFOs bearing the Elohim and the thirty-nine immortal prophets including Jesus, Buddha, Mohammed, and Joseph Smith.* Rael asserted that these prophets were born from the union of a mortal woman and an Elohim.

Members of the movement, which has been described as "world affirming" in its orientation toward society (as opposed to other religions that are afterlife–otherworld–oriented), are encouraged to achieve success in their careers, to have a better health by avoiding all recreational drugs and stimulants, and to develop their capacity to experience pleasure. Rael compares men and women to biological robots who are programmed to give each other pleasure. Members who find total self-fulfillment will become immortal through cloning.

Rael, whose version of free love resembles that of Fourier, John Humphrey Noyes, and Rajneesh, encourages members of his movement not to marry or to maintain longterm relationships, but rather to commune with others by exploring sexuality with the opposite sex, the same sex, and any other lifeform. An annual sensual medi-

---

*Smith founded the Church of Jesus Christ and Latter Day Saints–the Mormon Church.

tation workshop features fasting, nudity, sensory awareness exercises, and sexual experimentation in order for the participants to achieve the "cosmic orgasm." According to Rael, these sexual customs reflect those of the space aliens that he observed.

Rael condones abortions and asserts that conceiving a child should be delayed until the individual is fulfilled. He suggests birth control, and allows women to be unmarried mothers, single mothers, and sexually active single mothers. He also gives women permission to give their children away. The symbol of the Raelian movement, a swastika inside a Star of David, is claimed to represent infinity.

THE ODYSSEY OF SISTER THEDRA*

For many years, the contactee movement attracted little attention from the larger world. For the most part, only those who were interested in UFOs were aware of the small but growing army of believers in Space Brothers. Press coverage was scant except for scattered articles in local newspapers, predominantly in southern California where the movement was most active. All of this would change, however, with a strange episode which began in a Chicago suburb in 1954.

Like most who become contactees, Dorothy Martin had long been drawn to unorthodox ideas. She was introduced to occultism while living in New York City in the late 1930s, when she attended a lecture on theosophy. She began reading a variety esoteric works and became active in dianetics, later called scientology. She turned to the works of Guy Warren Ballard, who as Godfré Ray King created the I AM movement, arguably the first religious group to make extraterrestrial contacts a central tenet. (Among other claims Ballard reported meeting twelve Venusians—"Lords of the Flame"—in California's Teton Mountains. Ballard essentially created the image of the golden-haired, angelic Venusian that Adamski would bring into the saucer age.) Martin also read *Oahspe*, based on the channelings of John Ballou Newbrough and first published in 1882. *Oahspe* depicts a complex, richly

---

*This section relies heavily on the work of Jerome Clark (1997).

populated spiritual cosmos whose inhabitants included guardian angels known as "ashars" who sail the universe in etheric ships.

One day in late 1952 or early 1953 Mrs. Martin, fifty, awoke in her home in Oak Park, Illinois, with "a kind of tingling or numbness in my arm, and my whole arm felt warm right up to the shoulder. . . . Without knowing why, I picked up a pencil and a pad that were lying on the table near my bed," and she started writing a message from her deceased father. The message was a trivial one—it consisted of instructions to his still-living wife on planting flowers—and her mother rejected it, but it was the beginning of an odyssey that eventually would catapult Martin into the headlines and shape the rest of her life (Clark 1997, pp. 205–206).

Meantime, a couple who would play a large role in the drama to come were also being swept up by events. For Charles and Lillian Laughead (pronounced *law*-head) it started in Egypt, where the couple had served as Protestant missionaries between 1946 and 1949. During that time Mrs. Laughead fell victim to recurring nightmares and irrational fears that she could not will to stop nor could her husband, a physician, treat successfully. Looking for a cure, they turned to esoteric literature and read many of the same books Martin was scrutinizing. When they returned to the United States, Dr. Laughead took up a staff position at the Michigan State College Hospital in East Lansing. By now the couple were full-fledged occult enthusiasts and inevitably soon incorporated flying saucers into their newly found faith.

On a trip to southern California to see the Rose Bowl game in January 1953, Dr. Laughead met George Adamski, whose recent meeting with Orthon was electrifying occultists and saucer buffs. Adamski told him that the Venusian had left tracks in the desert sand. Each contained within it a distinct set of mysterious symbols. Laughead took home a drawing of the prints, which he showed to his wife. Intrigued, Mrs. Laughead devoted the next five months to deciphering the symbols. She decided that the left track, in her interpretation, represented the sinking of the lost continents of Mu and Atlantis. (Mu, also known as Lemuria, is a mythical lost continent located somewhere in the Pacific Ocean and invented in nineteenth-century occult writing.) The symbols in the right track predicted their reemergence from the ocean floor following geological cataclysms that soon would befall the earth.

Another source of inspiration came not long after Laughead's visit with Adamski, through an automatic-writing message given to the doctor through a ministerial student. The message, according to Laughead, "was from the Elder Brother who later identified himself as being Jesus the Christ and also Sananda. In this message, I was told to keep telling the truth about the saucers. The Venusians, he said, would contact me, and I would work with them" (Clark 1997, p. 208).

For her part Martin was seeking to improve her automatic-writing skills. After her father proved boring and immature—trapped, she deduced, in the imbecilic region of the spirit world—she found her way to an entity who called himself the Elder Brother and then to other beings she would call the Guardians. One, who introduced himself in April 1954 as Sananda, now resident of the paradisiacal planet Clarion, was no less than Jesus in an earlier, earthly incarnation.

Though Martin got the name Clarion from Bethurum—or at least recycled it through her unconscious mind—her Clarion existed not on the other side of the moon but in an etheric (other-dimensional) realm. A companion planet, Cerus (sometimes confusingly referred to also as a constellation), housed other space people who kept Martin's arm and hand in furious motion as they acted on their promise to teach her cosmic wisdom. The Elder Brother said she would not be doing this alone: "We will teach them that seek and are ready to follow in the light. . . . Be patient and learn, for we are there preparing the work for you as a connoiter. That is an earthly liaison duty before I come. That will be soon. . . . They that have told you that they do not believe shall see us when the time is right" (Clark 1997, p. 208).

Soon a woman from a nearby town was typing up the messages for Martin and distributing them. Martin joined a local occult discussion group and talked about her experiences. She also passed them on to another group in Chicago. She spoke about them with John Otto, a Chicago-based but nationally known UFO enthusiast and lecturer. Thus the story of her space communications gradually became known to the larger "metaphysical" community.

The Laugheads met Otto in March 1954, when the latter attended a George Adamski lecture sponsored by the contactee-oriented Detroit Flying Saucer Club. Credulous and excitable by nature, Otto took space communications of all kinds very seriously. At some point, either in Detroit or in subsequent correspondence with the couple, he told the Laugheads about Dorothy Martin's messages and expressed the conviction that they represented something important. Intrigued, the Laugheads wrote Martin and recounted their own occult explorations.

Somewhere around this time Martin received a message urging her to go to East Lansing to seek "a child . . . to whom I am trying to get through with light." She took it to mean the Laugheads, since she had never heard of anyone else from that city. She quickly replied to the letter, and soon the three formed a tight association, based in part on Mrs. Laughead's conviction that she was the "child." For some time, she said, she had sensed overtures from the Guardians.

The Laugheads and Martin met for the first time in late June, when the couple drove down from Michigan to visit Martin's home. (Martin was married to a man who did not believe in space messages but who did not disparage her activities. He had little if anything to do with the events to come.) By this time Martin was receiving as many as ten messages a day, and they were taking an increasingly foreboding tone, warning of imminent disasters and cataclysms. Those who would "listen and believe," however, would enter a New Age of knowledge and happiness.

Gray Barker of Clarksburg, West Virginia, listened but did not believe. Barker was drawn to the UFO field in September 1952 through newspaper reports of a landing and encounter with a monstrous creature near the tiny town of Flatwoods in his native state. After interviewing the witnesses, he wrote an article on the incident for *Fate*, a popular magazine devoted to "true mysteries." Soon he was an active presence in ufology, and in September 1953 he started his own small-circulation bulletin, *The Saucerian*, which covered both seemingly credible sightings and saucerdom's most outlandish aspects.

Martin, also a native West Virginian, wrote Barker in early 1954 to subscribe to the publication. In follow-up letter in April, she wrote,

"I have apparently been contacting the visitors, but the messages are beyond my comprehension. . . . They told me once before they would land in Flatwoods. This time the contact was stronger and more positive." She enclosed a message addressed to Barker from a spaceman named Garcia Sai:

> I am in contact with the pilot of an active space craft in the vicinity of Flatwoods. We have made contact there and expect to land in May or June.
>
> At that time you will be contacted. The contact will be one of the space people. You will look for a scar on the left cheek the color of the hair.
>
> The last time there was so much confusion they [presumably the witnesses to what the press called the "Flatwoods monster"] failed to see what did happen. This time it will be planned so there will be a contact on earth to receive us. (Clark 1997, p. 208)

Barker pressed for more details, more out of idle curiosity than any conviction that Martin's messages signified anything but self-delusion. A few weeks later Barker did meet a young man with a scar on his face, but he knew him to be a local man whose injury had come about in a car accident.

Though privately skeptical—"amused" probably best characterizes his attitude—Barker continued to play along with Martin. He solicited further messages. After another space communicant, one Sara, assured him that contact was imminent, he concocted a story about meeting a strange man near the post office and seeing him vanish into thin air. Sara quickly assured Martin that "the young man who contacted Gray Barker was our contact and had a message for him."

Later, reflecting on these matters after Dorothy Martin had fallen victim to worldwide headlines and international ridicule, Barker would observe that from his point of view, "Mrs. Martin had contacted some rather inept extraterrestrials—or . . . the information was coming from quite a remarkable subconscious."

Meanwhile, the messages kept pouring into Oak Park. Though of course they purported to be from extraterrestrial/dimensional Guardians, their true source was later traceable to the occult literature to which Martin had exposed herself. For example, in a July 8 communication, the Guardians described themselves as "beings of the UN [mind of the High Self] . . . who can and do create by the UN the casement or vehicle they chose to use in the seen." Earlier N. Meade Layne had written, "The aeroforms [flying saucers] are thought-constructs, mind constructs. As such, they are, in effect, the vehicle of the actual entity who creates them." The similarity in concepts is not likely to be coincidence. Significantly, Martin subscribed to *Round Robin,* the bulletin of Layne's BSRA (Clark 1997, p. 210).

The messages from Sananda and other Guardians more and more took on a prophetic tone. Spaceships would land and make contact with earthlings in May or June. Selected people would be flown to other planets, along with space people who had been on secret earth assignment. The messages also alluded darkly to imminent nuclear holocaust: "The people of Earth are rushing, rushing toward the suicide of themselves. . . . To this we are answering with signs and wonders in the sky" (Clark 1997, p. 210). The space people would see to it that those responsible were brought to swift justice.

On several occasions Martin was instructed to go to different locations in the Chicago metropolitan area either to see spacecraft or to receive direct messages from extraterrestrials in physical form. Nothing came of these ventures, except—in Martin's judgment—on one occasion. A saucer was to land at a nearby military base at noon on August 1. "It will be as if the world was coming to an end at the field when the landing occurs," the Guardians declared. "The operators will not believe their senses when they see the craft of outer space in the midst of the field." They assured Martin that she could trust this message: "It is a very accurate cast that we give" (Clark 1997, pp. 210–11).

So at the appointed hour Martin, the Laugheads (who were visiting for the weekend), and nine other believers parked near the gate and awaited the arrival. No spaceship appeared, but Martin took comfort from the sudden appearance of a stranger who showed up unexpectedly along the highway. She thought he had "eyes that looked through my soul. . . . I knew something was going on that I didn't understand." He declined her offer of a sandwich and a glass of fruit juice, then wandered off saying nothing more. The next day, through automatic writing, Martin learned, "It was I, Sananda, who appeared on the roadside in the guise of the sice." "Sice," in extraterrestrialese, is "one who comes in disguise" (Festinger, Rieken, and Schachter, p. 63). It would not be the last time Martin would inflate a mundane incident into a signal from the cosmos. Nor would it be the last of the unfulfilled prophecies.

The most important of these came through on the same day Sananda pronounced himself the man on the road (August 2). He delivered these chilling words:

> The Earthling will awaken to the great casting [conditions to be fulfilled] of the lake seething and the great destruction of the tall buildings of the local city—the case that the lake bed is sinking to the degree that it will be as a great scoop of wind from the bottom of the lake throughout the countryside. You shall tell the world that this is to be, for such it is given. To you the date only is secret, for the panic of men knows no bounds. (Festinger, Rieken, and Schachter 1956)

In subsequent messages that month Sananda warned of enormous geological upheaval. North America would soon break in two:

> In the area of the Mississippi, in the region of Canada, Great Lakes and the Mississippi, to the Gulf of Mexico, into the Central America will be as changed. The great tilting of the land of the U.S. to the East will throw up mountains along the Central States, along the Great New Sea, along North and South—to the South. The new mountain range shall be called The Argone Range, which will signify the ones who have been there are gone—the old has gone past—the new is. This will be as a monument to the old races; to the new will be the Altar of the Rockies and the Alleghenies. (Festinger, Rieken, and Schachter 1956)

Not only North America would feel the full impact of the upheaval. The Egyptian desert would be transformed into a green valley. Much of Europe, from Britain to Russia, would sink under the sea, and the lost continent of Mu would rise.

Stunned and awed, Martin and the Laugheads reported these revelations to the larger world in a seven-page mimeographed document, "Open Letter to American Editors and Publishers," sent out on August 30. A handwritten addendum appended at the last minute cited December 20 as the "date of evacuation"—in other words, the final day on which human beings living in the affected areas could save themselves.

A second mailing two weeks later concerned the "terrific wave" that would rise from Lake Michigan at dawn on December 21 and overwhelm Chicago before spreading east and west:

> Glad are the actors who have awaited the coming of the Guardians. Amid the cries of anguish the question is heard: "Why didn't someone tell us that we might have moved to safety?" But in the days of the warnings they were told of the safe places—the eastern slopes of the Rockies, the Catskills, and the Allegheny Mountains—but they said, "It can't happen here!" (Festinger, Rieken, and Schachter 1956)

The first press story to report the curious beliefs of Martin and her disciples appeared in a Chicago newspaper on September 23. The reporter missed another flying saucer-related apocalyptic prophecy that had been published six days earlier in a small Oklahoma paper, the *Clinton Daily News.* According to the *Daily News,* Gladys White Eagle, a Cheyenne woman, claimed to have seen a UFO land with a roaring sound on the north bank of the Canadian River a month or so earlier. A tall, thin man with a long beard stepped outside. Speaking in "twisted words" and with an unpleasant cackle, he declared that a great earthquake and atomic bombs would destroy the United States on October 13. He asked her to return to the same spot on September 17. "I'm not going back because I'm scared," White Eagle told the newspaper.

Though Martin saw no one emerge from a spacecraft, it was a spaceman, she believed, who came to her door in the wake of the press account of her prophecies. One man, who did all the talking, identified himself as an earthling, but went on to reveal that his companion was from another world. The man directed Martin to desist from further publicity and to await orders. It did not occur to Martin that these callers might be practical jokers. Her sole concern was whether they represented good extraterrestrials or bad ones trying to shut down the earth–Clarion link.

Among those who were congregating in Martin's home, besides the predictable coterie of occult seekers, the curious, and the gullible, were five psychologists, sociologists, and graduate students under the direction of the Laboratory for Research in Social Relations of the University of Minnesota. Learning of the ongoing saga from the newspaper story, three university professors–Leon Festinger, Henry W. Riecken, and Stanley Schachter–saw the chance to research firsthand a prophetic movement at work. They were especially interested in what would happen to its participants when the anticipated events did not occur–thus the title of the classic book they would write about the episode: *When Prophecy Fails.*

While Martin, Laughead, and the others waxed hot and cold on publicity and proselytization, it would have been impossible to conceal what was going on. For one thing, there were followers not just in the Chicago area but also in East Lansing and Detroit. In the former Laughead led a church-related group. He also had ties to the Detroit saucer community, dominated by contactees and mystics, including medium Rose Phillips, whose spirit guide–a discarnate physician–had his own cosmic sources. In fact, some of Martin's Michigan followers would go to Phillips to seek confirmation or disconfirmation of the December 21 prophecy. To the confusion or irritation of the inquirers, Phillips managed to provide both, agreeing that the described cataclysm would occur but offering conflicting testimony on the date.

In any case, as December 21 grew closer, the Laugheads spent more and more time away from their East Lansing home. Participants debated whether to quit their jobs and otherwise cut off earthly ties, and all awaited anxiously for further signs. As tension mounted, one member began channeling her own communications from "the Creator." For a time the often discordant testimony coming through the two women created a rift within the group, but soon Martin's strong personality—one manifestation of which was the greater relative clarity of Sananda's messages—won out.

All the while, however, the larger outside world was closing in. Besides pressure from disbelieving family members and friends, the believers experienced a particular jolt when Laughead lost his job.

On November 22, 1954, Laughead had been asked to resign his position (effective December 1) with the college health service, though word of the firing would be withheld for another three weeks. On December 17, Michigan State College president John A. Hannah told the Associated Press that students had complained about Laughead's "propagandizing" them "on a peculiar set of beliefs of questionable validity" which would "affect adversely the quality of their college work." But before this public announcement, only school officials, the Laugheads, and—when Laughead confided to them a week later—members of the Martin group knew why Laughead had been fired.

With time running out, the Laugheads moved into the Martin residence and prepared for the coming landing. Each member received a "passport" consisting of a sheet of blank paper inside a stamped envelope. This, along with the "password" ("I left my hat at home"), assured each believer a seat on the flying saucer.

On December 17 the relative privacy that had shielded the group from ridicule ended when a Chicago paper exposed Martin's strange beliefs and reported Laughead's loss of employment. Papers across the country, and soon afterwards the world, picked up the story, and over the next few days Martin and Laughead did their best to convince journalists, who were playing the episode for laughs, that they were not crazy. Laughead did most of the talking, trying to come across as a reasonable man who simply followed the evidence—unlike the reporters, who "are very, very confused and far behind the times on flying saucer knowledge" (Clark 1997, p. 214).

The publicity left the relentlessly gullible group open to the most obvious pranks, including phone calls from self-identified space people. The most absurd of these came from "Captain Video"—the hero of a popular television series for children—who on the day of the newspaper article's appearance informed Martin of a spaceship landing to occur at four o'clock that afternoon in her own backyard.

Incredibly, Martin directed the group to prepare for the pickup. Only Mrs. Laughead suspected a joke, but Martin would have none of it.

Soon after the call everyone was busy ripping the metal out of his or her clothes—the space people had warned that metal could not safely be worn aboard a saucer—and scanning the sky. At four the believers walked out the door, often in mid-conversation with reporters and curiosity-seekers, in full expectation that within moments they would be whisked into space.

After an hour and a half of no saucer, they trooped back and watched Captain Video—the real one—on television. Martin suspected that the space people would send a coded message through the show, but even with her considerable imaginative powers she discerned none.

Late that evening Martin received a psychic message that a spaceship was on its way; anyone who wasn't ready when it arrived would be left behind. For more than three hours, until about 3:20 in the morning, the small band shivered outside in the frigid cold. Finally a message arrived from the space people praising the believers' patience and commitment and releasing them from the vigil.

Not everybody was able to sustain the faith, and the ranks dwindled as one by one those who could not contain their growing doubts slipped away. The others let themselves be persuaded that the space people were merely testing them to prove that they were worthy of rescue from the coming cataclysm.

On the morning of December 20, less than twenty-four hours before the tidal wave would wipe Chicago off the face of the earth and forever reshape the earth's geography, Martin got these words from the Guardians:

> At the hour of midnight you shall be put into parked cars and taken to a place where ye shall be put aboard a porch [flying saucer] and ye shall be purposed by the time you are there. At that time you shall have the fortuned ones forget the few who have not come—and at no time are they to be called for, they are but enacting a scene and not a person who should be there will fail to be there and at the time you are to say "What is your question?" . . . and at no time are you to ask

what is what and not a plan shall go astray and for the time being be glad and be fortuned to be among the favored. And be ye ready for further instructions. (Festinger, Riecken, and Schachter 1956)

Martin and the others spent the day rehearsing the passwords and rituals that would enable them to board the spaceship when it arrived. One message revealed that the escape from earth would begin precisely at midnight, when a spaceman would knock at the door. He was to be greeted with these words: "What is your question?"

When no spaceman showed up at the designated hour, one member began intermittent channeling from the Creator, who promised a miracle. None happened. For the first time even the most hardened believers were facing the possibility that maybe nothing was going to happen, at least any time soon. Martin lamely suggested that maybe "it was this little group spreading light here that prevented the flood." Not long afterwards, not surprisingly, a message from Sananda confirmed that interpretation.

Laughead took over the phone to call reporters and wire services with the happy news: The earth had been saved. The result was a fresh round of ridicule-filled news stories. Even worse, group members who had given up jobs and cut ties with skeptical family members faced uncertain immediate futures.

But as the day went by and the press and the curious marched in and out of Martin's door, there was growing anxiety that members were missing hidden messages from the space people. At 9 that evening Martin took a call from someone identifying himself as a spaceman. Taking him at his word, she engaged him in prolonged conversation. Another prank call sent her off on a brief, embarrassing venture to a boy's house. A teenaged UFO buff who came to the house was assumed to be a spaceman and pressed for orders.

Martin also claimed that earthquakes which had occurred in Italy and California validated her prophecy. By now she was grasping at anything. The next day, when Sananda directed her to turn on her tape recorder at 8 P.M. so that a flying saucer could beam down a song sung by an extraterrestrial "boys' glee club," all that came of it was a blank tape.

As if things were not already farcical enough, a message on December 23 ordered everyone to stand in front of the Martin home at 6 P.M. and to sing Christmas carols. At that moment–what else?–a flying saucer would land and spacemen would talk with the carolers in person. The message further directed the group to publicize the new prophecy and to encourage anyone who wanted to be there. Interviewed that evening about this yet one more failed prophecy, Laughead could only offer this feeble explanation: "There may have been spacemen there in disguise." On Christmas Day one of the sociologist-observers called on Martin. Taking him to be a spaceman, she asked him what orders he had for her.

Of the group, only Martin and the Laugheads, bottomlessly faithful, managed to sustain belief in extraterrestrials who promised much and delivered nothing beyond ever more lame rationalizations for each successive failed prophecy. Laughead survived a psychiatric hearing initiated by his sister, who was trying to take custody of his three daughters. But as late as May, acting on instructions channeled through Rose Phillips, the Laugheads and the Detroit medium waited at a hotel garage ramp in East Lansing for a saucer landing.

For Martin things were even worse. To her Oak Park neighbors the caroling episode, which had precipitated a near riot and brought police to the scene to quell an unruly crowd, was the final irritation. Community pressure forced the police to draw up a warrant against Martin and Laughead, charging them with disturbing the peace and contributing to the delinquency of minors. Though clearly reluctant to act on the warrant, the police warned the Martins to shut down the meetings. They also intimated that if there were any further problems, Mrs. Martin would face psychiatric examination and possible institutionalization.

Early in January, Dorothy Martin slipped out of town. Under an alias she flew to Arizona. (Or, as one sympathetic account has it, "Sananda told her to burn her bridges behind her. Just minutes before a sanity warrant was to be served, committing her for 'observation,' Sananda sent ones who whisked her away to a place of safety, never to return to her home again" [Clark 1997, p. 217]) In her new residence she found herself much closer to the hub of contactee activity. Both Truman Bethurum and George Hunt Williamson lived in Arizona. The Laugheads, now living in southern California, dropped in from time to time.

Through Williamson's channelings the Laugheads and Martin, who now thought of herself (at Sananda's urging) as "Sister Thedra," learned of the Brotherhood of the Seven Rays. According to an extraterrestrial named Aramu-Muru:

> The Brotherhood of the Seven Rays traces its origin back many thousands of years to the post-Lemurian period. It really goes back further than that, but it knew its monastery in post-Lemurian times at Lake Titicaca, Peru. It worked then and it continues to work now with other Brotherhoods throughout the world. It is in close association with Master Koot Hoomi Lah Singh at Shigatse, Tibet, and with the master teacher of the great White Brotherhood at Mt. Shasta, California. There are several others located throughout the world that work in fellowship with the Brotherhood of the Seven Rays. (Clark 1997, p. 217)

In another session, on February 19, 1956, the planetary spirit of Venus, Sanat Kumara, who ordinarily communicated with Martin but this time spoke through Williamson (aka "Brother Philip"), assured Martin that her apocalyptic prophecy would prove true after all:

> Very soon, beloved of my being, the winds shall howl, sooner than we realize. It is already upon us, for I have witnessed it in the plane which is just above that of physical expression upon the earth, and that means that if it descends one more plane, it shall find reality. And that which you knew must come on a December not many months ago shall find its reality, for it is in the plane ready to descend into form and motion upon the earth. (Clark 1997, p. 218)

Guided by such prophecies, Martin, Williamson, and others moved to Lake Titicaca to establish the Priority of All Saints in the remote northern Peruvian town Moyobamba. From Hemet, California, the Laugheads kept the North American faithful abreast of developments. A bulletin reported day-to-day activities there. Each report was accompanied by a transcript of channeled or automatically written messages, often with apocalyptic overtones.

Soon, these messages said, cataclysmic changes would bring flying saucers down from the skies and Atlantis and Lemuria up from the ocean depths.

By the summer of 1957, however, nearly all of the spiritual pilgrims were back in the United States. The exception was Martin, whom Sananda directed to stay behind.

Living under the most primitive conditions, suffering from poverty and ill health, Martin barely survived. She felt that her colleagues had betrayed her. She spent a portion of her meager income on postage for mailings to North America, but no one seemed to listen or to care. Even so, the messages continued to come at a furious pace. Now they included dramatic visionary encounters with various space people, angels, and religious figures.

Though expecting to spend the rest of her life in the Andes, Martin was surprised to receive instructions in 1961 to return to the United States. She moved to southern California and was there for nearly a year before heading to the northern part of the state and Mount Shasta, long an attraction to America's mystically minded. Occult legend held that a colony of Lemurians (survivors of a lost city akin to Atlantis) lived inside or under the mountain. The Lemurians maintained contacts with extraterrestrials who regularly arrived in UFOs.

Sananda and Sanat Kumara told Martin to establish the Association of Sananda and Sanat Kumara. Finding peace and stability at last, Martin took up residence in the Shasta area and worked with a small but devoted group of followers who carefully recorded and circulated the messages she received daily.

By 1988, with Sedona, Arizona, now the New Age center of North America, the space people dictated yet another move. It was here, on June 13, 1992, that Sister Thedra's long, strange trip ended. Just before her death Sananda told her of his plans for her in the next world. As her body failed, her hand guided a pen one last time to write the final message from her beloved cosmic friend: "It is now come the time that ye come out of the place wherein ye are. . . . Let it be, for many shall greet thee with glad shouts!" (Clark 1997, p. 219).

7

NEW AGE DOOMSDAYS

Many great deluges have taken place during the last nine thousand years, for that is the number of years which have elapsed since the time of which I am speaking; and in all the ages and changes of things there has never been any settlement of the earth flowing down from the mountains, as in other places, which is worth speaking of; it has always been carried round in a circle, and disappeared in the depths below. The consequence is that, in comparison of what then was, there are remaining in small islets only the bones of the wasted body, as they may be called, all the richer and softer parts of the soil having fallen away, and the mere skeletons of the country being left. . . .

—Plato, *Critias*

The last traces of sunlight from another lazy Santa Barbara day had just faded out of the western sky. From the darkened street some twenty yards away, we heard occasional car noises and the muffled voices of passing pedestrians, but these sounds felt somehow distant, as if our little gathering was mysteriously insulated from the outer world. A large, low window along the wall we were facing made the office room in which this meeting was held seem less businesslike than usual, a transformation enhanced by the dim lighting that created a séancelike atmosphere. Seated on folding chairs in a loose semicircle around an entranced, heavy-set medium, we relaxed as best we could in what was supposed to approximate a meditative state. Our outward calm, however, belied the intense expectancy with which we awaited the arrival of the spirit who would soon possess the sleeping channel's body.

Soon she began to twitch, a sign that a disembodied entity had taken control of her body. Gradually opening her eyes, the possessed medium began by addressing us in the unidentifiable accent so common to most New Age channels: "Greetings to you, Masters! How are you in your bodies this evening?" This odd salutation was the lead-in to a lively session in which the medium channeled a number of entities, from St. Germain to the Archangel Michael. Judging from the dialogue, these elevated beings showed remarkable interest in the mundane affairs of our small group of less than a dozen participants.

The claims of elevated spiritual authority, the unnatural accents, and the uncanny impression that we might actually be communicating with discarnate spirits were all pretty standard fare. These accoutrements, familiar to anybody who has experienced New Age spiritualism firsthand, recalled similar performances from channeling's heyday in the late 1980s. In those heady days, when the premier medium/entity J. Z. Knight/Ramtha could chum around with Merv Griffin on national television, channelers' messages were bolder and their prophecies more dramatic: Rather than picturing the New Age dawn in fuzzy pastels, Ramtha and others painted the future with stark colors of apocalyptic destruction. In particular, imminent "earth changes" were confidently predicted—earthquakes and other natural disasters that would radically change the face of the planet, and usher in a New Age civilization. The New Age's primary source for this sort of doomsday prophecy appears to have been the work of Edgar Cayce.

EDGAR CAYCE AND EARTH CHANGES

Cayce was born in 1877 near Hopkinsville, Kentucky, the son of Leslie B. Cayce, a businessman and tobacco farmer, and Carrie Elizabeth Cayce. Raised in the Christian Church (Disciples of Christ), he eventually taught Sunday school. He dropped out of school to became a photographer's apprentice and made his living as a photographer. Married to Gertrude Evans in 1903, he fathered two sons. As a young man he discovered he had the ability to sleep on a book and wake up with a photographic memory of its contents.

Cayce developed severe laryngitis in 1900. During this crisis, an acquaintance hypnotized Cayce, although according to some accounts, the trance was self-induced. During the trance, Cayce diagnosed his own health problem and prescribed a cure. Soon after this experience, he began to perform the same trance prescriptions for others and his reputation gradually grew.

It was at this point that Cayce discovered he had what was called at the time "traveling clairvoyance." He could put himself into a trance (he did not need a hypnotist), and psychically reach inside another person, even at a distance, to "see" any problematic health condition and then prescribe a cure. He was one of the few psychics in the early twentieth century to do this kind of "reading," which had been far more popular in the nineteenth century, and his success with it led other psychics to revive it in the late twentieth century.

In 1909, Cayce met a homeopathic physician, Dr. Wesley Ketchum, who requested that Cayce give him a reading. Ketchum's illness was cured, and he publicized his story and the story of other Cayce cures widely. Some of Ketchum's remarks about Cayce were quoted in a sensational article that appeared in the *New York Times* in September 1910. Following this exposure, Cayce, now widely known as the "Sleeping Prophet," was sought after by thousands of ailing people. His prescriptions varied from psychic treatments to home remedies to advising the patient to see a particular medical doctor.

A turning point in Cayce's readings occurred in 1923 when Cayce met Arthur Lammers, a wealthy printer and student of theosophy and Eastern religions. Cayce traveled to Dayton, Ohio, to conduct a series of private readings. One of Lammers's central articles of faith was belief in reincarnation, and Cayce mentioned Lammers's past lives in one of the private readings. Cayce subsequently began to explore the past lives of his other clients, including past lives on the lost continent of Atlantis. He soon added past-life readings to his health readings. This new "ability" was enough to make Cayce a sensation. Not long after his sessions with Lammers, he closed his photography studio and moved to Ohio.

After Lammers suffered some financial reverses, Morton Blumenthal, a New York stockbroker, offered to finance a center and hospital on the East Coast to be headed by Cayce. Cayce then moved to Virginia Beach, where he resided for the rest of his life. The hospital opened in 1928 and Atlantic University in 1930. In 1931, however, Blumenthal's business failed, a casualty of the Great Depression. Without Blumenthal, both the hospital and the university had to be shut down.

In 1929, prior to the shutdown, Cayce and his family began a newsletter, *The New Tomorrow*, to advertise his activities and spread the knowledge gained from his trances. In 1931 Cayce formally founded the Association for Research and Enlightenment (A.R.E.) to promote and study his work. The A.R.E., besides running the newsletter, recorded all of Cayce's readings; very few psychics have been subject to such thorough documentation. By the time of Cayce's death in 1945, the A.R.E. had compiled over 14,000 readings given to more than 8,000 people.

After Cayce's death, two compilations of material on Atlantis were released by the Association for Research and Enlightenment: *Atlantis: Fact or Fiction?* and *Edgar Cayce on Atlantis.* These two paperbacks were the source for most beliefs about Atlantis held by members of the New Age movement. Cayce predicted that evidence for the historical existence of Atlantis would be found off the East Coast of North America in the 1960s. To date, however, the most that has been discovered is a roadwaylike series of stones on the ocean floor—stones that might be a natural phenomenon rather than an artifact of human design.

During the 1970s A.R.E. wedded itself to the developing New Age movement and became a major promoter of New Age–related health therapies, spiritual practices, and trance-channeling. The group also began to sponsor workshops and seminars that focused on the theme of a coming new age of spiritual illumination. This millenarian theme complemented Cayce's earlier prophecies of cataclysmic earth changes during the late twentieth century.

In particular, he anticipated that a sudden reversal of the earth's axis–a pole shift–would be responsible for the worst damage. This final cataclysm would occur around the year 2000. The notion exists that the earth has undergone such pole shifts in the past, based on a geological theory that proposed to explain why different layers of rock are polarized in different directions. There are, however, alternate hypotheses for explaining such layering, making the prediction of future pole shifts problematic. In any event, this notion was picked up by later New Age prophets, such as Ruth Montgomery, who is primarily responsible for making the pole shift idea a core assumption of New Age apocalypticism.

In Cayce's view, these catastrophic earth changes would be the heralds of a better age. It is not difficult to see how Cayce's thinking about the end of the century and the emergence of a new world after the pole shift unconsciously reflects the basic structure of traditional Christian millennialism: A series of smaller catastrophes lead up to apocalyptic earth changes at the end of the millennium. In the wake of this destruction, a new, edenic era of love and peace is ushered in. This scenario would seem rather natural to a former Sunday school teacher.

Specifically, Cayce prophesied a sixty-year period of cataclysmic activity prior to the "big one" at the end of the second millennium. A sense of what this will entail was expressed in a 1934 reading, in which he outlined these events as follows:

- major upheavals in western North America;
- most of Japan will sink into the ocean;
- dramatic changes in Northern Europe will take place "in the twinkling of an eye";

- land will rise out of the Atlantic off the eastern shore of North America;
- open waters will appear in Greenland;
- cataclysmic upheaval at the poles and volcanic activity in the tropics;
- land rising between Antarctica and Terra del Fuego, the southernmost tip of South America;
- a pole shift (Mann, pp. 86–88).

Cayce made many more predictions about earth changes beyond these—so many, in fact, that Cayce enthusiasts have been able to draw maps of how the earth will look after the shift. Such "earth change maps" have caught on among more recent prophets of terrestrial cataclysms.

Some of Cayce's more specific predictions have already been disconfirmed. For example, prior to the World War II, Cayce asserted in a reading that Hitler was "good" for the German people. With respect to earth changes, he also predicted that in the late 1960s new land would rise in the eastern Caribbean/western Atlantic that would contain some of the remains of ancient Atlantis. As with other prophets whose predictions have proven incorrect, followers of the Edgar Cayce teachings have disregarded or explained away such mistakes.

In addition to his biblical background, it is evident that the other paradigm for Cayce's earth changes prophecies was the story of the destruction of Atlantis. In particular, Cayce predicted that major land areas in North America would sink into the oceans—precisely the fate ascribed to ancient Atlantis. The Atlantis legend, in turn, goes back to Plato.

PLATO'S ATLANTIS

Plato is widely acknowledged as the greatest philosopher of the Western tradition. A student of the Greek thinker Socrates, Plato was the teacher of Aristotle. A number of passages in Plato's surviving works are important sources for the legend of the lost island kingdom of Atlantis. In the Atlantis passages and elsewhere, Plato alludes to a series of floods that have affected the earth. His mention of deluges is articulated within a larger discussion of terrestrial cataclysms–a discussion to which few writers, either scholarly or popular, have called attention.

Plato's description of Atlantis and his reference to cataclysmic geological cycles have been almost completely overshadowed by his contributions to Western thought. The particular manner in which he posed key philosophical questions, from the issue of knowledge (How do we know what we know?) to the issue of ethics (How do we determine right action?), set the agenda for the ongoing discussion and debate that we refer to as Western philosophy. This is so much the case that the twentieth-century philosopher and mathematician Alfred North Whitehead once remarked that all of Western philosophy is a series of footnotes to Plato.

Plato was born in Athens, Greece, in about 428 B.C.E. to an important family. He lived during a time of turmoil and transition, when the city-states of classical Greece were crumbling. (Aristotle's pupil Alexander the Great would later conquer all of Greece.) After the city of Athens tried and ordered the death of his teacher, Socrates, in 399 B.C.E., Plato left his native city and traveled widely through Greece, Egypt, and Italy. During his travels, he met a Pythagorean mathematician, Archytas of Tarentum, and became convinced of the value of mathematics. Plato returned to Athens and founded his school, the Academy, in 387 B.C.E. Later occultists would assert that he was initiated into mystery religions in Egypt in the Great Pyramid during his travels.

The surviving works of Plato are his semipopular works, which were cast in the form of dialogues. The spokesperson for Plato's views in these writings was his friend and tutor, Socrates. The earliest dialogues appear to reflect the personality and views of Socrates, while the ideas expressed in the later dialogues are Plato's own. In the middle group of dialogues, it is difficult to tell where Socrates' ideas end and Plato's begin. References to Atlantis occur in the dialogues *Timaeus* and the *Critias*, with the most extended treatment in the latter work.

Commentators on Plato's Atlantis passages have tended to ignore the cataclysmic view of geological history articulated by an unnamed Egyptian priest who recounted the tale of Atlantis to the Greek poet Solon. In response to Solon's recounting of the Greek version of the flood story, the priest chides Solon regarding the Greeks' state of knowledge, which is confined to the cultural memory of but one deluge: "There have been, and there will be again, many destructions of mankind arising out of many causes." In addition to floods, a declination of the heavenly bodies cause

> a great conflagration of things upon the earth recurring at long intervals of time: when this happens, those who live upon the mountains and in dry and lofty places are more liable to destruction than those who dwell by rivers or on the sea-shore. (Cited in Hope, p. 14)

Specific cataclysms affect individual groups of people differently. Floods tend to affect large cities, leaving only herdsmen as survivors:

> When, on the other hand, the gods purge the earth with a deluge of water, among you herdsmen and shepherds on the mountains are the survivors, whereas those of you who live in cities are carried by the rivers into the sea. (Hope, p. 14)

A similar discussion about mountaintop herdsmen surviving the deluge is found in Plato's *Laws*. Like Plato's discussion of Atlantis (which will be detailed shortly), the passage from the *Laws* is interesting because of the cataclysmic view of history that the Greek philosopher is apparently putting forward–a dynamic perspective that stands in sharp contrast to his unchanging view of the realm of the archetypes:

> Athenian: Do you consider that there is any truth in the ancient tales?
> Clinias: What tales?
> Athenian: The world of men has often been destroyed by floods, plagues, and many other things, in such a way that only a small portion of the human race has survived.

Clinias: Everyone would regard such accounts as perfectly credible.

Athenian: Come now, let us picture to ourselves one of the many catastrophes—namely, that which occurred once upon a time through the Deluge.

Clinias: And what are we to imagine about it?

Athenian: That the men who then escaped destruction must have been mostly herdsmen of the hill, scanty embers of the human race preserved somewhere on the mountaintops.

Clinias: Evidently. . . .

Athenian: Shall we assume that the cities situated in the plains and near the sea were totally destroyed at the time?

Clinias: Let us assume it. . . .

Athenian: Shall we, then, state that, at the time when the destruction took place, human affairs were in this position: there was fearful and widespread desolation over a vast tract of land; most of the animals were destroyed; and the few herds of oxen and flocks of goats that happened to survive afforded at the first but scanty sustenance to their herdsmen? (Plato, pp. 167–73)

A significant aspect of this passage is its relative realism: had a dramatic flood actually occurred in the distant past, herdsmen in high altitudes would have been one of the few groups of people equipped to survive in a post-deluge world. It is also noteworthy that the passage is unconnected with any discussion of antediluvian civilization, indicating that Plato's adherence to a cataclysmic view of history was broader than his interest in the Atlantis legend.

The Atlantis story is part ancient myth and part modern legend. Atlantis, as an island in the Atlantic, first appears as a parable in two of Plato's dialogues. Plato asserted that the story of Atlantis had been brought to Athens from Egypt by the Greek poet Solon, so many people have supposed there may have been some historical basis for Plato's tale. However, it could also be that Plato was simply using the legend of Atlantis as a narrative lead-in to the meat of his analysis—without being particularly concerned about the legend's historical truth—as he does with other myths elsewhere in his dialogues. For the Greek philosopher, the story of Atlantis was primarily a morality tale: In many ways parallel to the biblical flood story, Plato's narrative Atlantis was a kind of earthly paradise that was destroyed by the gods after its rulers became puffed up and greedy. Thus, as with many other versions of the flood myth that is told worldwide, the Atlantean deluge was explained as a form of divine punishment.

However, it should also be noted that the cataclysm which destroyed Atlantis was not just confined to the island nation, but devastated other areas of the world as well. In particular, in the dialogue *Critias*, Plato indicates that the Athenian army which threw back the Atlantean invaders was destroyed in the same cataclysm:

> But afterward there occurred violent earthquakes and floods, and in a single day and night of rain all your warlike men in a body sank into the earth, and the island of Atlantis in like manner disappeared, and was sunk beneath the sea. (Cited in Hope, p. 18)

Thus the Atlantean cataclysm was presumably also a universal cataclysm which had an impact on the entire world, or at least on the entire "world" with which Plato was familiar, namely the eastern Mediterranean.

A number of contemporary scholars have proposed alternate sites for the legendary isle. Most compelling is the theory originally advanced early in the twentieth century that Plato's story of Atlantis actually describes the destruction of Cretan civilization by a volcanic explosion in 1470 B.C.E. An alternative argument, put forward by Eberhard Zangger in *The Flood from Heaven* (1992), is that the myth refers to the Achaean destruction of Troy in the fourteenth century B.C.E.

There has been some interest in Atlantis over the centuries, but the Christian civilization of traditional Europe tended to discourage such speculation. After the Americas were encountered by Europeans, a number of writers penned works arguing that the newly discovered continents were Plato's Atlantis. Subsequently, interest in the ancient tale of a sunken isle waned. In terms of belief in the existence of an antediluvian world, Atlantis is more of a modern than a traditional myth–a myth that did not achieve widespread currency until late in the nineteenth century, over two millennia after Plato's time.

Contemporary interest in the legend began with Ignatius Donnelly's *Atlantis: The Antediluvian World* (1882), in which he proposed that the human race and human civilization had begun on that island, and had initially spread elsewhere by colonization, and then by refugees when the island was destroyed by a natural cataclysm. Donnelly's ideas were adopted as an integral element of theosophy in Helena Petrovna Blavatsky's *The Secret Doctrine*. The most important author who spread interest in Atlantis was, however, Lewis Spence (1874–1955), a Scottish occult scholar who wrote five books on Atlantis between 1924 and 1943.

From these sources, the focus on Atlantis passed to Edgar Cayce. Through books built around his psychic readings that were published after his death, Cayce was responsible for popularizing the notion that apocalyptic "earth changes" would occur at the end of the millennium. This idea would later become an article of faith in the New Age movement. Speculation on Atlantis within the New Age subculture did not, however, end with Cayce.

In the early 1980s, Frank Alper, in *Exploring Atlantis*, extensively discussed the material he claimed to have channeled on how the Atlanteans used crystals to power their civilization. Discussions such as Alper's further served to secure a place for the Atlantis legend in New Age thinking. For many contemporary "metaphysical" writers, Atlantis was a highly technological society that, through misuse of its technology–perhaps even through misuse of its crystal technology–destroyed itself.

In the late 1990s, however, these views are undergoing modification as the result of a new school of "Atlantology" which champions the view that Antarctica was the site of the ancient nation. The assumption at work here, based on the geological theories of the late Charles Hapgood, is that the earth's crust has been displaced in such a way that Antarctica was shifted from a temperate climate zone to its present location at the South Pole.

This perspective has been popularized by the relatively recent *Fingerprints of the Gods* (1995), which argues for the existence of a technologically advanced civilization—i.e., Atlantis—in the time period preceding the earliest known cited societies. To support his point, author Graham Hancock examines the many artifacts and architectural monuments that are difficult to account for within the limits of our currently accepted scheme of history. Like Donnelly before them, for Hancock and other Atlantologists the ancient civilizations of Egypt and Mesoamerica (Central America) were either Atlantean colonies or areas where survivors fled after sinking of Atlantis.

The advantage of this new site for Atlantis is that it avoids the problem of the nonpresence of ancient ruins in the Atlantic oceanbeds: Whatever remains of Atlantis is hidden beneath the South Polar ice cap. Given the inaccessibility of this new site for the antediluvian world, Plato's Atlantis is likely to continue to provide fuel for the human imagination until well into the next millennium. Meanwhile, the vision of apocalyptic earth changes that ultimately originated Cayce's appropriation of the Atlantis legend has become an article of faith within a sizable segment of the New Age subculture. It should thus come as no surprise that a doomsday scenario should be part of the ideology of the group known as Heaven's Gate.

HEAVEN'S GATE

Like the New Age more generally, UFO religions and messages from the Space Brothers have been treated a laughable and unworthy of serious attention. This situation changed rather abruptly on March 26, 1997, when the bodies of thirty-nine men and women were found in a posh mansion outside San Diego, all victims of an apparent mass suicide. Messages left by the group indicate that they believed they were stepping out of their "physical containers" in order to ascend to a UFO that was arriving in the wake of the Hale-Bopp comet. They also asserted that this comet, or parts of it, would subsequently crash into the earth and cause widespread destruction.

Heaven's Gate—formerly known as Human Individual Metamorphosis (HIM)—originally made headlines in September 1975 when, following a public lecture in Waldport, Oregon, more than thirty people vanished overnight. This disappearance became the occasion for a media event. For the next several months, reporters generated story after story about glassy-eyed cult groupies abandoning the everyday lives to follow the strange couple who alternately referred to themselves as "Bo and Peep," "the Two," "Do and Ti," and other bizarre monikers.

Bo and Peep founded one of the most unusual flying saucer religions ever to emerge out of the occult-metaphysical subculture. Bo (Marshall Herff Applewhite) and Peep (Bonnie Lu Nettles) met in 1972. In 1973, they had an experience that convinced them that they were two witnesses mentioned in Revelation 11 who would be martyred and then resurrected three and a half days later—an event they later referred to as the Demonstration. Preaching an unusual synthesis of occult spirituality and UFO soteriology, they began recruiting in New Age circles in the spring of 1975. Followers were required to abandon friends and family, detach themselves completely from human emotions as well as material possessions, and focus exclusively on perfecting themselves in preparation for a physical transition (i.e., beaming up) to the next kingdom (in the form of a flying saucer)—a metamorphosis that would be facilitated by ufonauts.

Bo and Peep were surprisingly effective at recruiting people to their strange gospel, though their activities did not attract much attention until the Waldport meeting. Six weeks later, the group was infiltrated by University of Montana sociologist Robert Balch and a research assistant, David Taylor. In a violation of professional ethics, Balch and Taylor presented themselves as interested seekers and became pseudofollowers in order to clandestinely conduct field research.* As they would later report in subsequent papers, the great majority of the people who became involved with Bo and Peep were either marginal individuals† living on the fringes of society or people who had been deeply involved with occult spirituality for some time before their affiliation with the Two (Balch 1995).

---

*Professional ethics require social scientists to inform people that they are being studied, especially in participant-observer research.

†People without careers, without family, without a community, who don't own their home—in short, people who are not "tied down" and who are thus free to experiment with a radical group.

UFOs, an unusually fascinating form of rejected knowledge that mainstream scientists tend to classify as paranormal, have attracted considerable interest within the occult-metaphysical subculture. Almost from the beginning, however, this subculture transformed flying saucers and their presumed extraterrestrial pilots into spiritual beings who came to earth to help us along the path to salvation. To accomplish the transformation of E.T.s into wise, esoteric beings, "ufonauts" were assimilated into earlier models of spiritual sages, particularly the so-called Ascended Masters.

The concept of Ascended Masters or the Great White Brotherhood was codified within theosophy by Helena Petrovna Blavatsky in the 1880s, and from there has been derived by the various religious groups that descend from the Theosophical Society. Many people in the New Age movement believe that such Masters guide the spiritual progress of humanity. Equating Ascended Masters with ufonauts seems to have developed out of the earlier idea that at least some of the Masters were from other planets in our solar system, such as Venus.

In contrast to the modern UFO era, which began with Kenneth Arnold's sightings on June 24, 1947, the theosophical claim of extraterrestrial contact goes back to the late nineteenth century. A useful, somewhat later example of such contact claims can be found in the story of the "I AM" Religious Activity, a popularized form of theosophy, reformulated to appeal to a broader audience than earlier theosophical organizations. The founder of the movement was Guy Ballard, who had long been interested in occultism and had studied theosophical teachings.

Ballard was engaged in mining exploration and promotion. In 1930, while he was working near Mt. Shasta—a giant volcanic cone in northern California where strange occult events had been said to occur—he had his first contact with the Ascended Master Saint Germain. One New Year's Eve, the Master and Ballard joined a gathering inside a cavern in Royal Teton Mountain. The individuals at this assembly played host to twelve Venusians who appeared in their midst in a blaze of light, not unlike a *Star Trek* beam-in. These Venusian "Lords of the Flame" played harp and violin music, and, using a great mirror, showed the gathered terrestrials scenes of advanced technological achievements from their home world. These events from the early 1930s were reported in Ballard's *Unveiled Mysteries*, which was published a dozen years before Kenneth Arnold's celebrated encounter.

The first noteworthy prophet to emerge in the wake of postwar flying saucer sightings was George Adamski. Adamski's encounters were reported in *Flying Saucers Have Landed*, one of the most popular flying saucer books ever written. Adamski gained a broad following and was a much sought-after lecturer. As we can see from Ballard's report of the Royal Teton gathering, religious and other revelations from Venusians were nothing new. Adamski was thus not an innovator in this regard. Rather, his contribution was to connect the earlier notion of receiving information from extraterrestrials with the emergent interest in flying saucers. The Ballard example of "Venusian Masters" also allows us to see that the human imagination had a predisposition to respond to flying saucers–viewed as alien spacecraft–in religious terms.

Even much "secular" thinking about UFOs embodies quasireligious themes, such as the cryptoreligious notion that the world is on the verge of destruction and that ufonauts are somehow going to rescue humanity. As we have already noted, psychologist Carl Jung referred to the latter portrayal of ufonauts as "technological angels." Jung interpreted the phenomenon of flying saucers–which often appear in the form of circular disks–as mandala symbols, reflecting the human mind's desire for stability in a confused world. From a psychological point of view, it is thus no coincidence that the chariots of the gods should manifest in the form of a circle, a symbol of wholeness.

But if UFOs are the chariots of the gods, then why don't the Space Brothers just land and communicate their ideas to humanity in person? The same question has sometimes been asked with respect to the Great White Brotherhood. One of the salient characteristics of the Ascended Masters was that they preferred to communicate their occult teachings through the medium of telepathic messages sent to select individuals. These chosen vessels then relayed the Masters' messages to the larger public, either vocally in a form of mediumship later called "channeling" or in written form via a process usually referred to as automatic writing. Because the Ascended Masters are the primary model for the Space Brothers, it comes as no surprise that later-day UFO prophets should employ the same methods for communicating the wisdom of the ufonauts to the larger public.

George King, founder of the Aetherius Society, a UFO "religion," proposed that these Masters were actually extraterrestrials who were members of a "space command" managing the affairs of the solar system. This concept has been built upon by other channelers and groups, such as Michael and Aurora El-Legion, who channel the "Ashtar Command." It was from this tradition that Applewhite and Nettles took the basic idea of spiritually advanced ufonauts. And it is easy to connect the Two to the theosophical tradition: before meeting Applewhite, Nettles had belonged to the Theosophical Society and had attended New Age channeling sessions at which extraterrestrial beings may have been channeled.

In addition to teaching that ufonauts were spiritually advanced beings, Applewhite and Nettles also taught that aliens had come to pick up spiritually evolved human beings who would join the ranks of flying saucer crews. Only a select few members of humanity will be chosen to advance to this transhuman state. The rest will be left to wallow in the spiritually poisoned atmosphere of a corrupt world. Applewhite would later teach that after the elect had been picked up by the Space Brothers, the planet would be engulfed in cataclysmic destruction. When, in 1993, under the name of Total Overcomers Anonymous, the group ran an advertisement in *USA Today*, their portrayal of the post-rapture world was far more apocalyptic than Applewhite and Nettles had taught in the 1970s:

> The Earth's present "civilization" is about to be recycled–"spaded under." Its inhabitants are refusing to evolve. The "weeds" have taken over the garden and disturbed its usefulness beyond repair. (Cited in Balch, p. 163)

For followers of the Two, the focus of day-to-day existence was to follow a disciplined regimen referred to as the overcoming process or, simply, the process. The goal of this process was to overcome human weaknesses—a goal not dissimilar to that of certain spiritual practices followed by more mainstream monastic communities. For Applewhite, however, it appears that stamping out one's sexuality was the core issue. Furthermore, it is clear that his focus on sexual issues was tied to the problems he had experienced in the past as a direct result of his own sexuality.

Despite the outward success of Applewhite's early academic and musical career, he had been deeply troubled. Married and the father of two children, he secretly carried on a double life as a homosexual (Clark 1998). Guilty and confused, he is said to have longed for a platonic relationship within which he could develop his full potential without being troubled by his sexual urges. He eventually divorced his wife and, in 1970, was terminated by St. Thomas University, located in Texas. Devastated, Applewhite became bitter and depressed.

He met Nettles in 1972 at a hospital where he was seeking help for his sexual and psychological problems. Nettles was a nurse, and she and Applewhite quickly became inseparable. For a short while they together operated a metaphysical center. After the center folded, they continued holding classes in a house they called "Knowplace." In 1973 they began traveling in search of a higher purpose. They eventually camped out in an isolated spot near the Oregon coast and, after six weeks, came to the realization that they were the two witnesses prophesied in Revelation 11.

In the spring of 1975 they recruited their first followers, beginning with a metaphysical teacher named Clarence Klug and twenty-three of his students. As the first step in the transformational process taught by the Two, their followers abandoned everything that tied them to their everyday life, including their jobs, families, and most of their possessions except for cars and camping supplies (necessary for leading a quasinomadic lifestyle). Mirroring their own relationship, they placed males and females together in nonsexual partnerships in which each was instructed to assist his or her partner in the overcoming process. They also attempted to tune in to the next level, again reflecting the process that Applewhite and Nettles had experienced during their six-week retreat.

The group developed quietly until the media interest evoked in the wake of the Waldport, Oregon, meeting. This new attention awakened fears that Bo and Peep might be assassinated before they could fulfill their mission. (Their paranoid worldview postulated various hostile forces.) They subsequently canceled a planned meeting in Chicago and split the group into a number of autonomous "families" consisting of a dozen or more individuals. These families were then sent on their way, traveling, camping out, begging food, and occasionally recruiting new members. Many of the faithful fell away during this period. Around the end of 1975 or the beginning of 1976, the Two re-emerged, gathered together the remnants of their followers, and eventually began a new round of recruiting activities.

In the face of strong ridicule, however, Nettles abruptly announced that "the doors to the next level are closed," and their missionary activity ceased (Balch 1995). The harvest had ended, with less than a hundred individuals engaged in the overcoming process. Another change was the subsequent announcement that the Demonstration had been canceled because their followers had not been making rapid enough progress in the overcoming process. Rather than focusing on the time when they would be taken up by the saucers, the group must concentrate on their own development.

To this end, the Two developed more practices and disciplines to help their followers overcome their human weaknesses. For example, in one exercise known as "tomb time," followers would go for days without saying anything except "yes," "no," or "I don't know" making the community "as quiet as a tomb" (other communications took place via written notes). Followers also began to wear uniform clothing.

The seminomadic period ended within a few years when two followers inherited approximately $300,000. The group then rented houses, initially in Denver and later in the Dallas–Fort Worth area. Each house, which they called a "craft," had the windows covered to prevent the neighbors from watching their activities. Followers adhered to a strict routine. Immersed in the intensity of their structured lifestyle, the teachings of the Two became more and more real to members.

The group's strict segregation from society was suddenly altered in 1983 when many followers visited their families on Mother's Day and informed their relatives that they were learning computer technology. However, these members dropped out of contact again as soon as they left their parents' homes. Another change took place in 1985, when Nettles died of cancer. The group surfaced again in 1994 when, thinking the lift-off would begin in a year or two, they held another series of public meetings. It was during this new cycle of missionary activity that the *USA Today* ad appeared.

Details about how the group came to attach apocalyptic significance to the Comet Hale-Bopp are tantalizingly scanty. For whatever reason, someone outside the group had come to the conclusion that a giant UFO was coming to earth, "hidden" in the wake of Hale-Bopp. This individual then placed his opinion on the Internet. When Heaven's Gate retrieved this information, Applewhite took it as an indication that the long-awaited pick-up of his group by aliens was finally about to take place. The decision that the time had come to make their final exit could not have been made more than a few weeks before the mass suicide. Applewhite may have begun to rethink his theology after his beloved partner died because, in order to be reunited with Nettles, her spirit would have to acquire a new body aboard the spacecraft. While the death of Nettles may or may not have been the decisive influence, Applewhite later adopted the view that Heaven's Gate would ascend together spiritually rather than physically.

The idea that the group might depart via suicide had emerged in Applewhite's thinking only within the last few years. The earlier idea—an idea that had set Heaven's Gate apart from everyone else—was that group of individuals selected to move to the next level would bodily ascend to the saucers in a kind of "technological rapture." Applewhite and Nettles had originally taught that the goal of the process they were teaching their followers was to prepare them to be physically taken aboard the spacecraft where they would enter a cocoonlike state, eventually being reborn in a transformed physical body.

Christianity's view of resurrection reflects the influence of the cultures in which it originated and spread during its first centuries in the Mediterranean basin. The idea of resurrection, which was originally formulated within Zoroastrianism, was introduced in Christianity from Judaism. This idea developed in tandem with an apocalyptic vision of history that entailed the end of the world as we know it and which resulted in the defeat of death and evil.

The notion of resurrection is also central to chapter 11 of the Book of Revelation, the biblical passage Applewhite and Nettles came to view as describing their particular ministry. This chapter recounts the story of two prophets who will be slain. Then, three and a half days later, they will be resurrected and taken up in a cloud:

> At the end of the three days and a half the breath of life from God came into them; and they stood up on their feet to the terror of all who saw it. Then a loud voice was heard speaking to them from heaven, which said, "Come up here!" And they went up to heaven in a cloud, in full view of their enemies. At that same moment there was a violent earthquake. (Rev. 11:11–13)

In the early phase of their movement, Applewhite and Nettles prophesied that they would soon be assassinated. Using the above passage as a script for future events, they further predicted that they would be resurrected three and a half days later and taken up into a flying saucer. The Two asserted that this event—which they called the Demonstration—would prove the truth of their teachings. As for their followers, they taught that Heaven was the literal, physical heavens, and those few people chosen to depart with the Two would, after their physical transformation, become crew members aboard UFOs.

While the basic teachings seem to have remained constant, the details of their ideology were flexible enough to undergo modification over time. For example, in the early days, Applewhite and Nettles taught their followers that they were extraterrestrial beings. However, after the notion of walk-ins became popular within the New Age subculture, the Two changed their tune and began describing themselves as extraterrestrial walk-ins.

A walk-in is an entity who occupies a body that has been vacated by its original soul. An extraterrestrial walk-in is one supposedly from another planet. The walk-in situation is somewhat similar to possession, although in possession the original soul is merely over-shadowed rather than completely supplanted by the possessing entity. The walk-in concept seems to be related to certain traditional South Asian tales about aging yoga masters taking over the bodies of young people who die prematurely. Another possible source for the notion is the teaching well-known in theosophical circles that Jesus and Christ were separate souls. According to this teaching, Jesus prepared his physical body to receive Christ and, at a certain point in his career, vacated his body so as to allow Christ to take it over and preach to the world. An underlying notion here is that Christ was such a highly evolved soul that it would have been difficult if not impossible for him to have incarnated as a baby. And, even if he could have done so, it would have been a waste of precious time for such a highly developed soul to have to go through childhood.

The modern notion of walk-ins was popularized by Ruth Mont-gomery, who developed it in her 1979 book, *Strangers among Us*. According to Montgomery, walk-ins are usually highly evolved souls here to help humanity. In order to avoid the delay of incarnating as a baby, and thus having to spend two decades maturing to adult-hood, they contact living people who, because of the frustrating cir-cumstances of life or for some other reason, no longer desire to remain in their body. The discarnate entity finds such people, per-suades them to hand over their body, and then begins life as a walk-in. Montgomery describes the phenomenon rather dramatically:

> There are Walk-ins on this planet. Tens of thousands of them. Enlightened beings, who, after successfully completing numerous incarnations, have attained sufficient awareness of the meaning of life that they can forego the time-consuming process of birth and childhood, returning directly the adult bodies. A Walk-in is a high-minded entity who is permitted to take over the body of another human being who wishes to depart. . . . The motivation of a Walk-in is humanitarian. He returns to physical being in order to help others help themselves, planting seed-concepts that will grow and flourish for the benefit of mankind. (1979, pp. 11–12)

In 1983 Montgomery published another book, *Threshold to Tomorrow*, containing case histories of seventeen walk-ins. According to Montgomery, history is full of walk-ins, including such famous historical figures as Moses, Jesus, Muhammad, Christopher Columbus, Abraham Lincoln, Mary Baker Eddy, Gandhi, George Washington, Benjamin Franklin, Thomas Jefferson, Alexander Hamilton, and James Madison. In fact, it seems that almost everyone manifesting exceptional creativity and leadership would be identified by Montgomery as a walk-in. In her words, "Some of the world's greatest spiritual and political leaders, scientists, and philosophers in ages past are said to have been Walk-ins" (1983, p. 12).

In a later book, *Aliens among Us* (1985), Montgomery developed the notion of extraterrestrial walk-ins—the idea that souls from other planets have come to earth to take over the bodies of human beings. This notion dovetailed with popular interest in UFOs, which had already been incorporated into New Age spirituality. Following Montgomery, the New Age movement came to view extraterrestrial walk-ins as part of the larger community of advanced souls that have come to earth to help humanity through a period of crisis. It is easy to see how this basic notion fit nicely into the Two's ideology, explaining away their human personal histories as the histories of the souls who formerly occupied the bodies of Applewhite and Nettles.

It should be noted that the walk-in idea—a notion implying a radical disjunction between soul and body—would have provided Applewhite with an essential ideological component in his rethinking of the ascension scenario. In other words, after the death of Nettles, Applewhite had to come to grips with the fact that—under the physical ascension scenario that had been a cornerstone of their teachings for almost two decades—his spiritual partner would miss the chance to escape the planet with the rest of the group. This option was, however, unimaginable to Applewhite. Hence, by the time of the mass suicide, Applewhite had reconceptualized the ascension as an event in which Heaven's Gate members let go of their physical containers and ascended *spiritually* to the waiting saucers. Once on board, they would consciously "walk-into" a new physical body and join the crew of the Next Level spacecraft. This scenario is related in one of the group's Internet statements:

Their final separation is the willful separation from their human body, when they have changed enough to identify as the spirit/mind/soul–ready to put on a biological body belonging to the Kingdom of Heaven. (This entering into their "glorified" or heavenly body takes place aboard a Next Level spacecraft, above the Earth's surface.)

Presumably, these new physical bodies would be supplied to Heaven's Gate members out of some sort of "cloning bank" kept aboard the spaceships.

Another notion the Two picked up from the metaphysical subculture of their day was the ancient astronaut hypothesis. The term "ancient astronauts" is used to refer to various forms of the concept that ufonauts visited our planet in the distant past. The basic idea that many, if not all, of the powerful sky gods of traditional religions were really extraterrestrial visitors intervening in human history had been around for many decades. However, it was not until a series of books about the "chariots of the gods" authored by Erich van Däniken in the 1970s that this notion was popularized. While later writers such as Zecharia Sitchin have developed this view with greater sophistication, none has been as influential as van Däniken.

This view, which seems to call into question the validity of religion, has been adopted by large segments of the New Age culture in a way that is not seen as contradicting metaphysical spirituality. Instead, believers view the Space Brothers as working in cooperation with spiritual forces to stimulate the spiritual evolution of this planet. One aspect of the ancient astronaut hypothesis is the idea that the contemporary human race is the offspring of a union between aliens and native terrestrials. Some even believe that a distorted record of this event can be found in a few enigmatic verses in the book of Genesis about the sons of God copulating with the daughters of men (Gen. 6:1–4). This union produced an intermediate species that Genesis calls the "Nephilim." In a different version of the same idea, ancient ufonauts stimulated the evolution of our apelike forebears to produce present-day humanity. Our space "fathers" have subsequently been watching over us, and will, according to some New Age notions, return to mingle with their distant offspring during the imminent New Age.

Applewhite and Nettles taught a slightly modified version of the ancient astronaut hypothesis: Aliens planted the seeds of current humanity millions of years ago, and have come to reap the harvest of their work in the form of spiritually evolved individuals who will join the ranks of flying saucer crews. Only a select few members of humanity will be chosen to advance to this transhuman state. The rest will be left to wallow in the spiritually poisoned atmosphere of a corrupt world.

Applewhite would later teach that after the elect had been picked up by the Space Brothers, the planet would be engulfed in cataclysmic destruction. While Applewhite's apocalyptic teachings might at first appear to be derived entirely from his biblical background, his decidedly "this-worldly" vision of our planet's end suggests that his ideology was influenced by the New Age subculture and by the more recent discussion of colliding asteroids found in contemporary popular culture.

Particularly in the teachings of New Age channels, one often finds the theme of apocalyptic "earth changes" that are supposed to take place around the end of the millennium. Furthermore, these upheavals in the earth's crust are often thought of as coming about as a direct result of a planetary "pole shift," a subsidiary notion that was popularized by Ruth Montgomery. In sharp contrast to Applewhite, however, New Age thinkers postulate that these dramatic earth changes will herald a terrestrial Golden Age. The idea that global destruction would come about as the result of a wandering asteroid is a more recent notion that has been popularized in magazine articles and television specials only within the last half-dozen years or so.

Yet another theme Applewhite and Nettles absorbed from the metaphysical subculture was the view that the spiritual life is a series of learning experiences culminating—in the case of Heaven's Gate—in a "graduation" to the next evolutionary kingdom. Members of the group thought of themselves as "students," their fellows as "classmates," and Applewhite as their "tutor." These educational metaphors would have been particularly comfortable and natural for a man who had been a popular university teacher during the first part of his adult life.

Like other religious and cultural systems, the worldview of the contemporary New Age movement is held together by a shared set of symbols and metaphors—shared images of life reflected in the discourse of participants as a set of commonly used terms. For example, due partly to a vision of metaphysical unity inherited from theosophy and from Asian religious philosophy—but also due to this subculture's reaction against the perceived fragmentation and alienation of mainstream society—the New Age movement emphasizes the values of unity and relatedness. These values find expression in such common terms as "holistic," "oneness," "wholeness," and "community." This spiritual subculture also values growth and dynamism—an evaluation expressed in discourse about "evolution," "transformation," "process," and so forth.

The image of education is related to the growth metaphor (e.g., one of our linguistic conventions is that education allows a person to "grow"). If we examine the metaphysical subculture through the lens of the education theme, we discover that, in contrast to so many other religious movements, the dominant New Age "ceremonies" are workshops, lectures, and classes rather than worship ceremonies. Even large New Age gatherings such as the Whole Life Expo resemble academic conferences more than they resemble camp meetings.

It is also interesting to note the extent to which educational metaphors inform New Age thought: The Western metaphysical tradition has interpreted the ongoing process of reincarnation, spiritual growth, and even life itself as learning experiences. To cite some of examples of this, Katar, a New Age medium, channels such messages as, "Here on Earth, you are your teacher, your books, your lessons and the classroom as well as the student" (Clark 1988, p. 7) This message is amplified by J. L. Simmons, a sociologist, who, in his *The Emerging New Age*, describes life on the physical plane as the "Earth School," and asserts that "we are here to learn . . . and will continue to return until we 'do the course' and 'graduate' " (Simmons, p. 73).

Similar images are reflected in an essay titled "The Role of the Esoteric in Planetary Culture," in which David Spangler argues that spiritual wisdom is esoteric "only because so few people expend the time, the energy, the effort, the openness and the love to gain it, just as only a few are willing to invest what is required to become a nuclear physicist or a neurosurgeon" (1977a, p. 193). It would not be going too far to assert that, in the New Age vision of things, the image of the whole of human life—particularly when that life is directed toward spiritual goals—can be summed up as a learning experience:

> Each of us has an Inner Teacher, a part of ourselves which knows exactly what we need to learn, and constantly creates the opportunity for us to learn just that. We have the choice either to cooperate with this part of ourselves or to ignore it. If we decide to cooperate, we can see lessons constantly in front of us; every challenge is a chance to grow and develop. If, on the other hand, we try to ignore this Inner Teacher, we can find ourselves hitting the same problem again and again, because we are not perceiving and responding to the lesson we have created for ourselves. [It] is, however, the daily awareness of and cooperation with spirit [that] pulls humanity upwards on the evolutionary spiral, and the constant invocation and evocation of spirit enables a rapid unfolding of human potential. When the Inner Teacher and the evolutionary force of the Universe are able to work together with our full cooperation, wonders unfold. (From a flyer put out by the Findhorn Foundation in 1986)

In these passages, we see not only the decisive role of the educational metaphor, but also how this metaphor has itself been reshaped by the spiritual subculture's emphasis on holism and growth. In other words, the kind of education this subculture values is the "education of the whole person," sometimes termed "holistic education," and this form of education is an expression of the "evolutionary force of the Universe" (a parallel to what, in more traditional language, might be called the redemptive activity of the Holy Spirit). Thus, despite the marked tendency to deploy images drawn from the sphere of formal education—a tendency that has created a realm of discourse saturated with metaphors of "classrooms," "graduations," and the like—the metaphysical subculture's sense of the educational process has tended to be more informal (more or less equivalent to learning in the most general sense), as well as more continuous—a process from which there may be periodic graduations, but from which there is never a final graduation after which the learning process ceases. Even for Heaven's Gate members, graduation from the earth plane represented entering a new sphere of never-ending personal evolution—The Evolutionary Kingdom Level above Human.

While some aspects of this view of the spiritual life as a learning experience are based on tradition, the widespread appeal of this image of spirituality is the result of the manner in which modern society's emphasis on education informs our consciousness. The various social, economic, and historical forces that have led to the increased stress on education in the contemporary world are too complex to develop here. Obvious factors are such things as the increasing complexity of technology and of the socioeconomic system. Less obvious factors are such considerations as the need to delay the entry of new workers into the economy. But whatever the forces at work in the larger society, by the time the Baby Boom generation began attending college in the 1960s, formal educational institutions had come to assume their present role as major socializing forces in Western societies. Being a college graduate and achieving higher, particularly professional, degrees became associated with increased prestige and the potential for increased levels of income. In other words, to a greater extent than previously, education and educational accomplishments became symbols of wealth and status.

Because the generation from which the majority of participants in the spiritual subculture have been recruited is the Baby Boom generation, the majority of participants in that subculture have been socialized to place a high value on education. Baby Boomers, however, also tend to have been participants in the counterculture of the 1960s, which means that they come from a generation that was highly critical of traditional, formal education.

While some members of that generation revolted against the educational establishment by denying the value of education altogether, other college students of the time reacted against what they saw as an irrelevant education by setting up alternative educational structures such as the so-called free schools. These educational enterprises, which could offer students nothing in terms of degrees or certifications, were viable, at least for a time, because they offered courses on subjects people found intrinsically interesting–including such metaphysical topics as yoga, meditation, and so forth. The free school movement, in combination with the adult education programs that emerged in the 1970s, provided the paradigms for the form many independent, metaphysical educational programs would eventually take.

As is evident from even the most casual perusal of the group's writings, Heaven's Gate was dominated by the educational imagery found in the contemporaneous New Age subculture. As has already been noted, Applewhite viewed himself as a teacher, his followers were students, their spiritual growth was likened to an educational process (in their "metamorphic classroom"), and their goal was frequently referred to as a graduation. In the group's writings published on the Internet, they discussed how their "Teachers" on the Next Level had an "extremely detailed lesson plan" designed for their personal growth. Then, toward the end, they received signals that their "classroom time" was over and that they were ready to graduate to the next level.

The same basic images can be found in the teachings of innumerable contemporary spiritual teachers. For example, John-Roger (1980), the founder of the Movement of Spiritual Inner Awareness (MSIA), asserts that

> The earth has been designated as the classroom where you learn lessons. You're . . . in a continual learning process, which will bring forth that which is for your highest good. When you have finished your lessons, you graduate to other levels of consciousness.

This is not, of course, to imply that MSIA is another potential Heaven's Gate, but rather that the basic images at work in Applewhite's teachings were derived more or less directly out of the same metaphysical subculture that shaped MSIA and certain other emergent religions.

Thus, with the exceptions of (1) suicide being the means by which the transition to the next evolutionary sphere is to take place and (2) the belief that the next sphere is a literal, physical realm (a spacecraft), the basic concepts informing Heaven's Gate's thought world would be recognizable to any serious seeker of the metaphysical. However, even the notion of a physical spaceship as a quasi-heavenly realm is implicit in the marked tendency of the New Age movement to portray ufonauts as spiritual beings. Furthermore, the widely accepted walk-in notion provides a readily understandable mechanism by which such a transition could be accomplished.

This leaves only suicide as the one anomalous component of Applewhite's synthesis. We should note, however, that there are many aspects of the New Age movement that portray death–if not suicide–in a positive light. For example, the basic metaphysical/New Age afterlife notion is reincarnation, although this process is regarded somewhat differently by the New Age than by Asian religions from which the notion is derived. Whereas in a tradition like Buddhism, reincarnation is viewed negatively, as a process that brings one back into the world to suffer, in the metaphysical subculture reincarnation is viewed as part of an extended education program stretched across many lifetimes, and is thus part of a positive process. In the same vein, the interest many participants in occult-metaphysical spirituality have displayed in learning about their past lifetimes in the hope of discovering that they were some famous or otherwise exalted personality would be anathema to a traditional Buddhist.

The New Age movement is also home to advocates of conscious dying. The term "conscious dying" refers to an approach to dying in which death is regarded as a means of liberation of one's own consciousness–as a means of achieving enlightenment. This approach, ultimately inspired by Tibetan Buddhism, was popularized in the New Age subculture through the work of Baba Ram Das and Stephen Levine. In line with the New Age emphasis on spiritual-unfolding-as-education, dying thus acquires a positive value as part of the larger learning process.

Finally, it is within the metaphysical subculture that one finds the most interest in the near-death experience. The term "near-death experience" (NDE), sometimes also called the "pseudodeath" experience, refers to the seemingly supernatural experiences often undergone by individuals who have suffered apparent death and have been restored to life. The main impetus for modern studies on NDEs was the publication in 1975 of the book *Life after Life*, by psychiatrist Raymond A. Moody, which followed earlier researches on this topic by other physicians such as Elisabeth Kübler-Ross and Russell Noyes.

Moody's work describes the results of more than eleven years of inquiry into near-death experiences and is based on a sample of about 150 cases. He outlines nine elements that seem to occur generally (but not universally) in the NDE experiencers:

1. Hearing a buzzing or ringing noise, while having a sense of being dead. At this initial stage of the NDE, the experiencers are confused and try, unsuccessfully, to communicate with other people at the scene of their death.

2. Peace and painlessness. While people are dying they may be in intense pain, but, as soon as they leave the body, the pain vanishes and they experience peace.

3. Out-of-body experience. Those undergoing an NDE often have the experience of rising up and floating above their own body and watching it down below, surrounded by a medical team, while feeling very detached and comfortable. They experience the feeling of being in a spiritual body that resembles a living energy field.

4. The tunnel experience. The person having an NDE then experiences being drawn into darkness through a tunnel, at an extremely high speed, or going up a stairway (or some other symbol of crossing a threshold) until he or she achieves a realm of radiant, golden-white light.

5. Rising rapidly into the heavens. Instead of a tunnel, some NDEers report an experience of rising suddenly into the heavens, and seeing the earth and the celestial sphere as if they were astronauts in space.

6. People of light. Once on the other side of the tunnel, or after they have risen into the heavens, those experiencing near-death meet people who glow with an inner light. Often they find that friends and relatives who have already died are there to greet them.

7. The being of light. After connecting with these beings, the next phase of an NDE is a meeting with a powerful, spiritual being whom some have called an angel, God, or Jesus.

8. The life review. This higher being presents the person with a panoramic review of everything he or she has done. In particular, victims experience the effects of every act they have ever done to other people, and come away feeling that love is the most important thing in life.

9. Reluctance to return. The higher being sometimes says that the NDEer must return to life. In other experiences, the NDEer is given a choice of staying or returning. In either case, there is a reluctance to return. The people who choose to return do so only because of loved ones they do not wish to leave behind.

The near-death experience has attracted extensive public interest because of its seeming support for the notion of life after death. As reflected in the above list of characteristics, it is clear that the overall picture of the dying process to emerge from NDE studies is quite positive, even attractive. Furthermore, with respect to our larger discussion, it should also be noted that trait number five sounds like it could have been (though I actually doubt that it was) the immediate source of Applewhite's idea that his group could die and ascend to a waiting spacecraft.

In this regard, Moody mentions, in another of his books, an ecstatic vision Carl Jung experienced during an apparent NDE. Following a heart attack, Jung found himself a thousand miles above the surface of the earth, on the threshold of entering a floating temple in which he would finally discover the answers to all of his questions. In this vision, Jung vividly describes the terrestrial globe, his sense of letting go of everything associated with earthly life, and his sense of anticipation of the glories awaiting him upon his entrance into the temple. Finally, Jung notes his profound disappointment when his doctor brings him back to his body before he has a chance to cross the threshold.

Again, with only a little interpretation (e.g., temple = spacecraft), the whole experience could be taken as almost a blueprint for what Heaven's Gate members believed would happened after their deaths. This is not, of course, to assert that either NDE research or the writings of Carl Jung encourage people to take their own lives. It is, however, clear that, if taken seriously, reports of near-death experiences paint a positive enough portrait of dying to take the sting out of death. Thus, far from being crazy or irrational, even the final dramatic exit of Heaven's Gate becomes understandable in terms of the metaphysical subculture from which Applewhite drew his theological synthesis.

8

THE END OF THE WORLD
Consigning Doomsayers
to the Flames

Classic millenarians, from self-flagellating medieval peasants to Sioux Ghost Dancers, are often people who, if not clinically mad, have reached what George Rosen has called "The wilder shores of sanity."

—Damian Thompson, *The End of Time*

As the millennial clock ticks toward the 2000 mark, we might well wonder how the Doomsayers will react to the nonevent of the Apocalypse. Some skeptical observers predict widespread hysteria that will prompt millenarians to engage in mass suicides, bombings, and other radical acts of violence. Others hope that the uneventful arrival of the year 2001 will at last dampen the flames of apocalyptic enthusiasm, so that scientific "rationality" can at last gain the upper hand in the struggle against religion. From a historically informed perspective, however, either outcome is highly unlikely. Endtime enthusiasm springs eternal in the human breast, and even the most disappointed millennialists tend to reformulate, spiritualize, or otherwise reinterpret failed prophecies and continue living within a "tamed" apocalyptic vision, as did the early Christians. The classic case in point is the Millerite movement.

No discussion of American doomsday thinking would be complete without some mention of William Miller, who founded the Millerite movement, one of the more colorful events in American religious history. Miller's followers were so convinced of the truth of the "Rapture"–the doctrine that, at the end of time, the saved would spring off the ground and meet Jesus in the air–that, on the date predicted for Christ's return, Millerites sat on the roofs of their houses in order to avoid bumping their heads on their ceilings. The Millerites gave birth to what is known as the Adventist movement.

Adventism shares many of its theological perspectives with other Christian denominations. There is general agreement with doctrines concerning the Bible, God, Christ, and the sacraments. Its Baptist origins are reflected in the idea of ordinances–instead of sacraments–baptism by immersion, and the practice of washing each other's feet. Sabbatarianism was transmitted directly by the Seventh-Day Baptists.

The distinctive doctrine of Adventism is the belief that the Second Coming of Christ (the *Advent*) is imminent. It is from this tenet the name "Adventism" derives. Besides the emphasis on adventism, Adventists are distinguished from many other Christians by the doctrine of *Conditional Immortality*. According to this tenet, only God has immortality, and mortals possess a nature inherently sinful and dying. No conscious entity survives death, and the state after death is one of silence, inactivity, and complete unconsciousness, the grave being a place of darkness. All people, good and evil, remain in the grave from their death until the final resurrection, which is believed to be the resurrection of the whole person.

Only corporeal resurrection can bring humankind out of the prison of the grave. Resurrection occurs at the second advent of Christ for the righteous, and a thousand years thereafter for the impenitent wicked. The immortalized righteous are then taken to Heaven, the New Jerusalem, where they reign with Christ for a thousand years, judging the world and fallen angels. During this time the earth is believed to be in a chaotic condition, a bottomless pit where Satan, the author of sin, is confined and finally destroyed.

At the end of this period, fire, which flows out of Heaven from God to Gehenna, the lake of fire, devours and annihilates the wicked dead. The wicked, being raised only to undergo judgment and to meet everlasting punishment, disappear and become as though they had not been. Therefore, Hell is not perceived as an unending torment, but, rather, as a final destruction of evil. It is also believed that a new Heaven will stem from the ashes of the old earth, which will be purged of the curse of sin, and will be the place where the righteous shall evermore dwell.

The immediate source for the Adventist tradition can be found in the teachings of Baptist layman William Miller, who became involved with the study of the Bible. He became more and more convinced that he was living near the end of his age and that he had to preach about it. He began preaching in several cities, and published his first work—a series of sixteen articles—in the *Vermont Telegraph* in 1832.

After the Baptists gave him a license to preach in September 1833, Miller dedicated ten years of his life to his message of the imminent return of Jesus. He also published his lectures in his first book, *Evidences from Scripture and History of the Second Coming of Christ about the Year 1843: Exhibited in a Course of Lectures*, greatly stimulating the movement.

Central to Miller's belief was his conviction that, through studying Daniel and Revelation, he had deciphered the chronology concerning the end of the age. He claimed that the end of the seventy weeks mentioned in Daniel 19:24 was 33 C.E., at the cross of Jesus, and the beginning of the earth was, therefore, 457 B.C.E. His view, upheld by several computations, also included 1843 as the year of the cleansing of the sanctuary, i.e., the end of the world. Miller published his chronology of prophetic history, which covered the Old Testament period and showed that 1843 was the end of the sixth millennium since creation in a number of books.

Among several others who began to join Miller was Joshua Himes, who invited Miller to preach in his Boston church, and who started to publish the movement's first periodical, *Signs of the Times*, in 1840. The first conference of the growing movement was held on October 13, 1840, at Charon Street Church in Boston. Several leaders attended it, including Josiah Litch, Joseph Bates, and Henry Dana Ward.

After the Boston conference, which was very successful, other conferences propounding Miller's message, known as "the midnight cry," were held in other cities. However, the movement began to face opposition by established denominations, which began to counteract Miller's influence. Several ministers and laymen were expelled from formerly cooperative churches, and a series of articles against Millerism were published in the *New York Christian Advocate* in 1843.

The first camp meeting of the movement was held at East Kingston, New Hampshire, in 1843. In November of the same year the second periodical, *The Midnight Cry*, started publication. During the same period, Miller also perfected his view concerning the second coming, which, according to his new stance, would occur somewhere between March 21, 1843, and March 21, 1844. Although a large comet as well as other spectacular phenomena appeared in the sky in late February 1844, the second coming did not occur.

The outburst of increased opposition of the churches, as well as the lack of prior religious connection from which disappointed Adventists could gain nourishment, led Charles Fitch to start the "come out" movement. Although Fitch was opposed by Miller, many believers in Christ's imminent return started to "come out" of their denominational churches and form new religions.

Soon new adjustments in Miller's chronology were made by Samuel S. Snow, who looked to October 22, 1844, as the real date of Christ's return. But again, nothing happened, and a "great disappointment" arose, leaving the movement in chaos. After a short period of despair, Miller continued to speak of a near return, but argued against any further date-setting. He eventually retired from active leadership in the movement, while the believers were organized into a number of denominational bodies. As his health declined he lectured less and died a few years later.

THE MEDICALIZATION OF HERESY

Under the sacred garb of religion, sensual feelings are, I fear, too frequently concealed. The expressions and behavior of some of these heated enthusiasts, evince to the eye of sober reason, that they are devoured by carnal rather than by spiritual fires—that their glowing mystical love is lighted at the flames of earth, not heaven. This pretended spiritual love consumes the body more than if the patients really gave themselves up to the appetite of the senses, because the orgasm which excites it lasts continually. I have observed that many of these unhappy people have become hypochondriacal, hysterical, stupid, and even maniacal.

                   –William Sweetser, *Mental Hygiene*

The Millerite "craze" was regarded with extreme disdain by the larger part of the population who refused to get caught up in the enthusiasm. Like many contemporary secularists, the "enlightened" classes of the nineteenth century regarded emotional religiosity as crazy. In the nineteenth century, however, someone infected with the disease of "Millerism" or some other form of "religious insanity" could actually be locked up in an asylum.

Although madness has long been attributed to certain forms of religious expression, it was only in the late eighteenth and early nineteenth centuries that "religious enthusiasm" or "religious insanity" began to be generally accepted as a diagnostic category for a disorder treatable by medical means. It was in an atmosphere that favored such a view that William Perfect, a doctor who specialized in mental illness, published a compilation in 1798 of his more "curious and interesting" cases, including four anecdotal accounts of religious enthusiasm. The full title of Perfect's book was *Annals of Insanity, Comprising a Selection of Curious and Interesting Cases in the Different Species of Lunacy, Melancholy, or Madness, with the Modes of Practice in the Medical and Moral Treatment, as Adopted in the Cure of Each.* Included in this compilation was the case of one "Mrs. E.H.," who

had for some time been made a proselyte to a prevailing system of
religion, that like an epidemic disease had long spread its baneful influence through many ranks of people, to the excitement of the most
daring outrages, and the wildest extravagancies. (p. 87)

While Perfect's observation effectively conveys his distaste for
revivalist religion, it is less clear how Mrs. E.H.'s "enthusiasm" had
led to a state of madness. In this regard, Perfect asserted that,

> So humiliating a degradation of our reasoning faculties owes much
> of its accession to the absurd and ill-founded prejudices of that epi-
> demic enthusiasm, which naturally excites the attention of weak
> minds to the discussion of religious points, which they too eagerly
> contemplate, without the power of clear comprehension, to the
> entire subversion of their intellectual discernment. Amongst this
> description was the unfortunate subject of this case; religious studies
> having so far gained the ascendancy over her reason, as to impel
> her to words and actions of a maniacal tendency. In this dangerous
> state of fanaticism she was committed to my care. (pp. 89–90)

From the scanty evidence available to us from his description of the
case, it is difficult to determine with certainty whether Mrs. E.H. was
genuinely unbalanced. Perfect superficially described a few of the
unhealthy beliefs and behaviors that she had "contracted," but there is
nothing in his description that would strike the modern reader as pathological. One is thus inclined to assume that she was committed to the
good doctor's care because her family disapproved of her new faith.

Mrs. E.H. was subjected to a physiological course of treatment
that included a new diet, regular bleedings, and laxatives. This treatment program may strike the reader as naive and even amusing, but
a perusal of the medical literature of earlier centuries turns up many
instances where religious ravings were attributed to physiological
problems; for example, the following from an 1869 article by Joseph
Workman: "His bowels were obstinately constipated. Purgatives had
a calming effect, but still his religious delusions persisted" (pp.
45–46). Dr. Perfect noted, however, that the abatement of his
patient's symptoms was "in great measure to be attributed to her

sanctified sectaries not having it in their power to procure access to her person as usual" (p. 92). (In other words, Perfect had her locked up.) It was this isolation from her coreligionists, in combination with the heavily disapproving atmosphere of her treatment environment, that eventually brought about a "cure":

> No one being permitted to pay the least attention to her enthusiastic extasies [*sic*] and raptures, they began gradually to lose their influence on her mind; and in about eight months appeared to be nearly forgotten. Her reason thus completely restored, she returned home to her family, who carefully guarded against a future relapse by a firm and steady resolution to prohibit the visits of those zealous devotees, through whose principles she derived the first impression of her terrible affliction. (Perfect, p. 239)

When interpreting descriptions of religious insanity, we must be careful to distinguish between cases where a medical diagnosis was being used to express disapproval of sectarian religion and cases of genuine disturbance. Perfect's compilation is a useful text in this regard because his unconcealed prejudices allow us to perceive that most of the instances of religious enthusiasm he cited belong to the former. For example, in the case of "Mrs. S.J.," on which his advice was consulted via the mail, his correspondent noted that the patient "converses rationally, but reluctantly, on any other subject [than religion]." The "apparent rationality" of victims of religious insanity on other topics, a tendency that was noted in a number of nineteenth-century studies, reinforces the impression that many of these individuals were not actually unbalanced.

Perfect's anthology is also useful because his etiology (study of the cause of disease) overtly contains a marked disapproval of sectarian belief in its native conceptualization of the connection between false belief and disease. For example, although a certain "Mr. G.L." had a natural "disposition to melancholy," this predisposition did not become pathological until he became "acquainted with a gloomy fanatic teacher of the Methodist order" (pp. 295–96). After imbibing the "poisonous tenets of his doctrine, he soon became enthusiastically mad."

Such a naive etiology implies a similarly naive course of treatment, namely that one should attempt to dislodge diseased beliefs. Perfect soon discovered, however, that religious enthusiasts were unusually resistant to therapy. When responding to his correspondent in the case of S.J., for instance, Perfect observed that,

> If she could be conversed with on any regular basis, her mistaken notions of religion might probably be corrected; but in religious melancholy I have repeatedly found that argument has but little weight, for it seems to be the nature of the disorder to involve the mind in the most miserable and inextricable mysteries. The patients thus influenced resist or evade every argument which the most sensible person can adduce from the most rational ground, to undeceive their blinded judgement and deluded mind. (p. 240)

Hence, rather than recommending a direct assault on S.J.'s deluded beliefs, Perfect prescribed a course of physiological treatments combined with advice on how to distract her from thoughts and conversation on religion:

> Perhaps she is not altogether inclined to company, although she may be to business or amusement. The mind, if possible, should be diverted, and kept in a calm unruffled state; and all conversation on her favorite topic be carefully avoided. (p. 240)

In yet another case, Perfect prescribed "a change of residence, prohibiting all intercourse with her *religious* friend" as a way of weakening his patient's pernicious belief system (p. 365). In this particular instance, a mainstream minister was called in to conduct what we in the twentieth century might refer to as a "deprogramming" session:

> At this crisis a truly pious divine of her acquaintance had free access to her, and succeeded in endeavouring to enlighten the dark gloom that had involved her mind, and brought it back to a clear sense of religious duties; and after the patient had continued completely rational for six weeks, . . . she became in every respect as well as at the period before her illness. (p. 366)

Whatever one might think about Dr. Perfect's opinions, we can be grateful for his admirable candidness, which allows us to reconstruct a very different state of affairs underneath his medical discourse. In most, if not all, of the instances cited above, a medical model was being used to interpret deviations from accepted norms where a heresy model would have been utilized less than a hundred years earlier. Instead of being burned at the stake, these "deviants" were sent to hospitals to be "cured" of their heretical notions. Despite the various physiological treatments to which the patients were subjected, it was obvious even to Perfect that separation from fellow believers was the key element of therapy.

The plausibility of any given symbolic universe is maintained by the ongoing process of conversation with coinhabitants of a particular belief system. When our conversation partners change, and especially when we are entirely cut off from former associates, there is a natural (though not inevitable) tendency for our beliefs to undergo a process of modification in the direction of the beliefs of our new friends. This process is particularly effective when, as in this case, the desired change is in the direction of *re*socialization into the norms of mainstream society. Something of this sort almost certainly took place in the cases recounted by Perfect.

Despite the fascinating nature of the notion of religious insanity, few studies have done more than scratch the surface of this topic, and only one has dealt exclusively with it: William Sims Bainbridge's article "Religious Insanity in America: The Official Nineteenth-Century Theory." Because of the dearth of relevant studies, it might be useful to briefly lay out the theory of religious insanity that one finds in the medical literature of the late eighteenth and early nineteenth centuries. Although the conception of mental illness gradually changed over the course of the nineteenth century, the generally accepted theory was firmly physiological:

> Insanity is a disease of the physical organism, principally of the brain and nervous system, though disease of the physical organism may be *brought* on by a thousand "causes," whether of the kind we logically distinguish as "efficient" causes, or "occasional" causes, and these too both moral and physical. ("Religious Insanity," 1876)

In the early part of the nineteenth century, one finds the notion that insanity is correlated with lesions in the brain, whereas later in the century the tendency is more to see mental (as well as many physical) illnesses as resulting from a deficiency of "nerve force." Nonetheless, the etiology of insanity was remarkably constant: While acknowledging certain predisposing factors such as heredity, the actual initiating cause was portrayed as some kind of "shock" to the system—either physical, as in the case of a blow to the head, or through what nineteenth-century alienists (the older term for psychiatrists) referred to as "moral" causes—bereavement, loss of employment, etc. Within this schema, religious enthusiasm was viewed as a moral factor which, when taken to extremes, could result in physiological damage; in the words of Amariah Brigham, one early nineteenth-century theorist of religious insanity,

> All long continued or violent excitement of the mind is dangerous, because it is likely to injure the brain and nervous system. Religious excitement, therefore, like all mental excitement, by affecting the brain, may cause insanity or other diseases. (pp. 284–85)

Revivals were the paradigmatic context in which this "violent excitement of mind" was experienced. For instance, William Sweetser, another nineteenth-century psychiatrist, observes that,

> At the field-meetings that are annually held among us I have been witness to the most frightful nervous affections, as convulsions, epilepsy, hysteria, distressing spasms, violent contortions of the body, not only in females in whom, from their more sensitive and sympathetic temperament, such affections are most readily excited, but also in the more hardy and robust of our own sex. Even spectators, such as attend for the purpose of amusement or merriment, will oftentimes be overtaken by the same nervous disorders. (p. 196)

Many alienists, however, continued to echo William Perfect's opinion that pernicious doctrines in and of themselves could induce insanity.

Such a vague and imprecise etiology was, however, only superficially physiological. With no way of measuring depleted nerve force, and no pre-mortem way of discovering brain lesions, the de facto criterion for determining mental illness was verbal and behavioral expression. The obvious problem with such a criterion was that any unusual expression of belief or conduct could be labeled crazy and result in incarceration. This actually seems to have been the case with the majority of religious enthusiasts committed to asylums. As Bainbridge observes, the "high reported cure rate for religious insanity" as contrasted with other forms of insanity indicates that incarceration was probably being "used by families to punish deviant members" and bring them back into line with accepted norms (p. 235). This is not to say that either families or physicians cynically deployed medical labels they knew were spurious, but rather asserts that a medical explanation was seized upon because it "made sense"–it seemed to substantiate popular prejudice as well as to legitimate a vigorous response.

This kind of "medicalization of deviance" perspective seems especially likely when we consider some of the more unusual causes of insanity mentioned in the psychiatric literature of the nineteenth century: masturbation, spermatorrhea ("involuntary seminal discharges"), intemperance, hashish intoxication, novel reading, "effeminate education," tobacco use, onset of puberty, and dealing in lottery tickets. Even more to the point are the psychiatric disorders "discovered" among slaves by Samuel A. Cartwright, a Southern physician: Drapetomania–the mental illness "that induces the negro to run away from service"–and "Dysestheia Ethiopis, or hebetude of mind and obtuse sensibility of body–a disease peculiar to negroes–called by overseers, 'rascality' " (pp. 707, 709). The recommended therapy for the latter was

> to have the patient well washed with warm water and soap; then, to anoint it all over with oil, and to slap the oil in with a broad leather strap; then to put the patient to some hard kind of work. (p. 712)

Needless to say, the same course of treatment, minus water, soap, and oil, had been applied by overseers long before Dr. Cartwright's remarkable investigations.

There had been enough speculation about religious insanity by the beginning of the second quarter of the nineteenth century that another physician, George Man Burrows, could devote considerable space to discussion of the subject in his 1828 study, *Commentaries on the Causes, Forms, Symptoms and Treatment, Moral and Medical, of Insanity.* The second chapter of that work, "Religion in Reference to Insanity," is one of the best treatments of its kind, and thus provides a useful point of reference for gaining a better sense of the intricacies of the theory of religious insanity. Burrows begins by noting that the excessive emotion associated with religion is the chief causal factor:

> As there is no single passion, when excited to excess, that may not induce mental derangement, so we may readily believe that religion, which influences the internal man more than the passions collectively, may be the cause of insanity. (p. 25)

Burrows immediately notes, however, that causality may be falsely attributed to religion merely because the lunatic raves about religious matters. He further points out that the whole subject has been brought into a state of confusion because of the tendency of physicians to attribute pathological consequences to religious systems with which they disagreed.

Early in the chapter, Burrows makes an important disclaimer that one finds in almost every extended treatment of religious insanity:

> It is not, however, from the agency of the Christian faith, in its pure and intelligible form, but from the perversion of it, that many become victims of insanity. (p. 26)

This appears to be an innocent enough statement in itself, but the mere admission that there can be perverted versions of the Christian faith indicates that Burrows has his own axe to grind.

Toward the end of the chapter, after he has gone over a number of case studies, Burrows observes that "misused" religion may be only the initiating cause in people who are otherwise predisposed to derangement:

Each of them certainly possessed a constitutional temperament highly susceptible of excitement, and consequently favourable to derangement. Religion, therefore, in these instances, can be considered as the agent only; and, as may be the case with any other agent, the effect was consequent on the misuse, and not on the fair and proper application of it. (p. 54)

Burrows observes that most theories impute causal efficacy to one of three factors:

Firstly, to the mysticism of the tenets inculcated; secondly, to the intenseness with which abstract theology has been studied or followed; and thirdly, from religion being over-ardently impressed on minds too tender or uninformed to comprehend it. (p. 38)

His own opinion, however, is that the transitional state from one religious system to another is the efficient cause:

I do not recollect an instance of insanity implying a religious source in any person stedfast [sic] in his ancient opinions. Wherever it was suspected to emanate from such a cause, it was clearly to be traced to circumstances which had diverted the lunatic from the authority of primary principles, to the adoption of new tenets, which he had not comprehended, and therefore had misapplied. The Maniacal action appeared always to originate during the conflict in deciding between opposite doctrines; and the exacerbation arrived before conviction was determined. (p. 39)

From this statement and most of the other passages cited above, it can be seen that Burrows is more careful than many of his contemporaries. He, however, is not immune from the prejudices of his age. For example, he attributes the higher percentage of women infected with religious excitement to the natural weakness of the female sex—a very common observation in the literature on the subject. To his credit, however, and in marked contrast to many other writers on this topic, Burrows *also* notes certain differences between the socialization and occupations of males and females as explanatory factors:

Many causes combine to make women more prone to such impressions. Physically, man is more robust, and has less sensibility, or irritability, than women; morally, his education is more solid, and his pursuits more active and definite. The education of females is generally showy, rather than substantial; and as they naturally possess more ardent and susceptible minds, want of active occupation becomes a most dangerous enemy to them. (p. 55)

This passage may not strike the reader as exceptional, but Burrows's remarks are enlightened when contrasted with statements from other medical doctors of the time, for example,

History, as well as the experience of physicians of the present day, teaches us that in certain highly emotional women, religious sentiment and venereal desires are convertible passions. Religious sexual delusions are common occurrences and even certain diseases, such as epilepsy and hysteria, predispose to abnormal fervor. ("Brinton," p. 491)

Burrows is, however, less cautious when expressing his opinions about certain specific religions. Despite his assertion that "in these enlightened times, it is to be hoped" that just "because a deranged person is a Papist, or a Protestant of the established church, or a sectarian, or even a Pagan" it should not be imputed that he or she is consequently more prone to insanity (p. 32), Burrows's own bias comes forward in the context of some of his case studies. For example, his dislike of Catholicism is ill-disguised in the following:

Upon going out, she witnessed, for the first time, the ceremonies of the Romish church with which she appeared much struck. From that moment she lost all her zeal for the Protestant faith; and nothing would satisfy her but that she would be a catholic. She was brought home. No care, however, removed this conceit; and she still continued so wild and unmanageable, that she was sent to a lunatic asylum. (Burrows, p. 51)

Nonetheless, it should be noted that the deprecating tone of his remarks contrasts favorably with those of his contemporaries. One of the reasons Burrows was selected for detailed examination here is because his analysis is relatively cautious and reflective. He was, however, only slightly less guilty of medicalizing religious groups he disliked. We have tended to speak kindly of Dr. Burrows because of his comparative moderation; few of his contemporaries exercised such restraint. To cite an example:

> Superstition, which was noticed by Areteus as being sometimes a symptom of insanity, was the principal instrument, as it has always been the most prominent feature, of the Roman Catholic Church. It is no wonder, then that that church should be of all others, the most prolific parent of superstitious insanity. (Arnold, p. 220)

Finally, we might note a general lack of restraint among nineteenth-century psychiatrists that is evident in the wide variety of groups that were at one time or another accused of inducing mental derangement: Mormons, Methodists, Catholics, Anabaptists, Quakers, Spiritualists, Presbyterians, Millerites, and Christian Scientists.

From the standpoint of the late twentieth century, it is easy to be amused by the perceptions and formulations of our predecessors. Our amusement should be tempered, however, by the realization that the notion of religious insanity was devised and promulgated by some of the more thoughtful and liberal minds of the age. Much like Dr. Perfect, we moderns are not immune to the propensity to label ideas with which we disagree, or behaviors of which we disapprove, as sick or crazy. For example, in a recent (1996) book on millennialism, *The End of Time*, the author confidently asserts that:

> All millenarian movements are distinguished by the abnormal behaviour of their adherents, which can range from retreat to the wilderness to await the End to acts of unimaginable violence designed to bring it about. (Thompson 1996, p. xii)

This attitude seems to be particularly prevalent among certain members of the mental health profession toward doomsday "cults." When, for example, one prominent anticult psychiatrist can seriously assert that the question motivating his work is "What kind of nutty people get into these crazy groups?" and commit patients he has never examined to medical institutions on the basis of their membership in alternative religions, we should suspect that contemporary "cult disease" is a close relative of nineteenth century "religious insanity."

As in the nineteenth century, the contemporary "scientific" attacks on alternative religious groups are attempts to psychologize–to *medicalize*–a controversy which, on deeper examination, is clearly ideologically based. Opponents of religious innovation have been so successful in their tactic of medicalizing the controversy that their viewpoint finds expression, and therefore legitimation, in the *Diagnostic and Statistical Manual of Mental Disorders,* the standard diagnostic reference for psychological disturbances. For example, under the category "Atypical Dissociative Disorder"–a disorder which the manual characterizes as a "residual category" for dissociative responses that do not fit other, more specific, categories–we find that prospective candidates include "persons who have been subjected to periods of prolonged and intense coercive persuasion (brainwashing, thought reform, and indoctrination while the captive of terrorists or cultists)." In addition to the totally unsupported assertion that all alternative religions utilize "coercive persuasion," this statement also places "cultists" on equal standing with terrorists. Or, again, under the category "Paranoid Personality Disorder"–a disorder which the manual confesses "rarely comes to clinical attention"–we find the authors *speculating* that "It seems likely that individuals with this disorder are overrepresented among leaders of mystical or esoteric religions." Like the nineteenth-century diagnostic category "religious insanity," such nonempirical speculation shows more about the biases of certain psychiatrists than about the personality of religious leaders.

This shifting from ideological to medical ground is a common tactic employed by members of dominant social groups against minorities. As a general phenomenon, it has regularly been studied by social scientists under the rubric "the medicalization of deviance." The use of psychological-medical labels to legitimate repression is, in other words, not unique to the contemporary cult controversy. Most everyone is aware, for example, that one of the methods by which the former Soviet Union dealt with dissidents was to commit them to mental asylums, through the use of such exotic diagnoses as "manic reformism" and "paranoia with counter-revolutionary delusions." Our earlier mention of drapetomania–the mental illness that deranged slaves so that they wanted to "run away from service"–is another vivid example of medicalizing a social conflict.

Most scholars who have studied the cult controversy have come to similar conclusions about the "mind control" and "brainwashing" accusations leveled against contemporary new religions. In other words, in the context of this controversy, it is fairly clear that parents become concerned about their children because they adopt eccentric lifestyles and beliefs, rather than because they exhibit genuinely pathological behavior. Such parents are literally unable to understand their adult children's rejection of secular career goals and conventional family life, and as a consequence readily believe that their offspring have gone crazy.

Thus, the role of our secular society in transforming a disagreement over lifestyles and beliefs into a psychological issue is twofold: On the one hand, parents of individuals who have joined new religious movements are often so secularized that they are unable to comprehend intense religious commitment as anything other than "crazy." On the other hand, attacks on religious innovation must be cloaked in secular garb because accusations of heresy are powerless to mobilize a secular culture's repressive agencies.

Mainstream Americans have always been disdainful of millennialist groups. In recent years, however, this disdain has turned to irritation and even anger. The antagonism toward doomsday cults was particularly evident in the general public's response to the Branch Davidians. The balance of this chapter examines this response, using events in Waco, Texas, as a lens through which to measure and try to understand this hostility.

THE DEMONS WITHIN

In America, conflicts and tragedies quickly find expression as slogans on bumper stickers and on T-shirts. The Branch Davidian fiasco was no exception. In Waco, and especially in the general vicinity of Mt. Carmel, one could find vendors hawking T-shirts boasting such mindless slogans as: "I SUPPORT THE ATF" (as if supporting the ATF was comparable to supporting Desert Storm). Another, with words drawn across an image of the burning community, said "HI VERN, WEIRD ASSHOLE, COME OUT." Yet another one, which pictured Koresh's face in the cross-hairs of a gun sight, sported the chilling assertion "A SIGHT WE'VE BEEN WAITING TO SEE."

Scholars who have studied new religious movements (NRMs) found the public response to the immolation of the Branch Davidians more disturbing than usual: Over 80 percent approved of the ill-conceived assault in which ninety men, women, and children were burned alive. Since at least the mid-1970s, part of the stereotype of alternative religions has been that members are brainwashed–a portrayal that clearly implies they should be regarded as innocent, duped victims of the leader rather than as conscious coconspirators. This was the case with the public's response to the Jonestown murder/suicides, in which only Jim Jones, the group's leader, was blamed.

The response to the Davidian tragedy, however, has been markedly different. While most Americans would still be willing to agree with the assertion that Koresh's followers were "brainwashed," many would also be willing to ascribe to the opposite, contradictory assertion that the Davidians have only themselves to blame for becoming involved with David Koresh. This is clear from a statement published in the letters to the editor of the May 24, 1993, issue of *Time* magazine about Koresh and his followers being "responsible for their own untimely death."

This self-contradictory position is reminiscent of the view Americans held toward communists during the Cold War era: Citizens of the Soviet Union were regarded as duped, brainwashed puppets of their leaders. Simultaneously they were "commies," a subhuman species that deserved to be exterminated rather than allowed to breed ("the only good commie is a dead commie"). As part of this odd, contradictory attitude toward communism, defectors from behind the iron curtain were hailed as heroes–similar to the manner in which certain former "cult" members are regarded.

The parallels between the ways in which cults and communism are regarded is more than coincidence. One of the more widely accepted dictums of sociology is that societies need enemies. External threats provide motivation for people to overcome internal divisiveness in order to work together as a unit. Having an enemy one can portray as evil and perverse also provides support for the normative values and institutions of one's society: "They" are communists; "we" are capitalists. "They" are totalitarian; "we" are democratic. And so forth and so on.

One of the more interesting corollaries of this general line of thinking is that in situations where external enemies no longer threaten, a society will find groups or individuals within itself that it can construe as threatening and evil. Such enemies become particularly important to communities passing through a crisis in which fundamental values are being called into question; in the words of Albert Bergesen, taken from his important study, *The Sacred and the Subversive*, "a community will commence to ritually persecute imaginary enemies—conduct a witchhunt—to manufacture moral deviants as a means of ritually reaffirming the group's problematical values and collective purposes" (p. vii).

As unusual as this notion may appear to readers at first glance, it has been effectively supported by certain social historical studies. For example, in an interesting and creative study of New England witchcraft, *Entertaining Satan*, John Demos demonstrates that the persecution and execution of people—usually unsocial, crabby, old ladies—as witches abated during periods of war, and reappeared after peace had returned. This sheds considerable light on our current social situation.

As a potent international threat, communism has largely disappeared. The only significant remaining communist power is the People's Republic of China, and the Chinese are more interested in cooperating with the West than in challenging it. Other, non-Communist, threats, such as Iraq, flare up and pass rather quickly. The lack of pressing external enemies in combination with our current, ongoing social crisis would lead the sociologically informed observer to anticipate that our culture will seek out groups within society to take the place of the "commies."

Unless there are groups that are consciously antisocial or criminal, such as the Mafia, the deviations from the norm that a community chooses to perceive as threatening are somewhat arbitrary. The people that our culture have traditionally construed as "deviants" have been racial (e.g., blacks), ethnic (e.g., Jews), and sexual (e.g., homosexuals) minorities. In recent years, however, it has become "politically incorrect" to persecute these traditional groups, at least in the overt manner in which they have been attacked in the past. This leaves few groups of any significant size to persecute.

One of the few minorities that liberals have been slow to defend are nontraditional religions. This is due to a number of different factors, including the resistance of established, conservative religions to liberal change. The failure of normally open-minded people to protect religious pluralism has allowed contemporary witchhunters to declare open season on cults. The media response to Waco has also served to make nontraditional religions the preferred object of attack.

EXORCISING OUR PROJECTIONS

Groups of people who are believed to be threatening frequently become screens onto which a society projects its anxieties. If, for example, a culture is troubled by sexual issues (as is often the case), then its enemies are perceived as perverse, sexually deviant, and so forth. Racial minorities, who have often been viewed as "loose" and sexually aggressive, have suffered from this projection. This was also a dominant theme in nineteenth-century anti-Catholic and anti-Mormon literature. Contemporary "cults," of course, suffer from the same projection.

In the classical formulation of psychological projection, Sigmund Freud, who was especially concerned with sex and violence, viewed projection as a defense mechanism against unacceptable inner urges. Thus, in a society with strict sexual mores, an individual constantly keeping a lid on his desires might perceive rather ordinary dancing, let us say, as sexually suggestive. Becoming enraged at such "loose" behavior, he might then attempt to lead a movement to have all of the dance halls in town closed down. It should be clear that this hypothetical individual's *inner* struggle is being "projected" outward to provide a script for an *outer* struggle. In other words, internally he is repressing his desires while he symbolically battles the same desires in the outer world. The same process is at work in the collective mind of society, perceiving marginal groups as sexually deviant. For instance, the stereotype of the sexually abusive cult leader, routinely forcing devotees to satisfy his or her sexual whims, captures perfectly the fantasy of many members of our society who desire to have sexually any person he or she wishes.

The same sort of thing happens with repressed aggressive urges. We live in a society with strict sanctions against overt violence; simultaneously, violence is glorified in the entertainment media. This sets up a cultural contradiction that is projected onto enemies and deviant groups, with the result that minorities are often perceived as violent and belligerent. This accusation is also regularly projected onto nontraditional religions. In particular, the radical actions of a tiny handful of alternative religions is mistakenly taken to indicate a widespread tendency among all such groups.

We can generalize beyond Freudian psychology's emphasis on sex and aggression to see that many other cultural anxieties/contradictions are projected onto minority groups. For instance, our society gives us contradictory messages about the relative importance of money and possessions. On the one hand we are taught that economic pursuits are supposed to be secondary to social and spiritual activities. On the other, we receive many messages from the surrounding society that the single-minded pursuit of wealth is the be-all and end-all of life. This contradiction is projected onto alternative religions in the stereotype of the money-hungry cult leader who demands that her or his followers lead lives of poverty while the leader wallows in riches.

Similarly, the frequent accusations of child abuse and contemporary society's seeming obsession with child abuse flow out of another cultural contradiction. Our cultural heritage as well as many modern psychologists hold out the ideal of a child who is constantly under the wing of a loving parent, usually the mother. Current economic conditions, however, often require both parents to work full time, which usually entails leaving young children in the care of strangers. This results in a good deal of guilt, which is easily displaced onto "deviant" groups, such as cults. Like the accusation of violence, the radical actions of a tiny handful of alternative religions that have abused children is mistakenly taken to indicate a widespread tendency among all such groups. Despite the outcry against the Branch Davidians, for example, our best current information is that, while strict, the Davidians did *not* abuse their children. However, the readiness of people to buy into the stereotype of child-abusing cultists convicted David Koresh and sentenced him to death before he was able to receive a fair hearing.

One of the more important cultural contradictions that gets projected onto alternative religions is tied up in the brainwashing/mind control notion that is the core accusation leveled against such groups. Discourse that glorifies American society usually does so in terms of a rhetoric of liberty and freedom–e.g., What makes America great? Our Freedom! However, while holding liberty as a ideal, we experience a social environment that is often quite restrictive. Most citizens work as employees in highly disciplined jobs where the only real freedom is the freedom to quit. Also, we are bombarded by advertising designed to influence our decisions and even to create new "needs." Our frustration with these forms of influence and control is easily displaced and projected onto the separated societies of alternative religions, which offer distorted reflections of the situation we experience as members of the dominant society.

The "control" accusation is interesting because of its role in the Waco debacle. Readers who followed the siege on Mt. Carmel may recall the FBI spokesman who complained that David Koresh was in "total control" of the situation. Koresh in total control? Here was a community pinned down by a small army of federal agents. The FBI had cut off Mt. Carmel's water, electricity, and sewage. Tanks had run over and crushed the community's vegetable garden and the children's toys. An audio and visual assault dominated the night. Finally, the flow of information to reporters was tightly controlled by isolating the news media and feeding them only the information the FBI saw fit to share. The feds, not Koresh, had total control over the situation, a reflection of the tendency of FBI agents to be—in 1960s idiom—"control freaks." But the G-men were frustrated by their inability to control David Koresh enough to force him to surrender, and, in the heat of their frustration, leveled the accusation of "being in total control" onto him—not realizing how ridiculous they sounded.

CHILD ABUSE AT WACO

According to Attorney General Janet Reno, nobody high up in government said "don't do it" as she considered the disastrous plan. But it is not mere hindsight to say that someone should have. On March 10th the Houston Chronicle *reported that former Houston police SWAT commander Lieutenant Jim Gunn had advised that, considering the variety and firepower of weapons Koresh and his followers were alleged to have, "About the only thing you could do is go in there with the M-1 tanks and start knocking down walls, and they are not going to do that with the children in there." And use of tear gas was not a feasible alternative, according to Gunn, because "tear gas can get into a child's lungs and cause congestion and kill them."*

—Robert W. Lee, *New American Magazine*

Lieutenant Jim Gunn, it turned out, was terribly wrong about the authorities' concern for the children. The tear gas used in the FBI attack—a white, crystalline powder called CS (O-chlorobenzylidene malonitrile)—is such an inhumane form of tear gas that it has been banned from military use. It causes nausea, disorientation, dizziness, shortness of breath, tightness in the chest, burning of the skin, and intense tearing, coughing, and vomiting. In January 1993, the United States and 130 other nations signed the Chemical Weapons Convention agreement prohibiting CS gas. This treaty does not, however, govern domestic uses, such as quelling internal disturbances.

On April 23, 1993, Benjamin C. Garrett, director of the Chemical and Biological Arms Control Institute in Alexandria, Virginia, was quoted in the *Washington Times* as saying that CS gas would have had the greatest impact on the children at Mt. Carmel. "The reaction would have intensified for the children," Garrett said, because "the smaller you are, the sooner you would feel response" (cited in Lewis and Melton 1994, p. 160). According to the FBI, the anticipated scenario was that mothers, in an effort to protect their children, would leave the building with their offspring when the gas saturated the inside of the buildings. White House spokesman George Stephanopoulos, speaking at a news conference, was unwilling (or unable) to account for why such a deadly form of tear gas—one that temporarily blinds and disables a person—was selected over other possibilities.

Also, despite claims by the FBI that the community had not tried to save its children during the final fire, a May 14 report issued by the Associated Press revealed that, "Most of the children were found huddled in the concrete bunker, enveloped in the protective embraces of their mothers," in what had clearly been an attempt to avoid the flames (Lewis and Melton 1994, p. 160). These and many other particulars that could be cited indicate both that the Davidians were not planning a mass suicide and that they were not child abusers.

About the fortieth day of the Mt. Carmel siege, David Koresh informed his attackers that the community's babies and children had run out of milk. A number of different efforts to respond to this call for aid were repulsed by authorities. (While it was okay to provide humanitarian aid to Contras, U.S. citizens are clearly a different matter.) Linda Thompson, an attorney from Indiana who drove to Waco in a vain but admirable attempt to head off the holocaust, tried to deliver baby food and baby supplies on April 3 and 4. She and her husband were detained for questioning, and then turned back. At FBI headquarters, she posed the question, "Has it come to this? Does the United States government want babies to starve to death?" The answer she received was yes. Exasperated, the Thompsons finally placed the food alongside the roadblock at the press entrance with a sign that read, "Please take this food to the Mt. Carmel babies. The FBI says, 'Let them starve.' " Moments later, an ATF agent drove up in a pickup truck and stole the food.

A man named Gary Spaulding and another person from South Bend, Indiana, were arrested the following week for attempting to take food to the Mt. Carmel children. Spaulding pointedly suggested to the arresting officer that he should perhaps "check with his high command to be sure that the officer was doing what the high command wanted." The response he received was, "I can assure you that I speak for high command when I say that food is not going to those babies."

Although child abuse is technically the jurisdiction of the state rather than the federal government, concern that the Davidian children were being abused has been one of the principal reasons cited by authorities as justification for both the initial ATF attack and for the concluding FBI assault. On April 21, George Stephanopoulos, defending the holocaust, asserted that there "is absolutely no question that there's overwhelming evidence of child abuse in the Waco compound." This was a very odd line of defense, as if the assertion that the Davidians practiced such abuse justified gassing and incinerating the entire community.

However, on the very day Stephanopoulos was putting his foot in his mouth, the Justice Department publicly acknowledged that they had no solid evidence of child abuse—only *speculation* by mental health professions who had been studying Koresh from a distance. On the same day, 1,100 pages of unsealed documents relevant to the case were released. These included only two allegations of child abuse by disgruntled former members. Nothing else was reported, certainly nothing like credible evidence.

Certainly during the siege itself, the FBI showed little regard for the children. The weird light and sound show, which included recordings of dentists' drills and dying rabbits, would hardly have promoted any child's sense of well-being. Deteriorating sanitary conditions, caused by decaying bodies and the buildup of sewage, were also given as a justification for attacking Mt. Carmel on April 19. Attorney General Janet Reno told Larry King on national television that she feared that "if I delayed, without sanitation or toilets there . . . I could go in there in two months and find children dead from any number of things." Yet if this had truly been an overriding consideration, Why didn't the FBI restore the water and utilities it had shut off in March?

The Texas Department of Human Services had investigated Mt. Carmel on child abuse allegations brought by Mark Breault and others on at least three different occasions. No credible evidence for such accusations was found. The same can be said for the twenty-one children released from Mt. Carmel between the ATF raid and the FBI assault–no hard evidence of child abuse. On March 5, Janice Caldwell, director of the Texas Department of Protective and Regulatory Services, stated that, "They're in remarkably good shape considering what they have been through. No signs of physical abuse have been found." The March 6 edition of the *Houston Post* noted that "all the youths appear to be in good condition psychologically and physically." In the same article, a social worker asserted that "the children are remarkably well-educated and they're fascinated by the books in the residence where they're staying."

The only relevant accusation of child abuse originated with the chief of psychiatry at a Texas medical school who examined several of the children released between February 28 and April 19. In the words of psychologist Lawrence Lilliston, a widely recognized expert on children in nontraditional religions,

> This psychiatrist's conclusions were widely reported in the media, including a lengthy article in the *New York Times*. He concluded that the children had been abused, and cited as evidence marks on their bodies. These physical marks, described as round red marks on the skin of several children, comprised the only specific evidence reported. The psychiatrist otherwise described the children as being friendly, happy, and likable, and as having good interpersonal skills and being open to others. They were also described as generally being bright and above average on cognitive and educational tasks. This picture is clearly not consistent with expectations for children who have been abused. (pp. 171–72)

The lack of any solid evidence for Davidian child abuse probably explains the reason why the attorney general and the FBI dropped this explanation as soon as reporters began to raise questions about specific evidence for abuse. But, as Professor Lilliston further points out, there *was* child abuse in Waco:

> Consider the following. Knowing that there were many children inside, federal agents conducted a raid on the compound, firing a fusillade of bullets through windows and walls, killing one child and surely terrifying the others. Knowing that there were many children inside, federal agents cut off electricity and other utilities necessary to the maintenance of health and safety standards for these children, and then, incredibly, criticized the adults because children had to perform elimination functions in buckets. Knowing that there were many children inside, federal agents bombarded the building with spotlights twenty-four hours a day in an admitted attempt to disrupt sleep and rest. Knowing that there were many children inside, federal agents incessantly assaulted the building with loud music and bizarre sounds, such as rabbits being killed. Knowing that there were many children inside, federal agents used tanks as battering rams, crashing into the building and punching holes in the walls even though they were aware that the building was a potential tinder box and that the people inside were using lanterns which could easily be knocked over. Knowing that there were many children inside, federal agents pumped in tear gas–tear gas of such strength and capacity for producing pain, it has been banned by international law–and they did this, knowing that there were no gas masks inside small enough to protect children. Certainly these children's last living moments must have been filled with unbelievable horror and agony.
>
> Who, considering these facts, could dispute the charge of child abuse in Waco? If firing bullets at them, disregarding and disturbing their health and tranquility, destroying their home while placing them in clear danger, and intentionally inflicting intense pain on them is not abusive to children, what is? (pp. 172–73)

In short, it is clear that the charge of child abuse leveled against the Davidians was little more than a pretext that legitimated the drastic actions of April 19, 1993.

Child abuse is an issue, like AIDS or the plight of the homeless, that has been uppermost in the public consciousness during the last decade or so. As a consequence, accusations of child abuse are more effective at attracting attention than other kinds of charges, particularly if the media can be persuaded to pick up the story. Although one of the principles of our legal system is that a person is innocent until proven guilty, the media present information so that merely reporting sensationalistic accusations is often sufficient to convict the accused in the mind of the general public. If it later turns out that the accused was innocent, this item of corrective information rarely gets reported, and the public is usually left with the impression that the accused is guilty.

What this means is that nontraditional religions accused of child abuse lose their chance for a fair hearing as soon as the media label them cults. Cults are, by definition, abusive, so that to attempt assert that such-and-such a "cult group" is *non*-abusive sounds like a contradiction in terms. Thus simply succeeding in getting the cult label to stick to any given religious community is to succeed in "demonizing" the group. Once effectively demonized, the enforcement agencies of the state are free to undertake otherwise unthinkably repressive actions against the target group, even, as in the case of the Davidians, incinerating an entire community with scarcely a peep of protest from the American public.

FANNING THE FLAMES OF SUSPICION

On April 19, 1993, the FBI's workday began somewhat prior to the gas attack. As reported by a nurse who was interviewed on two different radio programs—one in Laport and the other in Waco—the FBI had dropped by the local hospital at 5:00 A.M. Monday morning to find out how it was equipped to handle burn victims. This indicates that the FBI fully *expected* Mt. Carmel to catch fire, and stands in sharp contrast to the agency's *apparent* lack of preparedness for the final fiery holocaust. The nurse's radio interview is, however, only the most glaring item of information in a rather lengthy laundry list of suspicious events and situations—bits of information that, while insignificant in isolation, together appear to indicate that the Mt. Carmel fire was intentionally set by government officials.

Consider, for example, that, tactically, the best times for tear gas attacks are days on which the wind is still, allowing the gas to hang in the air around its target rather than being blown away. Instead of waiting for such conditions, the feds chose to move on a day when the wind was blowing at a brisk thirty miles per hour. On top of that, they called the Davidians at 5:50 A.M., and casually informed them, "Well, we got tired of waiting, so we decided we were going to gas you instead" (or words to that effect). Now, it doesn't take a genius to figure out that the people inside the community would respond by opening up the windows and doors to allow the wind simply to blow the gas through the building and out the other end. This would have created a wind-tunnel effect—an effect *increased* by the large, gaping holes the tanks had created as they ripped into the building. Clearly these were *poor* conditions for a tear gas attack, but *ideal* for setting fire to a wood frame structure.

The potential for Mt. Carmel to go up in flames should have been readily apparent. Electricity had been cut off on March 12, compelling the community to use gasoline-powered generators, propane, and kerosene lamps. The building itself was a crudely built firetrap, constructed from plywood and new lumber and tacked together with tar paper. Bales of hay had been pushed against windows to help stop bullets.

On April 26, a team of "independent" arson investigators led by Paul Gray, the assistant chief investigator for the Houston Fire Department who had confidently asserted that his group of experts was "independent of any federal law enforcement agency," issued their report. Gray and his team concluded that the blaze must have been initiated by people inside the building in two or more different locations at about the same time (Kopel and Blackman, pp. 226–27). (Defending the scenario of several simultaneous starting points was an important point in eliminating the possibility that one of the tanks tipped over a lamp that set the building on fire—the Davidian version of the story.) However, other authoritative sources assert that flames broke out at different points *within 50 to 120 seconds* of each other—

not exactly "simultaneous" when we take into consideration a thirty-mile-per-hour wind in a firetrap that burned to the ground in less than forty-five minutes.

Suspicions were also raised on April 28 when *CBS News* correspondent Sarah Hughes broadcast the information that the "independent" arson team had "close ties with the FBI." It was also discovered that the wife of arson team leader Paul Gray was an employee of the ATF. Gray responded indignantly to these revelations with the assertion that to "even suggest that any information we may be getting from the FBI is somehow tainted is absolutely ridiculous." However, on *Nightline* that same evening, lawyer Jack Zimmermann posed the question "Why in the world did they bring in, as chief of this investigating team looking into the fire, a fellow who had been on an ATF joint task force for eight to ten years, out of the Houston office of the ATF, the office that planned and executed the raid?"

In a situation already reeking with the stench of dissimulation and cover-up, choosing an individual with close personal ties to the very agencies he was hired to exonerate could only have had the opposite effect, increasing rather than decreasing widely held suspicions. As if to *further* confirm critics' suspicions, the burned-out remains of Mt. Carmel—along with any remaining evidence—were bulldozed on May 12. This action, which assured that no *truly* independent arson investigator would be able to sift through the charred remains and construct an alternative scenario to the official version, was justified on the pretext of safety and health concerns—filling holes, burying trash, and so on.

The government's interpretation assumes that, like Jonestown, the Davidians had actually planned a mass suicide. Given this assumption, it is plausible that they set fire to Mt. Carmel rather than surrender to government forces. Otherwise, the contention that Koresh's followers torched their community is implausible. The only sources for asserting that Mt. Carmel was another Jonestown were Mark Breault (a rival prophet who claimed to be a disenchanted defector) and individuals associated with the Cult Awareness Network—neither reliable sources of information. There is far more evidence to support the alternative contention that the Davidians were not suicidal and that Koresh and company were planning on living into the future.

From as authoritative a source as William Sessions, then director of the FBI, we learn that the agency had concluded before the April 19 assault that Koresh was not suicidal. On April 20, during the *MacNeil/Lehrer Report* news program, Sessions noted that "every single analysis made of his writing, of what he had said, of what he had said to his lawyers, of what the behavioral science people said, what the psychologists thought, the psycholinguists thought, what the psychiatrists believed, was that this man was not suicidal, that he would not take his life."

On April 29, Dr. Murray Miron, one of the psychologists consulted by the FBI, informed newsman Tom Brokaw that, with respect to the letters authored by Koresh that he had been asked to analyze, "All of his communications were future oriented. He claimed to be working on a manuscript. He was talking about the publication rights to that manuscript through his lawyer. He was intent upon furthering his cause" (cited in Kopel and Blackman, p. 152). Koresh even went so far as to retain literary attorney Ken Burrows to handle his story. He also requested another attorney to prepare a will that would protect Davidian property rights, as well as establish a trust for his children to safeguard any future income from books or movies. These and many other particulars that could be cited indicate that the Davidians were not planning mass suicide.

Given the choice of the deadly CS tear gas, the question of how the fires started on the plains of east Texas that fateful day becomes all the more intriguing. All of the survivors, despite FBI claims to the contrary, denied that Davidians started the fire. Instead, they asserted that the tanks had knocked over lanterns, setting the blaze. The Davidians were, however, more generous to the FBI than the evidence indicates. As we have already noted, it seems that the FBI took steps to guarantee that flames would spread quickly, and could not be stopped once started. A dry, windy day was chosen for the assault—a day that, as we pointed out earlier, would have been terrible for a tear gas attack, but perfect for incinerating a building.

Despite the obvious risk of a fire, fire trucks were nowhere near the attack scene when the assault began. When smoke began to appear, the FBI waited at least ten minutes before calling 911 to request firefighters from Waco be dispatched. The McLennan County Sheriff's Department relayed the request to the fire station:

Dispatcher: Sheriff's office dispatch.
Fireman: Yes.
Dispatcher: Is this Hawthorne?
Fireman: Yeah, it is.
Dispatcher: They've got a fire at the compound.
Fireman: Tell me!
Dispatcher: Are y'all en route?
Fireman: No, we're looking at it. Just waitin' for you to call.
Dispatcher: Okay, take off then.

Clearly, stopping the fire was not a high priority on anyone's list. When fire trucks finally arrived, they were held at the checkpoint *under FBI order* for another sixteen minutes—more than enough time to guarantee that Mt. Carmel would be reduced to a pile of embers before a drop of water touched the flames. The FBI's explanation? "The reason the fire trucks were not allowed to go in immediately was the firemen's safety. It's that simple. There were people there with automatic weapons ready to fire." How individuals dying in the inferno could have posed a risk to firemen was not explained.

What does all of this indicate? Given the FBI's visit to the local hospital early that morning to inquire about burn facilities, that the conditions were less than ideal for a tear gas attack, the inadequate preparations for the possibility of a fire, and so on, we get the following as a possible scenario:

For whatever reason, the FBI had become impatient and decided that they were going to end the siege once and for all on April 19. They planned a two-stage assault. In stage one, they would pump Mt. Carmel full of tear gas—the worst possible, nonlethal gas they could find—and hope the Davidians, or at least the mothers and children, would be forced out of the building. If by noontime the tear gas attack failed—and, given the determination displayed by the Davidians up to that point, it is unlikely that they would have backed down from their resolve–the FBI would avoid embarrassment by setting the place on fire. Most of David Koresh's people would then vacate the building to save themselves and their children. The agency's intentional igniting of Mt. Carmel would effectively be disguised by the tear gas attack, and afterwards they could claim either that the Davidians had set the blaze, or that the fires had started accidentally.

The plan went terribly wrong, however, when the Davidians failed to run out, and the FBI has since been trying to hide any evidence of wrongdoing. Hiring an arson investigator with close links to the agency and bulldozing the site to destroy evidence were clumsy cover-up efforts unworthy of the FBI. If the fires were indeed set intentionally, the stupidity characterizing the cover-up indicates that the deaths of most community members had not been the anticipated result of the assault. While it is difficult to contemplate that an agency with the reputation of the FBI could have perpetrated the Mt. Carmel fire, it is a far more likely explanation–given the information currently available to us–than the notion that the Davidians committed mass suicide. The same conclusion was expressed in the final stanzas of a poem, "Christian Holocaust," composed by some of the children who were released before the FBI attack whose father perished in the blaze:

Thank you, Mr. President, Janet Reno too.
We mustn't forget the ATF, the FBI, all the men in blue.

How well did you sleep last night?
Did you toss and turn?
I myself didn't get much sleep.
Did you know I saw my father burn?

We don't know how you did it.
You really must be brave.
You sat through all their screaming,
without emotion as they entered their fiery grave.

Save the children.
Well, not this time.
For patience we have none.
Enough time has been wasted;
we were ordered, "Get this over, get this done."

Patience is a virtue.
Good things come to those who wait.
It took only 51 days for you to decide their fiery fate.
Deep down inside your heart, you know the truth;
you cannot hide.
Christians who believe in God don't contemplate suicide.

The day will come we'll all be judged
as we stand before the Lord.
Koresh may have thought himself as Christ,
But you thought yourself as God.

> The Family of Floyd Houtman
> *We Love and Miss You, Dad.*

9

EPILOGUE
A New Armageddon?

The night is far gone, the day is at hand. Let us cast off the works of darkness.

—Romans 13:12

While the advent of the third millennium is unlikely to signal either the demise or the "explosion" of religion, it *is* likely to leave an altered religious landscape in its wake. There have been a variety of historical periods during which religious innovation flourished. In the West, there was a proliferation of a new religious consciousness in the late classical period, as well as in the wake of the Reformation. In the United States, historians have noted a recurring pattern of religious awakenings, beginning with the Great Awakening of the 1740s.

The most general observation we can make in this regard is that periods of renewed spiritual activity occur in the wake of disruptive social and economic changes: The established vision of "how things work" no longer seems to apply, and people begin searching for new visions. In previous cycles of American religious experimentation, innovative forms of Protestantism often formed the basis for these new visions. As revivalist fervor died down, new or reinvigorated Protestant denominations became the pillars of a new cultural hegemony.

The most recent period of American religious innovation occurred in the decades following the demise of the 1960s counter-culture. However, unlike previous cycles of revival, the religious explosion that occurred in the 1970s and 1980s has not provided a basis for a new spiritual and cultural synthesis. While there has been a growth in conservative Protestant denominations during this period (a growth parallel to the pattern of earlier Awakenings), there has also been a marked growth in "metaphysical" religion. The most visible manifestation of this latter strand of spirituality has been the New Age movement, which offers a vision of the world fundamentally at odds with that of traditional Christianity. Thus, during this most recent cycle of religious enthusiasm, Protestantism has failed to re-establish its traditional hegemony over American culture.

It has been asserted by some alarmists that the simultaneous expansion of conservative Christianity and the New Age movement is, in and of itself, a development with potentially "apocalyptic" implications. These two subcultures seem to be on a collision course with each other, and, to certain observers, it appears inevitable that some sort of violent Armageddon will emerge from this clash of worldviews. If this perspective is to be believed, then one of the first skirmishes in the coming Armageddon took place in 1990, in connection with a more recent series of revivals. It is with an account of this "endtime" event that we bring the present volume to a close.

CHRISTIAN AND NEW AGE APOCALYPSES MEET

On Halloween night 1990, Evangelist Larry Lea led an assault on San Francisco's local demons. A popular televangelist and leading proponent of "spiritual warfare," Lea ordered his prayer warriors to descend on the city to do battle with the ruling spirits of witchcraft, drugs, and sexual perversion. The San Francisco assault had been preceded by earlier campaigns in Anaheim, California, where 6,000 angry freelance exorcists had attended a three-day crusade in order to "inflict serious damage" on the forces of darkness in southern California. Seven thousand Christian warriors had turned up at another such meeting to "clobber the devil" in Chicago, where they shouted, stomped, brandished imaginary swords, and spoke in tongues. While even Christian critics have described Lea's dramatic campaigns as "supernatural sideshows," and while his campaigns have not yet inflicted noticeable damage on the powers of darkness, his tactics *have* been highly successful at packing auditoriums. The sense of high drama in the war against Satan is heightened when Lea wears military fatigues. The pastor-warrior also distributes "prayer army dog tags" to his soldiers so they can feel they have been officially enlisted into the ranks of his Christian regiments.

Bay area neopagans and an ad hoc group called GHOST (Grand Homosexual Outrage at Sickening Televangelists) organized to oppose Lea's crusade. Eric Pryor, high priest of the New Earth Temple, was quoted as saying, "We came to the United States to escape religious persecution. The witch-hunts are over, and I, for one, don't intend to be burned at the stake" (Lewis 1996, p. 340). GHOST organizer Mark Pritchard asserted that Lea's "message is, 'Perverts are bad and we're going to destroy perversity.' People in San Francisco want a chance to stand up against fundamentalists. Larry Lea has made himself a convenient target."

Despite the preacher's claim that the angry militancy generated by his campaigns is "not directed at flesh and blood," in San Francisco it was widely rumored that Lea's prayer warriors were planning to roam the streets and physically assault witches and gays following the prayer meeting in the Civic Auditorium. Protests began on the day preceding the crusade, when approximately 100 people showed up for a "public cursing" of the controversial evangelist. Pagan leader Eric Pryor led the "cursing," burning and eventually decapitating a black candle representing pastor Lea. On the night of the crusade, charismatic Christians were forced to run a gauntlet of more than a thousand angry gays and pagans in order to reach the auditorium. Protesters "chanted, blew whistles, and occasionally tossed eggs" at the prayer warriors (Lewis 1996, p. 340). In Civic Center Plaza, across the street from the auditorium, a large banner reading "Born Again Bigots, Go Home" was raised over mock gravestones bearing the names of Lea and other conservative Christian evangelists. San Francisco police were barely able to prevent the opposing sides from coming to blows.

WORKS OF DARKNESS

Although the basic notion of "spiritual warfare" has biblical roots, Lea's campaign was directly inspired by the novels of bestselling Christian author Frank Peretti. Peretti's works, especially *This Present Darkness* and *Piercing the Darkness*, have fueled the imaginations of charismatics and fundamentalists with bloody visions of angelic crusades against demonic evil. The action in his novels moves back and forth between two interacting levels: While angels and devils cross swords in the spiritual realm, Peretti's this-worldly heroes and heroines do battle with New Agers, witches, psychologists, secular education, and the ACLU. One of the keys necessary for understanding the nature of Lea's crusades is Peretti's notion that the concentrated prayers of God's saints provides power and protection for warrior angels. This "prayer energy" tips the balance of power in the spiritual realm, enabling angels to defeat demons. A decisive rout of infernal legions in the spiritual realm then leads more or less immediately to a defeat of Satan's minions in the earthly sphere (i.e., to a defeat of everyone opposed to Christian fundamentalists), which in turn leads to their defeat.

The climax to the final confrontation in *This Present Darkness* provides a good example of how this "prayer power" is viewed as working. In the concluding scene of the battle, Tal, leader of the angelic host, crosses swords with Rafar, leader of the demonic forces. At the same time, God's human "warriors," the "Remnant," engaged in the earthly struggle, are distracted by the dramatic damage inflicted by their crusade. This distraction interrupts the flow of "power" to Tal, so that Rafar almost gets the better of him. At the last possible moment, these Christians are impressed by the Lord to direct their prayer power against the demonic presence they can sense but not see:

[*Event in spiritual realm:*]
Tal could only back away from the fearsome onslaught of the demon prince, his one good hand still holding his sword up for defense. Rafar kept swinging and slashing, the sparks flying from the blades as they met. Tal's arm sank lower with each blow. "The Lord . . . rebuke you!" Tal found the breath to say again.

[*Appropriate Christian "prayer" response, intuited by an elderly lady:*]
Edith Duster was on her feet and ready to shout it to the heavens. "Rafar, you wicked prince of evil, in the name of Jesus we rebuke you!"

[*Effect of "prayer energy" in spiritual realm:*]
Rafar's blade zinged over Tal's head. It missed.

[*Further "prayer" action in physical realm:*]
"We bind you!" shouted the Remnant.

[*Effect in spiritual realm:*]
The big yellow eyes winced.

[*Action in physical realm:*]
"We cast you out!" Andy said.

[*Effect in spiritual realm:*]
There was a puff of sulfur, and Rafar bent over. Tal leaped to his feet.

[*Action in physical realm:*]
"We rebuke you, Rafar!" Edith shouted again.

[*Effect in spiritual realm:*]
Rafar screamed. Tal's blade had torn him open.

Such melodramatic invocations of God's power—more reminiscent of exorcisms than of prayers—provide the paradigm for Lea's frenzied crusades. Whatever may be the effects of these tactics on the powers of darkness, Peretti's vision of the nature of spiritual combat has powerfully influenced certain segments of the conservative Christian community. In effect, Peretti's writings have encouraged charismatics and fundamentalists to adopt an attitude of greater hostility to the non-Christian world by providing quasitheological justifications and dramatized prayer tactics for *attacking* Satan's forces. How is the widespread appeal of these novels, which are reshaping the face of conservative Christianity, to be understood?

In the first place, Peretti, in sharp contrast with most other "Christian" authors, is a gifted writer. Even the harshest critics will find themselves drawn into the narrative action of the *Darkness* novels. In the second place, Peretti is able to weave together not unbelievable, this-worldly stories with fantastic, "Dungeons and Dragons" struggles between other-worldly angels and demons. The results of this skillful juxtaposition are novels with an eerie narrative landscape that Irving Hexham has described as "sanctified Stephen King." In the third place, Peretti chooses to portray the anti-Christian forces in his stories in terms of the single, most popular target of conservative Christian ire, namely the New Age movement. The summary of *This Present Darkness* on the book's back cover, for example, describes Peretti's story in the following manner:

> Ashton is just a typical small town. But when a skeptical reporter and a prayerful pastor begin to compare notes, they suddenly find themselves fighting a hideous New Age plot to subjugate the towns-people, and eventually the entire human race.

Unknown to people outside of the Christian subculture, "New Age" has become the catch-all category for everything despised by fundamentalists. The major steps by which this came to pass are not difficult to trace.

HAMMERING THE HERETICS

If one peruses the shelves of any Christian bookstore, one will almost always find a section devoted to volumes that critically analyze secular humanism, cults, and other heresies. As might be expected, these works run the gamut from even-handed treatments that discuss various groups and movements in terms of their deviations from correct doctrine, to hysterical books that portray everything outside of a rather sharply delimited circle of light as a demonic conspiracy aimed at destroying true Christianity. While the ostensible purpose of such volumes is to alert Christians and to equip them to convert the heathen, they are probably best viewed in terms of "boundary maintenance"–compositions that allow a community to strengthen its own sense of identity by contrasting itself with "others" who are portrayed as being the exact opposite of themselves.

The 1980s saw the emergence of a new topic for such works–the New Age movement. Beginning rather modestly in 1983 with the publication of Constance Cumbey's *The Hidden Dangers of the Rainbow*, the number of conservative Christian books on the New Age increased rapidly until a complete collection would now fill several library shelves. The event that appears to have crystallized the topic of the New Age as a target of attack was Benjamin Creme's highly public advertising campaign for Maitreya, the New Christ who Creme presented in terms of Alice Bailey's theosophy. Creme's widespread advertising began in 1982 and the first book-length responses directed explicitly at the New Age emerged in 1983. The one other clearly identifiable event that stimulated the growth of this genre was the televised version of Shirley MacLaine's book *Out on a Limb* in 1987. While Creme's campaign was important for giving birth to Christian anti–New Age literature, MacLaine's televised miniseries was responsible for establishing the New Age as *the* most popular topic for Christian polemics.

As the first of its kind, Constance Cumbey's book suggests itself as a useful focal point for analysis. *The Hidden Dangers of the Rainbow* is a mixed work in which one finds a few insightful criticisms juxtaposed with many accusations of the least responsible sort. As the earliest work in this genre, Cumbey set the agenda, both positive and negative, for later writers. For instance, her conspiracy theory and her focus on certain "buzz words" as identifying New Age conspirators (including certain Christian ministers) are points which most succeeding authors have felt compelled either to affirm or to deny.

The very vagueness of the New Age movement has allowed it to become a catch-all category for everything conservative Christians perceive as threatening. In Constance Cumbey's case, after asserting that "this Movement has infiltrated all of Christianity, as well as Judaism" (p. 37) she goes on to imply or to assert that the New Age conspiracy is the motivating force behind ecumenism, holistic health centers, New Thought, humanistic psychology, Montessori schools, modernism, secular humanism, and zero population growth. In her conspiratorial vision, Unitarian Churches and health food stores become "New Age recruiting centers," and the Guardian Angels become one of the New Age movement's "para-military" organizations. Her least cautious assertion is that "the New Age Movement has complete identity with the programs of Hitler" (p. 127) and the link to Nazism is a theme to which she returns over and over again throughout *Hidden Dangers.* The basis for this collapsing of boundaries between widely disparate phenomena is, with few exceptions, not empirical; rather, it is transparent that Cumbey is simply lumping together anything that departs from a rather strict interpretation of Christianity.

Peretti's writings draw much of their nourishment from this polemical literature. As one might anticipate, his novels reflect many of the characteristics of this literature, such as the tendency to lump together everything outside of conservative Christianity as part of a Satanic conspiracy:

> It's all a con game: Eastern meditation, witchcraft, divination, Science of Mind, psychic healing, holistic education–oh, the list goes on and on–it's all the same thing, nothing but a ruse to take over people's minds and spirits, even their bodies. (Peretti 1986, p. 314)

Over the course of the two *Darkness* novels, Peretti mentions many other facets of the satanic threat, such as environmentalism; feminism; channeling; sex education; humanism; the ACLU; liberal Christianity; yoga; psychology; belief in extraterrestrials, karma, and reincarnation; and belief in mother earth and mother goddesses. These various threats are woven together in such figures as Juleen Langstrat, the evil genius behind the plot to take over the town of Ashton in *This Present Darkness.*

As a woman with advanced degrees in psychology, Langstrat directly embodies two "fundamentalist bogey-men" (to once again borrow an expression from Hexham): feminism and secular education. While Peretti does not put strong feminist statements in her mouth, Langstrat's feminism comes across in the titles of some of the courses she teaches at the university, such as "In the Beginning Was the Goddess" (Peretti 1986, p. 94). Peretti's disdain for higher education comes through in the reflections of one of his chief protagonists, Marshall Hogan, who, while waiting for his daughter to get out of class, happens to overhear fragments of Langstrat's lecture. Hogan reflects,

> Yeah, here was more of that college stuff, that funny conglomeration of sixty-four-dollar words which impress people with your academic prowess but can't get you a paying job. Marshall smirked. (p. 37)

Not one for subtle distinctions, Peretti locates the central lair for the demons plotting to take over Ashton in a psychology department conference room—a room described in language suggesting that the department is an outpost of hell itself:

> In this dismal nether world the ceiling was low and oppressive, and crawling with water pipes and heat ducts that seemed like so many huge snakes waiting to drop. Everything—walls, ceiling, pipes, woodwork—was painted the same dirty beige, and light was scarce. (p. 48)

Beyond her already un-Christian status as a psychologist with feminist inclinations, Professor Langstrat teaches other courses on topics that serve to identify her more deeply with the dark forces. Such topics include how to meet your own spirit guides, how to experience past lives, spells and rituals, and Eastern meditation techniques. Langstrat is clearly a damned figure and she eventually meets an ignoble death at the hands of one of her own semipossessed henchman.

Peretti's narrative campaign against the forces of darkness does not, however, stop with attacks on obvious deviations from a rather narrowly circumscribed fundamentalism. While the psychology department's conference room may be the principal gathering place for demons in Ashton, lesser demons stalk such dens of iniquity as video arcades:

> Here were kids of all ages, with few other places to go, congregating after school and all through the weekends to hang out, hang on, play games, pair up, wander off, do drugs, do sex, do whatever. Hank [a minister] knew this place was a hell hole; it wasn't the machines, or the decor, or the dimness–it was just the pungent spiritual stench of demons having their heyday. He felt sick to his stomach. (Peretti 1986, p. 146)

Subjected to Peretti's discerning gaze, such superficially innocent events as the spring carnivals reveal their true nature as festivals of evil:

> Most would . . . take in the festivities, the street disco, the carnival rides, the nickel movies, and whatever else could be had, over or under the table, for kicks. It was a wild time, a chance to get drunk, pregnant, beat up, ripped off, and sick, all in the same night . . . On this warm summer night the roaming, cotton-candied masses were out to enjoy, enjoy, enjoy. . . . The streets, taverns, stores, alleys, and parking spots were jammed, anything was allowed, and the illegal was ignored. . . . The festival, reaching a crescendo now on its last night, was like a terrible storm that couldn't be stopped. (1986, pp. 9–10)

If even arcades and carnivals are hell holes, one might well ask what pleasures are left for good, God-fearing folk. Peretti obviously disapproves of the urge to "enjoy, enjoy, enjoy," and leaves very little to entertain weary spiritual pilgrims. Beyond the "righteous" pleasures of prayer and family life, the only excitement left is the joy of trouncing Satan's forces. The angel Guilo, for example, takes obvious pleasure in bloodying his sword with the gore of God's enemies:

> The demon warriors fell upon them like an avalanche, but for Guilo this was good sport. Tal and the General could hear his uproarious laughter through the thudding sounds of his blade going through demon after demon. (Peretti 1986, p. 358)

Spiritual combat is good, wholesome fun—the only enjoyment Peretti can unequivocally endorse. This explains much of the attraction of his writings within fundamentalist circles: Because of their edifying themes, the *Darkness* novels allow conservative Christians to indulge in reading good horror/adventure stories without the pangs of guilt they might feel reading secular stories. Much the same can be said about Larry Lea's campaigns: One can release one's emotions by cheering on the home team without the twinges of guilt one might feel getting worked up over a secular sporting event.

Peretti's art has created an exciting, imaginative world that enables Christians to understand and respond to the demonic threat, but the cost of this literary tour de force has been to bring conservative Christianity closer in spirit to the very phenomenon against which Peretti rails: His narratives have imaginatively transformed the realm of the ordinary and the everyday into a kind of real life Dungeons and Dragons game, replete with supernatural phenomena, psychic intuitions, quasimagical powers, and sword-swinging warriors. A fascination with the occult is evident in Peretti's descriptions of demons, for example:

> He was like a high-strung little gargoyle, his hide a slimy, bottomless black, his body thin and spiderlike: half humanoid, half animal, totally demon. Two huge yellow cat-eyes bulged out of his face, darting to and fro, peering, searching. His breath came in short, sulfurous gasps, visible as glowing yellow vapor. (1986, p. 36)

While Christians have always believed in the power of prayer, the *Darkness* novels picture prayer as having a fantastic, magical efficacy against demonic warriors:

> "Lord God," she said, and the warmth of the Holy Spirit flowed through them, "I build now a hedge around this young couple, and I bind the spirits in Jesus' name. Satan, whatever your plans for the town, I rebuke you in Jesus' name, and I bind you, and I cast you out!"

> CLUNK! Rafar's eyes darted toward the sound that had inter-
> rupted his talking and saw two swords fallen from their owners'
> hands. (Peretti 1986, p. 113)

While Christians have traditionally believed in the guidance of the Holy Spirit, the vivid picture Peretti draws of highly personal angels conveying guidance to the minds of God's saints makes "Christian" inspiration appear to be a close relative of spiritualistic psychism. Peretti also pictures angels as capable of materializing to help God's chosen, as when the angel Betsy materializes to give one of the heroines, Bernice Krueger, a short motorcycle ride. Once Bernice has reached her desti-nation, Betsy evaporates like some eerie figure out of an occult novel:

> She turned back to Betsy and stiffened. For a moment she felt she
> would stumble forward as if a wall had suddenly disappeared in
> front of her. Betsy was gone. The motorcycle was gone. It was like
> awakening from a dream and needing time to adjust one's mind to
> what was real and what was not. But Bernice knew it had not been
> a dream. The tracks of the motorcycle were still plainly visible in
> the gravel, leading from where it had left the highway to the spot
> directly in front of Bernice. There they ended. (Peretti 1986, p. 303)

As with many of the events that take place in the *Darkness* novels, such eerie encounters reflect a fascination with the supernatural and super-natural powers—a fascination Peretti's version of Christianity shares with the very phenomenon in which the hand of the Prince of Dark-ness is most evident: the New Age movement. In the final analysis, despite the macho, "stand by my God" rhetoric of the spiritual war-fare movement, the teachings of the Prince of Peace have been aban-doned. Instead, movement participants have fallen prey to a cheap, flashy imitation of true spirituality that substitutes angry, sword-waving militancy for the transforming power of Christian love.

The followers of Lea, Peretti, and the like appear to anticipate a Christian versus New Age Armageddon with much eagerness. But if Christians believe they must embrace the spiritual warfare move-ment's take-no-prisoners brand of spirituality in order to defeat the New Age movement, then the battle has already been fought—and lost.

BIBLIOGRAPHY

Adamski, George. 1949. *Pioneers of Space: A Trip to the Moon, Mars, and Venus.* Los Angeles: Leonard-Freefield Co.

Adler, Margot. 1989. *Drawing Down the Moon: Witches, Druids, Goddess-Worshippers, and Other Pagans in America Today,* 2d ed. Boston: Beacon Press.

Aetherius Society. 1982. *Temple Degree Study Courses.* Hollywood, Calif.: The Aetherius Society.

Alper, Frank. 1982. *Exploring Atlantis.* Farmingdale, N.Y.: Coleman Publishing.

American Psychiatric Association. 1994. *Diagnostic and Statistical Manual of Mental Disorders,* 4th ed. Washington, D.C.: American Psychiatric Association.

Apocalypse (magazine). N.d. Bulletin de Liaison du Mouvement Raelian.

Arberry, A. J. 1969. *The Koran Interpreted.* New York: Macmillan.

Arnold, Thomas. 1806. *Observations on the Nature, Kinds, Causes, and Prevention of Insanity,* 2d ed. London: Richard Phillips.

Asahara, Shoko. 1995. *Disaster Approaches the Land of the Rising Sun.* Shizuoka, Japan: AUM Publishing Co.

Bailey, Paul. 1957. *Wovoka: The Indian Messiah.* Los Angeles: Westernlore Press.

Bainbridge, William Sims. 1984. "Religious Insanity in America: The Official Nineteenth-Century Theory." *Sociological Analysis* 45, no. 3 (Fall).

Balch, Robert W. 1995. "Waiting for the Ships: Disillusionment and the

Revitalization of Faith in Bo and Peep's UFO Cult." In *The Gods Have Landed: New Religions from Other Worlds*, edited by James R. Lewis. Albany: State University of New York Press.

Ballard, Guy W. 1982. *Unveiled Mysteries*, 4th ed. Chicago: St. Germain Press.

Barker, Eileen. 1990. *New Religious Movements*. London: Her Majesty's Stationery Office.

Barker, Gray. 1956. *They Knew Too Much about Flying Saucers*. New York: University Books.

Barkun, Michael. 1998. "Christian Identity." In *The Encyclopedia of Cults, Sects and New Religions*, edited by James R. Lewis, pp. 114–17. Amherst, N.Y.: Prometheus Books.

———. 1997. *Religion and the Racist Right*. Rev. ed. Chapel Hill: University of North Carolina Press.

Bartholomew, Robert E. 1989. *Ufolore: A Social Psychological Study of a Modern Myth in the Making*. Stone Mountain, Ga.: Arcturus Book Service.

Beckford, James. 1994. "The Media and New Religious Movements." In *From the Ashes: Making Sense of Waco*, edited by James R. Lewis. Lanham, Md.: Rowman & Littlefield.

Bednaroski, Mary Farrell. 1989. *New Religions and the Theological Imagination in America*. Bloomington: Indiana University Press.

Bergesen, Albert. 1984. *The Sacred and the Subversive*. Storrs, Conn.: Society for the Scientific Study of Religion Monograph Series.

Bhagavad Gita. 1970. Juan Mascaro, trans. Baltimore: Penguin.

Billington, Ray Allen. 1938. *The Protestant Crusade 1800–1860: A Study of the Origins of American Nativism*. New York: Macmillan.

Black, Jeremy, and Anthony Green. 1992. *Gods, Demons and Symbols of Ancient Mesopotamia: An Illustrated Dictionary*. Austin: University of Texas Press.

Bliss, Sylvester. 1853. *Memoirs of William Miller*. Boston: Joshua V. Himes.

Brigham, Amariah. 1835. *Observations on the Influence of Religion upon the Health and Physical Welfare of Mankind*. Boston: Marsh, Capen and Lyon.

"Brinton: The Religious Sentiment." 1876. *Journal of Nervous and Mental Disease* 3.

Burrows, George Man. 1828. *Commentaries on the Causes, Forms, Symptoms and Treatment, Moral and Medical, of Insanity*. London: Thomas and George Underwood.

Cartwright, Samuel A. 1856. "Report on the Diseases and Physical Peculiarities of the Negro Race." *New Orleans Medical and Surgical Journal* 7 (May).

"Cases of Insanity–Illustrating the Importance of Early Treatment in Preventing Suicide." 1845. *American Journal of Insanity* 1 (January): 243–49.

Cayce, Edgar. 1968. *Edgar Cayce on Atlantis.* New York: Paperback Library.

Cayce, Hugh Lynn. 1980. *Earth Changes Update.* Virginia Beach: A.R.E. Press.

———. 1964. *Venture Inward.* New York: Harper & Row.

Circle Guide to Pagan Resources. 1987. Mt. Horeb, Wisc.: Circle.

Clark [channeled by Katar]. 1988. "Back to School–Earth Revisited." *Open Channel: A Journal with Spirit* 2 (November–December).

Clark, Jerome. 1997. "Sister Thedra." *Syzygy: Journal of Alterantive Religion and Culture* 6, no. 1.

———. 1990, 1992, 1996. *The UFO Encyclopedia.* 3 vols. Detroit: Omnigraphics.

Coates, James. 1987. *Armed and Dangerous.* New York: Hill and Wang.

Cohen, Daniel. 1977. *Myths of the Space Age.* New York: Dodd, Mead.

Cohn, Norman. 1993. *Cosmos, Chaos and the World to Come.* New Haven, Conn.: Yale University Press.

———. 1957. *The Pursuit of the Millennium.* London: Oxford University Press.

Cohn-Sherbok, Daniel. 1987. "Death and Immortality in the Jewish Tradition." In *Death and Immortality in the Religions of the World,* edited by Paul and Linda Badham, pp. 24–36. New York: Paragon House.

Conrad, Peter, and Joseph W. Schneider. 1980. *Deviance and Medicalization: From Badness to Sickness.* St. Louis: C. V. Mosby.

Cooper, Jerrold S. 1992. "The Fate of Mankind: Death and Afterlife in Ancient Mesopotamia." In *Death and Afterlife: Perspectives of World Religions,* edited by Hiroshi Obayashi. Westport, Conn.: Greenwood Press.

Cumbey, Constance. 1983. *The Hidden Dangers of the Rainbow.* Shreveport, La.: Huntington House.

Curran, Douglas. 1985. *In Advance of the Landing: Folk Concepts of Outer Space.* New York: Abbeville Press.

Dalley, Stephanie. 1989. *Myths from Mesopotamia.* New York: Oxford University Press.

Davis, Deborah (Linda Berg), with Bill Davis. 1984. *The Children of God: The Inside Story.* Grand Rapids, Mich.: Zondervan Books.

Derenberger, Woodrow W., and Harold W. Hubbard. 1971. *Visitors from Lanulos.* New York: Vantage Press.

Donnelly, Ignatius. 1882. *Atlantis: The Antediluvian World.* New York: Harper & Brothers.

Earle, Pliny. 1848. "On the Causes of Insanity." *American Journal of Insanity* 4 (January): 185–211.

Edmunds, R. David. 1983. *The Shawnee Prophet.* Lincoln: University of Nebraska Press.

Eliade, Mircea, ed. 1987. *Encyclopedia of Religion.* New York: Macmillan.

Ellwood, Robert S., and Harry B. Partin. 1988. *Religious and Spiritual Groups in Modern America.* Englewood Cliffs, N.J.: Prentice-Hall.

Evans, Hilary. 1983. *The Evidence for UFOs.* Wellingborough, U.K.: Aquarian.

———. 1984. *Visions, Apparitions, Alien Visitors.* Wellingborough, U.K.: Aquarian.

Farrar, Janet, and Stewart Farrar. 1989. *The Witches' God: Lord of the Dance.* London, Robert Hale, 1988. Reprint, Custer, Wash.: Phoenix Publishing.

Ferguson, Marilyn. 1980. *The Aquarian Conspiracy.* Los Angeles: Jeremy Tarcher.

Ferguson, William. 1954. *My Trip to Mars.* Chicago: Cosmic Circle of Fellowship.

Festinger, Leon, Henry W. Riecken, and Stanley Schachter. 1956. *When Prophecy Fails.* New York: Harper & Row.

Fiddleman, Thomas, and David Kopel. 1993. *Washington Times,* June 1.

Findhorn Community. 1975. *The Findhorn Garden.* New York: Harper & Row.

Findhorn Foundation. 1986–87. *Catalog.* Autumn–Winter.

Flem-Ath, Rand, and Rose Flem-Ath. 1995. *When the Sky Fell.* New York: St. Martin's Press.

Fort, Charles. 1999. *The Book of the Damned.* New York: Garland, 1975. Reprint, Amherst, N.Y.: Prometheus Books.

Frost, Gavin, and Yvonne Frost. 1991. *Who Speaks for the Witch.* New Bern, N.C.: Godolphin House.

Fundamental Beliefs and Directory of the Davidian Seventh-Day Adventists. 1943. Waco, Tex.: Universal Publishing Association.

Gallup, George. 1982. *Adventures in Immortality.* New York: MacGraw-Hill.

Gelberg, Steven, ed. 1983. *Hare Krishna, Hare Krishna.* New York: Grove Press.

Goldenberg, Robert. 1992. "Bound Up in the Bond of Life: Death and Afterlife in the Jewish Tradition." In *Death and Afterlife: Perspectives of World Religions,* edited by Hiroshi Obayashi, pp. 97–108. Westport, Conn.: Greenwood Press.

Goran, Morris. 1978 *The Modern Myth: Ancient Astronauts and UFOs.* New York: A. S. Barnes. Gowan, John Curtis.

Guffey, George R. 1987. "Aliens in the Supermarket: Science Fiction and Fantasy for 'Inquiring Minds.' " In *Aliens: The Anthropology of Science Fiction,* edited by George E. Slusser and Eric S. Rabkin. Carbondale: Southern Illinois University Press.

Guiley, Rosemary E. 1989. *Encyclopedia of Witchcraft and Witches.* New York: Facts on File.

Hall, John R. Forthcoming. "Public Narratives and the Apocalyptic Sect: From Jonestown to Mount Carmel." In *Armageddon in Mount Carmel,* edited by Stuart A. Wright. Chicago: University Chicago Press.

Hamilton, Edith, and Huntington Cairns, eds. 1961. *The Collected Dialogues of Plato.* Princeton, N.J.: Princeton University Press.

Hancock, Graham. 1995. *Fingerprints of the Gods.* New York: Crown.

Harrison, J. F. C. 1979. *The Second Coming, Popular Millenarianism 1780–1850.* London: n.p.

Heaven's Gate. 1996. "Time to Die for God?–The Imminent 'Holy War'– Which Side are You On?" Heaven's Gate Internet Statement. September 24.

Hexham, Irving. 1992. "The Evangelical Response to the New Age." In *Perspectives on the New Age,* edited by James R. Lewis and J. Gordon Melton, pp. 152–63. Albany: State University of New York Press.

Hope, Murray. 1991. *Atlantis: Myth or Reality?* London: Arkana.

Hopkins, Budd. 1987. *Intruders: The Incredible Visitations at Copley Woods.* New York: Random House.

———. 1981. *Missing Time.* New York: Richard Marek Publishers.

Hopkins, Thomas. 1992. "Hindu Views of Death and Afterlife." In *Death and Afterlife: Perspectives of World Religions,* edited by Hiroshi Obayashi, pp. 49–64. Westport, Conn.: Greenwood Press.

Houteff, Victor T. 1990. *The Shepherd's Rod Series.* Mt. Carmel, Tex.: Universal Printing, 1929–35. Reprint Salem, S.C.: General Association of Davidian Seventh-Day Adventists.

Hultkrantz, Ake. 1953. *Conceptions of the Soul Among North American Indians.* Stockholm: Ethnographic Museum of Sweden.

Introvigne, Massimo. 1997. *Heaven's Gate: Il paradiso non può attendere.* Turin, Italy: Editrice Elle Di Ci.

John-Roger. 1980. *The Way Out Book.* Los Angeles: Baraka Press.

Jung, Carl Gustav. 1965. *Memories, Dreams, Reflections.* New York: Vintage Books.

258   DOOMSDAY PROPHECIES

—. 1958. *Flying Saucers.* Princeton, N.J.: Princeton University Press.

Jwnody. 1996. "Overview of Present Mission." Heaven's Gate Internet Statement. April.

Kaplan, David E., and Andrew Marshall. 1996. *The Cult at the End of the World.* New York: Crown.

Keel, John. 1988. *Disneyland of the Gods.* New York: Amok Press.

—. 1975. *The Mothman Prophecies.* New York: Saturday Review Press.

Kehoe, Alice Beck. 1989. *The Ghost Dance: Ethnohistory and Revitalization.* New York: Holt, Rinehart and Winston.

Kelly, Aidan A. 1993. "An Update on Neopagan Witchcraft in America." In *Perspectives on the New Age,* edited by James R. Lewis. Albany: State University of New York Press.

—, ed. 1990. *Neo-Pagan Witchcraft.* New York: Garland.

King, George. 1964. *The Practices of Aetherius.* Hollywood, Calif.: Aetherius Society.

Kirkpatrick, R. George, and Diana Tumminia. 1992. "Space Magic, Techno-Animism, and the Cult of the Goddess in a Southern Californian UFO Contactee Group: A Case Study in Millenarianism." *Syzygy: Journal of Alternative Religion and Culture.* 1, no. 2: 159–72.

Klinek, Carl F., ed. 1961. *Tecumseh: Fact and Fiction in Early Records.* Englewood Cliffs, N.J.: Prentice-Hall.

Kopel, David B., and Paul H. Blackman. 1997. *No More Wacos: What's Wrong with Federal Law Enforcement and How to Fix It.* Amherst, N.Y.: Prometheus Books.

Kuhn, Thomas S. 1970. *The Structure of Scientific Revolutions.* Chicago: University of Chicago Press.

Lanternari, Vittorio. 1956. *The Religions of the Oppressed: A Study of Modern Messianic Cults.* New York: Mentor.

Lattin, Don. 1990. " 'New Age' Mysticism Strong in Bay Area." *San Francisco Chronicle.* April 24–25.

Lee, Robert W. 1993. "Truth and Cover-Up–Sorting Out the Waco Tragedy." *New American Magazine* 9, no. 12 (June 14).

Levine, Saul. 1984. *Radical Departures: Desperate Detours to Growing Up.* New York: Harcourt Brace Javanovich.

Lewis, James R. Forthcoming. "Edgar Cayce." In the *American National Biography.* New York: Oxford University Press.

—. Forthcoming. "L. Ron Hubbard." In *American National Biography.* New York: Oxford University Press.

———. 1999. *Peculiar Prophets: A Biographical Dictionary of New Religions.* St. Paul: Paragon House.

———. 1998a. *Cults in America.* Santa Barbara, Calif.: ABC-CLIO.

———. 1998b. *Seeking the Light: Uncovering the Truth about the Movement for Spiritual Inner Awareness.* Los Angeles: Mandeville Press.

———, ed. 1996. *Magical Religion and Modern Witchcraft.* Albany: State University of New York Press.

———. 1995a. *Encyclopedia of Afterlife Beliefs and Phenomena.* Detroit: Gale Research.

———, ed. 1995b. *The Gods Have Landed.* Albany: State University of New York Press.

———. 1994. *From the Ashes: Making Sense of Waco.* Lanham, Md.: Rowman & Littlefield.

———. 1991. "American Indian Prophets." In *When Prophets Die: The Postcharismatic Fate of New Religious Movements,* edited by Timothy Miller, pp. 47–57. Albany: State University of New York Press.

Lewis, James R., and J. Gordon Melton, eds. 1994. *Sex, Slander, and Salvation: Investigating The Family/Children of God.* Stanford, Calif.: Center for Academic Publication.

———. 1992. *Perspectives on the New Age.* Albany: State University of New York Press.

Lilliston, Lawrence. 1994. "Who Committed Child Abuse in Waco?" In *From the Ashes: Making Sense of Waco,* edited by James R. Lewis. Lanham, Md.: Rowman & Littlefield.

Macdonald, Andrew. 1978. *The Turner Diaries.* Washington, D.C.: The National Alliance.

Mack, John E. 1994. *Abduction: Human Encounters with Aliens.* New York: Ballantine.

Madigan, Tim. 1993. *See No Evil: Blind Devotion and Bloodshed in David Koresh's Holy War.* Ft. Worth, Tex.: Summit.

Mann, A. T. 1992. *Millennium Prophecies: Predictions for the Year 2000.* Rockport, Mass.: Element.

Marron, Kevin. 1989. *Witches, Pagans, and Magic in the New Age.* Toronto: Seal Books.

McCall, Henrietta. 1990. *Mesopotamian Myths.* Austin: University of Texas Press.

Melton, Gordon. 1993. *Encyclopedia of American Religions,* 4th ed. Detroit: Gale Research.

Melton, J. Gordon. 1992. *Encyclopedic Handbook of Cults in America.* Rev. ed. New York and London: Garland.

Melton, J. Gordon, Jerome Clark, and Aidan A. Kelly. 1990. *New Age Encyclopedia.* Detroit: Gale Research.

Mendenhall, George E. 1992. "From Witchcraft to Justice: Death and Afterlife in the Old Testament." In *Death and Afterlife: Perspectives of World Religions,* edited by Hiroshi Obayashi. Westport, Conn.: Greenwood Press.

Miller, Perry. 1956. *Errand into the Wilderness.* Cambridge, Mass.: Belknap.

Millikan, David. 1994. "The Children of God, The Family of Love, The Family." In *Sex, Slander and Salvation: Investigating The Family/Children of God,* edited by James R. Lewis and J. Gordon Melton. Stanford, Calif.: Center for Academic Publication.

MO Letters and other Children of God/Family literature:

Afflictions (#569, November 25, 1976).

Ban the Bomb! (#1434, April 1983).

The Book of the Future.

Child Brides! (#902, April 4, 1977).

Difficulty in Communications!–Have Mercy on the Departed Spirits! (DO 1846, September 18, 1984. *Daily Bread,* Vol. 11).

*Everything **YOU** want to know about **SEX!*** (undated *MO Letters,* Vol. 7).

A Father Applies the Rod!–Dad's Phone Call with Ho (DO 952–8, December 4, 1980, *MO Letters,* Vol. 8).

FF Tips (#548, May 4, 1976).

The FFers Handbook! (#559, January 1977).

FFing Behaviour! (#563, December 1976).

"Finish the Job!" (DO 1939, June 1985, DB3).

Fire & Ice! (#1213, October 2, 1982).

"Flatlanders" (GP 57, March 13, 1971, Vol. 1).

Four Fishing Failures (#533, April 6, 1976).

Glorify God in the Dance! (#1026, August 24, 1981).

Good News! (#554, July 1993).

Good News! (#486, November 1991).

Happy Daze!–Are you Still in *That Old House?*–or a *New House!* (DO 958 December 6, 1980, *MO Letters,* Vol. 8).

Here and Now for There and Then (DFO 1092, November 1, 1981).

Holy Ghosts (GP 620, January 27, 1974, *MO Letters,* Vol. 5).

Is Love Against the Law? (#648, January 1978).

Jesus Babies! (#739, June 24, 1976).

King Meets King! (#502, May 1976).

The Law of Love (#302C, March 21, 1974).

Law vs. Love (#647, July 23, 1977).

Male and Female (#529, September 5, 1976).

The Millennium! (#1197:93, May 1981).

More from Esther (DO 952-17, January 1, 1981, *MO Letters*, Vol. 8).

" 'Mountin' Maid!" (#240, December 27, 1970).

Mugshots! (#979, 1980).

New Year's Eve Praise! (DO 957, December 31, 1980, Vol. 8).

Nudity Can Be Beautiful (#1006, March 1981).

The Oil Shortage! What it Means to You! (DFO 938, September 29, 1980, *MO Letters*, Vol. 8).

Our Declaration of Love (#607, October 9, 1977).

The Real Victors of the Tribulation!–We're More Than Conquerors! (Rom. 8:37)–The *Other* Side of the Tribulation! (DFO 1624, September 1983, *Good News* Books 16 and 17).

Revolutionary Love-Making (#259, 1973).

Revolutionary Sex (#258, March 27, 1973).

Revolutionary Women (#250, June 20, 1973).

The 7 F's of FFing! (#1083, January 1, 1982).

The 7 Ways To Know God's Will!–At the Birth of The Family! (Huntington Beach GP 829, Summer 1968, *MO Letters*, Vol. 7).

Sex Questions and Answers, Parts 1–3 (#815–817, 1979).

The Spiritual Warfare Depends on Us! The Majesty of Choice! (DO 2327, June 1987).

The Story of Davidito. Zurich, Switz.: The Family of Love, 1982.

The Talisman!–Animism and the Sphinx!–A Family Emergency Just before Tim Concerned's Defection! (DFO 1369, January 23, 1979, *Lifelines*, Vol. 14).

Teen Sex! (#2061, September 1985).

Trust the Lord!–On Husband/Wife Relationships (DO 2135, November 2, 1983, DB3).

The Video Ministry (#977, March 1981).

Wars and Rumours of Wars! (DFO 1327, November 1982, *Lifelines*, Vol. 14).

What Did You Do Today to Save a Soul? (DO 2089, January 1986, DB3).

Why Disasters?–Is Death a Curse or Blessing? (DFO 959, November 26, 1980, *MO Letters*, Vol. 8.

Women in Love (#292, December 20, 1973).

You Are the Love of God! (#699, June 5, 1978).

Montgomery, Ruth. 1985. *Aliens among Us.* New York: Putnam's.

———. 1983. *Threshold to Tomorrow.* New York: G. P. Putnam's Sons.

———. 1979. *Strangers among Us: Enlightened Beings from a World to Come.* New York: Coward, McCann & Geoghegan.

———. 1974. *Companions Along the Way.* New York: Coward, McCann & Geoghegan.

Moody, Raymond A. 1989. *The Light Beyond.* New York: Bantam.

———. 1976. *Life after Life.* New York: Bantam.

Mooney, James. [1896] 1965. *The Ghost-Dance Religion and the Sioux Outbreak of 1890.* Chicago: University of Chicago Press.

Morgan, Edmund S. 1958. *The Puritan Dilemma.* Boston: Little, Brown & Co.

Nada-Yolanda [Pauline Sharpe]. 1974. *Visitors from Other Planets.* Miami: Mark-Age.

Neihardt, John G. 1961. *Black Elk Speaks.* Lincoln: University of Nebraska Press.

Nesheim, Eric, and Leif Nesheim. 1997. *Saucer Attack! Pop Culture in the Golden Age of Flying Saucers.* Los Angeles: Kitchen Sink Press.

Norman, Ernest L. 1956. *The Voice of Venus.* Los Angeles: New Age.

Norman, Ruth E., and Vaughan Spaegel. *The Conclave of Light Beings: Or the Affair of the Millennium.* El Cajon, Calif.: Unarius Publishers, 1973.

Oliver, Moorman, Jr. 1994. "Killed by Semantics." In *From the Ashes: Making Sense of Waco,* edited by James R. Lewis, pp. 71–86. Lanham, Md.: Roman & Littlefield.

"The Padrick 'Space Contact.'" 1965. *Little Listening Post* 12, no. 3.

Palmer, Susan J. 1995. *Moon Sisters, Krishna Mothers, Rajneesh Lovers: Women's Roles in New Religions.* Syracuse, N.Y.: Syracuse University Press.

———. 1992. "Woman as Playmate in the Raelian Movement: Power and Pantagamy in a New Religion." *Syzygy: Journal of Religion and Culture* 1, no. 3: 227–45.

Pate, James L. 1993. "Gun Gestapo's Day of Infamy." *Soldier of Fortune* (June).

Patrick, Ted, with Tom Dulack. 1976. *Let Our Children Go!* New York: E. P. Dutton.

Pavry, Jal Dastur Cursetji. 1926. *The Zoroastrian Doctrine of a Future Life.* New York: Columbia University Press.

Peretti, Frank E. 1989. *Piercing the Darkness.* Westchester, Ill.: Crossway Books.

———. 1986. *This Present Darkness.* Westchester, Ill.: Crossway Books.

Perfect, William. 1798. *Annals of Insanity, Comprising a Selection of Curious and Interesting Cases in the Different Species of Lunacy, Melancholy, or Madness, with the Modes of Practice in the Medical and Moral Treatment, as Adopted in the Cure of Each.* London: n.p.

Peterson, Scott. 1990. *Native American Prophecies.* New York: Paragon.

Pitts, Bill. 1995. "Davidians and Branch Davidians: 1929–1987." In *Armageddon in Mount Carmel,* edited by Stuart A. Wright. Chicago: University of Chicago Press.

Plato. 1926. *Laws,* trans. R. Bury. Cambridge, Mass.: Harvard University Press.

Pursglove, Paul David. 1995. *Zen in the Art of Close Encounters: Crazy Wisdom and UFOs.* Berkeley, Calif.: The New Being Project.

Randles, Jenny, and Peter Hough. *The Complete Book of UFOs: An Investigation into Alien Contacts and Encounters.* New York: Sterling, 1996.

"Religious Insanity." 1876. *American Journal of Insanity* 33 (July): 126–27.

Richardson, James T. 1994. "Lessons from Waco." In *From the Ashes: Making Sense of Waco,* edited by James R. Lewis, pp. 181–84. Lanham, Md.: Roman & Littlefield.

Ring, Kenneth. 1992. *The Omega Project.* New York: William Morrow & Co.

———. 1984. *Heading toward Omega.* New York: William Morrow & Co.

Robbins, Thomas, and Dick Anthony, eds. 1981. *In Gods We Trust: New Patterns of Religious Pluralism in America.* New Brunswick, N.J.: Transaction.

Saliba, John A. 1995. "Religious Dimensions of UFO Phenomena." In *The Gods Have Landed,* edited by James R. Lewis, pp. 15–64. Albany: State University of New York Press.

Sananda, as recorded by Sister Thedra. 1954. *I, the Lord God Say Unto Them.* Mt. Shasta, Calif.: Association of Sananda and Sanat Kumara.

Sandars, N. K., trans. 1971. *Poems of Heaven and Hell from Ancient Mesopotamia.* New York: Penguin.

———. [1960] 1972. *The Epic of Gilgamesh.* Rev. ed. New York: Penguin.

Schutz, Noel William, Jr., 1989. *The Study of Shawnee Myth in an Ethnographic and Ethnohistorical Perspective.* Ann Arbor: University Microfilms International.

Schwartz, Alan M., and Gail L. Gans. 1983. *The Identity Churches: a Theology of Hate.* In ADL Facts 28, 1–Spring.

Sebald, Hans. 1984. "New-Age Romanticism: The Quest for an Alternative Lifestyle as a Force of Social Change." *Humboldt Journal of Social Relations* 11, no. 2.

Shaw, David. 1993. "From Headline to Prime Time." *TV Guide.*

Shepard, Leslie A., ed. 1991. *Encyclopedia of Occultism & Parapsychology.* Detroit: Gale Research.

Silko, Leslie Marmon. 1977. *Ceremony.* New York: Signet.

Simmons, J. L. 1990. *The Emerging New Age.* Santa Fe, N.Mex.: Bear and Co.

Sitchin, Zecharia. 1976. *The Twelfth Planet.* New York: Avon.

Spangler, David. 1977a. "The Role of the Esoteric in Planetary Culture." In *Earth's Answer: Explorations of Planetary Culture at the Lindisfarne Conferences,* edited by Michael Katz, William P. Marsh, and Gail Gordon Thompson. New York: Harper & Row.

———. 1977b. *Towards a Planetary Vision.* Forres, Scotland: Findhorn Publications.

Speir, Dean. 1993. "Wither BATF in Future." *Gun Week.* June 11.

Starhawk. 1989. *The Spiral Dance: A Rebirth of the Ancient Religion of the Great Goddess,* 2d ed. San Francisco: Harper & Row.

Strieber, Whitley. 1987. *Communion.* New York: Morrow/Beech Tree Books.

Sweetser, William. 1850. *Mental Hygiene; or, an Examination of the Intellect and Passions.* New York: G. P. Putnam.

Tabor, James D. 1994. "The Waco Tragedy: An Autobiographical Account of One Attempt to Avert Diaster." In *From the Ashes: Making Sense of Waco,* edited by James R. Lewis. Lanham, Md.: Rowman & Littlefield.

Thedra, Sister. 1990. *Mine Intercome Messages from the Realms of Light.* Sedona, Ariz.: Association of Sananda and Sanat Kumara.

———. 1956. *Excerpts of Prophecies from Other Planets Concerning Our Earth.* Mt. Shasta, Calif.: Association of Sananda and Sanat Kumara.

Thomas, Evan. 1997. "The Next Level." *Newsweek Magazine,* April 7.

Thompson, Damian. 1996. *The End of Time.* Hanover, N.J.: University Press of New England.

Thompson, Keith. 1991. *Angels and Aliens: UFOs and the Mythic Imagination.* Reading, Mass.: Addison-Wesley.

Trafzer, Clifford E., ed. 1986. *American Indian Prophets.* Newcastle, Calif.: Sierra Oaks.

Tuella [Thelma B. Terrell]. 1985. *Ashtar: A Tribute.* Durango, Colo.: Guardian Action Publication.

———. 1982. *Project World Evacuation.* Salt Lake City, Utah: Guardian Action International.

Tumminia, Diana, and R. George Kirkpatrick. 1995. "Unarius: Emergent Aspects of a Flying Saucer Group." In *The Gods Have Landed: New Reli-*

gions from Other Worlds, edited by James R. Lewis. Albany: State University of New York Press.

Turner, Alice K. 1993. *The History of Hell.* New York: Harcourt, Brace & Co.

Valiente, Doreen. 1989. *The Rebirth of Witchcraft.* London: Robert Hale.

Vallee, Jacques. 1988. *Dimensions.* Chicago: Contemporary Books.

———. 1979. *Messengers of Deception.* Berkeley, Calif: And/Or Press.

———. 1969. *Passport to Magonia.* Chicago: Henry Regency Co.

Van Tassel, George. 1956. *I Rode a Flying Saucer.* Los Angeles: New Age Publishing Co.

Van Zandt, David E. 1991. *Living in the Children of God.* Princeton, N.J.: Princeton University Press.

Voegelin, C. F., and John Yegerlehner. 1957. "Toward a Definition of Formal Style, with Examples from Shawnee." In *Studies in Folklore,* edited by W. E. Richmond. Bloomington: University of Indiana Press.

Von Däniken, Erich. 1970. *Chariots of the Gods? Unsolved Mysteries of the Past.* New York: G. P. Putnam's Sons.

Vorilhon, Claude. 1986. *Extraterrestrials Took Me to Their Planet.* Brantome, France: l'Edition du Message.

Wallace, Anthony F. C. 1966. *Religion: An Anthropological View.* New York: Random House.

Winberg, Steven L., ed. 1986. *Ramtha.* Eastsound, Wash.: Sovereignty.

———. 1978. *Space Aliens Took Me to Their Planet: The Most Important Revelation in the History of Mankind.* Montreal: Canadian Raelian Movement.

Workman, Joseph. 1869. "Insanity of the Religious-Emotional Type, and Its Occasional Physical Relations." *American Journal of Insanity* 24 (July).

Wright, Stuart A., ed. 1995. *Armageddon in Mount Carmel.* Chicago: University of Chicago Press.

Zangger, Eberhard. 1992. *The Flood from Heaven.* New York: William Morrow & Co.

Zimmer, Heinrich. 1951. *Philosophies of India.* New York: Bollingen.

———. 1946. *Myths and Symbols in Indian Art and Civilization.* New York: Bollingen.

INDEX

267

268 **DOOMSDAY PROPHECIES**

Daniel, Book of, 44, 112, 125, 209

Family, The (Children of God), 22, 115–43. *See also* Berg, David Brandt
FBI, 10, 11, 79, 81, 95, 100, 102, 104, 105, 107, 108, 110–11, 112, 141, 228–29, 230, 232, 234, 236, 237, 238, 239
flying saucers, 12, 146–56, 160–62, 164, 166, 168, 169, 171, 173, 187, 188–90, 198. *See also* aliens; UFOs

Ghost Dance, 20, 69, 70–71, 72, 73, 207
Gilgamesh, 33–35

Handsome Lake, 55, 64–68, 69, 71
Harappan, 28–29
Heaven's Gate, 12–13, 22, 186–94, 196–99, 200, 202–203, 206
Hindu, Hinduism, 17, 25–32

Islam, 17, 18, 23, 33, 38, 39, 41, 42, 47–50, 130, 158

Jehovah's Witnesses, 18, 131, 137
Jones, Jim, 79, 224
Judaism, 17, 18, 23, 27, 33, 38, 39, 41, 42–46, 49, 50, 52, 126, 158, 194, 248

Koran, 49, 50
Koresh, David, 76, 78, 79, 81, 82, 86–87, 88, 89, 91, 92, 93, 94, 96, 97, 98, 99, 100, 101, 103, 104, 105, 106, 107, 108, 109–10, 111, 112–13, 224, 228, 229, 231, 236, 237, 239, 240

Lawmaster, Johnnie, 84–85, 101

Manicheism, 41
Matthews, Robert, 11
McVeigh, Timothy, 10
Mesopotamia, 32–38, 43
millenarian movement, 19–20, 23
Miller, William, 18, 209–10. *See also* Millerite movement.
Millerite movement, 18, 208, 211, 221. *See also* Miller, William
Mohammed, 18, 158, 196

Native Americans, 20, 54–74
New Age movement, 21, 22, 176, 178, 179, 185, 186, 187, 188, 190, 194, 196, 197, 198, 199–200, 202, 203, 242, 244, 246, 247, 248, 252
Nichols, Terry, 10
Nostradamus, 14

Oklahoma City bombing, 10, 13
Order, the, 11

Pierce, William L., 11
Plato, 180–85, 186

Raelian Movement, 156–59
"religious insanity," 211–23
Revelation, Book of, 18, 19, 20, 46, 100, 103, 104, 105–106, 107, 108, 109, 110, 111, 112, 124, 125, 127, 128, 130, 131, 132, 133, 138, 150, 156, 187, 191, 194, 209
Russell, Charles Taze, 18

Tenskwatawa, 55, 56, 57, 58, 60–61, 62, 63, 64, 65, 66, 69